First World War
and Army of Occupation
War Diary
France, Belgium and Germany

48 DIVISION
145 Infantry Brigade
Oxfordshire and Buckinghamshire Light Infantry
1/4 Battalion
27 March 1915 - 31 October 1917

WO95/2764/1

The Naval & Military Press Ltd
www.nmarchive.com
Published in association with The National Archives

Published by

The Naval & Military Press Ltd

Unit 10 Ridgewood Industrial Park,

Uckfield, East Sussex,

TN22 5QE England

Tel: +44 (0) 1825 749494

www.naval-military-press.com

www.nmarchive.com

This diary has been reprinted in facsimile from the original. Any imperfections are inevitably reproduced and the quality may fall short of modern type and cartographic standards.

© **Crown Copyright**
Images reproduced by permission of The National Archives, London, England, 2015.

Contents

Document type	Place/Title	Date From	Date To
Heading	1/4 Batt Ox At Buck Light Infantry April 1915 Oct 1917		
Heading	48th Division 145th Infy Bde 1-4th Bn Oxf & Bucks Lt Infy Apr 1915-1917 Oct		
Heading	145th Inf. Bde. 48th Div 1/4th Battn The Oxfordshire & Buckinghamshire Light Infantry March (27.3.15 To 3.4.15) 1915 Jan 19		
Heading	War Diary Of 1/4th Batt. Oxford & Bucks Light Infantry From 27th March 1915 To 31st March 1915		
War Diary	Writtle	27/03/1915	29/03/1915
War Diary	Boulogne	30/03/1915	30/03/1915
War Diary	Steenvoorde	02/04/1915	03/04/1915
Heading	145th Inf. Bde. 48th Div 1/4th Battn The Oxfordshire & Buckinghamshire Light Infantry April 1915		
Heading	War Diary Of 1/4th Battalion Oxfordshire & Buckinghamshire Light Infantry From 1st April 1915 To 30th April 1915 (Volume)		
Miscellaneous			
War Diary	Steenvoorde	01/04/1915	04/04/1915
War Diary	Moolenacker	05/04/1915	07/04/1915
War Diary	Oosthove Fm	08/04/1915	12/04/1915
War Diary	Billets 1 mile S. of Bailleul Station	13/04/1915	15/04/1915
War Diary	Nieppe	16/04/1915	17/04/1915
War Diary	Prowse Point Section	18/04/1915	19/04/1915
War Diary	Plugsteert	19/04/1915	23/04/1915
War Diary	Prowse Pt Section	24/04/1915	27/04/1915
War Diary	Romarin	27/04/1915	28/04/1915
War Diary	Plugsteert Wood	28/04/1915	30/04/1915
Heading	145th Inf. Bde. 48th Div. 1/4th Battn. The Oxfordshire & Buckinghamshire Light Infantry May 1915		
Heading	War Diary Of 1/4th Batt. Oxf. and Bucks Light Infantry From 1st May 1915 To 31st May 1915 (Volume)		
War Diary	Plugsteert Wood	01/05/1915	31/05/1915
Heading	145th Inf. Bde. 48th Div. 1/4th Battn. The Oxfordshire & Buckinghamshire Light Infantry June 1915		
Heading	War Diary Of 1/4th Battn. Oxfordshire & Buckinghamshire Light Infantry From 1 June 1915 To 30 June 1915 (Volume)		
War Diary	Pluegsteert Wood	01/06/1915	07/06/1915
War Diary	Pont De Nieppe	08/06/1915	11/06/1915
War Diary	Ash House	12/06/1915	15/06/1915
War Diary	White Lodge	16/06/1915	19/06/1915
War Diary	Hutments	20/06/1915	24/06/1915
War Diary	Bailleul	25/06/1915	25/06/1915
War Diary	Vieux Berquin	26/06/1915	26/06/1915
War Diary	Gonnehem	27/06/1915	27/06/1915
War Diary	Alouagne	28/06/1915	30/06/1915
Map	Map		
Heading	145th Inf. Bde. 48th Div. 1/4th Battn. The Oxfordshire & Buckinghamshire Light Infantry July 1915		

War Diary	Allouagne	01/07/1915	12/07/1915
War Diary	Noeux Les Mines	13/07/1915	16/07/1915
War Diary	Ames	17/07/1915	18/07/1915
War Diary	Terramesnil	19/07/1915	19/07/1915
War Diary	Coigneux	20/07/1915	20/07/1915
War Diary	Hebuterne	21/07/1915	31/07/1915
Heading	145th Inf. Bde. 48th Div. 1/4th Battn. The Oxfordshire & Buckinghamshire Light Infantry August 1915		
War Diary	Hebuterne	01/08/1915	05/08/1915
War Diary	Sailly	06/08/1915	13/08/1915
War Diary	Hebuterne Section J	14/08/1915	20/08/1915
War Diary	Hebuterne	21/08/1915	31/08/1915
Miscellaneous	Parade State (Fighting Strength)	31/08/1915	31/08/1915
Miscellaneous	Parade State (Fighting Strength)	21/08/1915	21/08/1915
Heading	145th Inf. Bde. 48th Div. 1/4th Battn. The Oxfordshire & Buckinghamshire Light Infantry September 1915		
Heading	War Diary Of 1/4th Battn. Oxf & Bucks Light Infantry From 1 Sept 1915 To 30 Sept 1915		
War Diary	Section G Hebuterne	01/09/1915	29/09/1915
War Diary	Courcelles	30/09/1915	30/09/1915
Miscellaneous	Parade State (Fighting Strength)	04/09/1916	04/09/1916
Miscellaneous	Other Officers On Strength		
Miscellaneous	Parade State (Fighting Strength)	11/09/1915	11/09/1915
Miscellaneous	Parade State (Fighting Strength)	18/09/1915	18/09/1915
Miscellaneous	Parade State (Fighting Strength)	25/09/1915	25/09/1915
Heading	145th Inf. Bde. 48th Div. 1/4th Battn. The Oxfordshire & Buckinghamshire Light Infantry October & November (1.10.15-1.12.15) 1915		
War Diary	Courcelles	01/10/1915	05/10/1915
War Diary	Sec Margin	08/10/1915	11/10/1915
War Diary	In The Trenches	12/10/1915	15/10/1915
War Diary	In The Trenches G. Section	16/10/1915	19/10/1915
War Diary	Courcelles	20/10/1915	27/10/1915
War Diary	G Section	28/10/1915	01/11/1915
War Diary	In The Trenches G Section Hebuterne	02/11/1915	04/11/1915
War Diary	Courcelles	05/11/1915	12/11/1915
War Diary	In The Trenches G. Section Hebuterne	13/11/1915	20/11/1915
War Diary	Courcelles	21/11/1915	28/11/1915
War Diary	In The Trenches G Section Hebuterne	29/11/1915	01/12/1915
Heading	War Diary Of 1/4th Batt Oxf & Bucks Lt Infy From 1/10/15 To 1/12/15		
Miscellaneous	Parade State (Fighting Strength)	27/11/1915	27/11/1915
Miscellaneous	Parade State (Fighting Strength)	02/10/1915	02/10/1915
Miscellaneous	Parade State (Fighting Strength)	09/10/1915	09/10/1915
Miscellaneous	Parade State (Fighting Strength)	16/10/1915	16/10/1915
Miscellaneous	Parade State (Fighting Strength)	20/11/1915	20/11/1915
Miscellaneous	Parade State (Fighting Strength)	13/11/1915	13/11/1915
Miscellaneous	Parade State (Fighting Strength)	06/11/1915	06/11/1915
Miscellaneous	Parade State (Fighting Strength)	30/10/1915	30/10/1915
Miscellaneous	Parade State (Fighting Strength)	23/10/1915	23/10/1915
Heading	145th Inf. Bde. 48th Div. 1/4th Battn. The Oxfordshire & Buckinghamshire Light Infantry December (2.12.15 To 31.12.15) 1915		
War Diary	In The Trenches G Section Hebuterne	02/12/1915	06/12/1915
War Diary	Billets Courcelles	07/12/1915	14/12/1915
War Diary	In The Trenches Hebuterne G Section	15/12/1915	22/12/1915

War Diary	Billets Courcelles	23/12/1915	28/12/1915
War Diary	In The Trenches Hebuterne G Section	29/12/1915	31/12/1915
Heading	War Diary Of 1/4th Battalion Oxfordshire and Buckinghamshire Light Infantry From 1st December 1915 To 31st December 1915 Volume IX		
Miscellaneous	Parade State (Fighting Strength)	18/12/1915	18/12/1915
Miscellaneous	Parade State (Fighting Strength)	11/12/1915	11/12/1915
Miscellaneous	Parade State (Fighting Strength)	25/12/1915	25/12/1915
Heading	145th Brigade 48th Division 1/4th Battalion Oxford & Bucks Light Infantry January 1916		
War Diary	In The Trenches Hebuterne G Section	01/01/1916	06/01/1916
War Diary	Courcelles	07/01/1916	08/01/1916
War Diary	Hebuterne	09/01/1916	15/01/1916
War Diary	Billets Courcelles	16/01/1916	21/01/1916
War Diary	In The Trenches K. Section Hebuterne	22/01/1916	27/01/1916
War Diary	Billets Courcelles	28/01/1916	31/01/1916
Miscellaneous	Parade State (Fighting Strength)	01/01/1916	01/01/1916
Miscellaneous	Parade State (Fighting Strength)	08/01/1916	08/01/1916
Miscellaneous	Parade State (Fighting Strength)	15/01/1916	15/01/1916
Miscellaneous	Parade State (Fighting Strength)	22/01/1916	22/01/1916
Miscellaneous	Parade State (Fighting Strength)	29/01/1916	29/01/1916
Heading	145th Brigade 48th Division 1/4th Battalion Oxford & Bucks Light Infantry February 1916		
War Diary	Billets Courcelles	01/02/1916	02/02/1916
War Diary	In The Trenches Hebuterne K Section	03/02/1916	15/02/1916
War Diary	In The Trenches Hebuterne Left Section	16/02/1916	17/02/1916
War Diary	In The Trenches Hebuterne K Section	18/02/1916	29/02/1916
Miscellaneous	Parade State	05/02/1916	05/02/1916
Miscellaneous	Parade State	13/02/1916	13/02/1916
Miscellaneous	Parade State	19/02/1916	19/02/1916
Miscellaneous	Parade State	26/02/1916	26/02/1916
Heading	145th Brigade 48th Division 1/4th Battalion Oxford & Bucks Light Infantry March 1916		
War Diary	In The Trenches Hebuterne K Section	01/03/1916	31/03/1916
Heading	145th Brigade 48th Division 1/4th Battalion Oxford & Bucks Light Infantry April 1916		
War Diary	In The Trenches Hebuterne K Section	01/04/1916	08/04/1916
War Diary	In Billets Bayencourt	08/04/1916	15/04/1916
War Diary	In Trenches Hebuterne K Section	16/04/1916	25/04/1916
War Diary	In Billets Bayencourt	26/04/1916	30/04/1916
Heading	145th Brigade 48th Division 1/4th Battalion Oxford & Bucks Light Infantry May 1916		
War Diary	Bayencourt In Billets	01/05/1916	01/05/1916
War Diary	Hebuterne In The Trenches G Section	02/05/1916	08/05/1916
War Diary	Couin (Huts)	08/05/1916	17/05/1916
War Diary	Beauval Billets	18/05/1916	30/05/1916
War Diary	Beauval To Oneux	31/05/1916	31/05/1916
Heading	145th Brigade 48th Division 1/4th Battalion Oxford & Bucks Light Infantry June 1916		
War Diary	Oneux In Billets	01/06/1916	03/06/1916
War Diary	Argenvillers in Billets	04/06/1916	09/06/1916
War Diary	March To Mezerolles (Billets)	10/06/1916	10/06/1916
War Diary	March To Couin (Bivouacs)	11/06/1916	11/06/1916
War Diary	Hebuterne Trenches G Section	12/06/1916	16/06/1916
War Diary	Bivouac W & Sailly	17/06/1916	21/06/1916
War Diary	Bivouacs between Couin and Coigneux	22/06/1916	26/06/1916

Type	Description	Start	End
War Diary	Bivouacs Between Couin & St Leger	27/06/1916	30/06/1916
Miscellaneous	Sports Programme	27/06/1916	27/06/1916
Heading	145th Inf. Bde. 48th Div War Diary 1/4th Battn. The Oxfordshire & Buckinghamshire Light Infantry July 1916		
Heading	War Diary Of The 1/4th Battalion Oxfordshire & Buckinghamshire Light Infantry (145th Infantry Brigade 48th Division) For The Month Of July 1916 Vol XVI		
War Diary	Bivouacs Between Couin St Leger	01/07/1916	01/07/1916
War Diary	Mailly-Maillet Bivouac	02/07/1916	02/07/1916
War Diary	Mesnil & Mailly	03/07/1916	03/07/1916
War Diary	Bivouacs Between Couin & St Leger	04/07/1916	04/07/1916
War Diary	In The Trenches Hebuterne G Section	05/07/1916	08/07/1916
War Diary	Bivouacs Between Sailly & Colqneux	09/07/1916	11/07/1916
War Diary	To Trenches Hebuterne G Section	12/07/1916	16/07/1916
War Diary	Bivouacs Between Couin & St Leger	17/07/1916	17/07/1916
War Diary	Huts Bouzincourt	18/07/1916	18/07/1916
War Diary	Between Ovillers & Pozieres	19/07/1916	19/07/1916
War Diary	Bouzincourt Huts	20/07/1916	20/07/1916
War Diary	Bivouacs 1/4 Mile NE Of Albert	21/07/1916	21/07/1916
War Diary	Bivouac Outside Albert	22/07/1916	22/07/1916
War Diary	In Action Front W Of Pozieres	23/07/1916	23/07/1916
War Diary	Bivouacs Outside Albert	24/07/1916	24/07/1916
War Diary	Huts Bouzincourt	25/07/1916	26/07/1916
War Diary	Billets Arqueves	27/07/1916	28/07/1916
War Diary	Billets Beauval	29/07/1916	29/07/1916
War Diary	Billets Aqenville	30/07/1916	31/07/1916
Heading	Appendices To Vol XVI (July 1916) Of War Diary Of 1/4 Batt Oxf & Bucks Infantry		
Miscellaneous			
Operation(al) Order(s)	145th Infantry Brigade Order No. 22	02/07/1916	02/07/1916
Miscellaneous	Extracts From 145th Infantry Brigade 1093	10/07/1916	10/07/1916
Map	Map		
Operation(al) Order(s)	145th Infantry Brigade Order No. 98	18/07/1916	18/07/1916
Miscellaneous	Report On Operation	19/07/1916	19/07/1916
Operation(al) Order(s)	145th Infantry Brigade Order No. 100	20/07/1916	20/07/1916
Miscellaneous	To:- Oxfords	20/07/1916	20/07/1916
Miscellaneous	48th Division G.X.1363	22/07/1916	22/07/1916
Operation(al) Order(s)	145th Inf. Bde. Order No. 101	23/07/1916	23/07/1916
Miscellaneous	Account Of Attack	23/07/1916	23/07/1916
Map	Map		
Miscellaneous	Formation In Attacks	23/07/1916	23/07/1916
Heading	145th Brigade 48th Division 1/4th Battalion Oxford & Buckinghamshire Light Infantry August 1916		
Miscellaneous	Headquarters 145 Infantry Brigade	01/09/1916	01/09/1916
War Diary	Aqenville In Billets	01/08/1916	09/08/1916
War Diary	Beauval Billets	10/08/1916	10/08/1916
War Diary	Varennes Billets	11/08/1916	11/08/1916
War Diary	Bivouac 1/2 Mile W Of Bouzincourt	12/08/1916	12/08/1916
War Diary	In The Line NE Of Ovillers	13/08/1916	14/08/1916
War Diary	Bivouacs Albert Bouzincourt Line	15/08/1916	16/08/1916
War Diary	In The Line NE Of Ovillers	16/08/1916	18/08/1916
War Diary	Usna Redoubt	19/08/1916	19/08/1916
War Diary	Albert Bouzincourt Line	19/08/1916	19/08/1916
War Diary	Bouzincourt	19/08/1916	19/08/1916
War Diary	Billet Bouzincourt	20/08/1916	21/08/1916

War Diary	Neighbourhood Of Usna Redoubt		22/08/1916	22/08/1916
War Diary	In The Line N Of Ovillers		23/08/1916	26/08/1916
War Diary	Ribble Street		27/08/1916	28/08/1916
War Diary	Bivouacs W Of Bouzincourt		28/08/1916	29/08/1916
War Diary	Huts In Bus Wood		29/08/1916	31/08/1916
Miscellaneous	Report Of Operation August 11th To 28th 1916		29/08/1916	29/08/1916
Map	Map			
Miscellaneous	Appendix II To Vol XVII War Diary 1/4th Oxford And Bucks Lt. Infantry			
Map	Map			
Miscellaneous	Military Cross			
Miscellaneous	Military Medals			
Heading	145th Brigade 48th Division 1/4th Battalion Oxford & Bucks Light Infantry September 1916			
War Diary	Huts Bus Wood		01/09/1916	05/09/1916
War Diary	In The Trenches E. Of Auchonvillers		05/09/1916	08/09/1916
War Diary	Billets Bus		09/09/1916	11/09/1916
War Diary	Billets Beauval		12/09/1916	18/09/1916
War Diary	Billets Fienvillers		19/09/1916	29/09/1916
War Diary	Billets Warluzel		30/09/1916	30/09/1916
Map	Map			
Heading	145th Brigade 48th Division 1/4th Battalion Oxford & Bucks Light Infantry October 1916			
War Diary	In Billets Warluzel		01/10/1916	01/10/1916
War Diary	Huts At Warlincourt		02/10/1916	05/10/1916
War Diary	Warlincourt		06/10/1916	14/10/1916
War Diary	Billets At Huts		15/10/1916	15/10/1916
War Diary	Warlincourt		16/10/1916	19/10/1916
War Diary	Billets Warluzel		20/10/1916	22/10/1916
War Diary	Billets Beauval		23/10/1916	23/10/1916
War Diary	Billets Talmas		24/10/1916	24/10/1916
War Diary	In Billets Lahoussoye		25/10/1916	31/10/1916
Heading	145th Infantry Brigade 48th Division 1/4th Battalion Oxford & Bucks Light Infantry November 1916			
War Diary	Millencourt		31/10/1916	01/11/1916
War Diary	Bivouacs Between Fricourt & Contalmaison		02/11/1916	02/11/1916
War Diary	Support Trenches Between Le Sars & Martin Puich		02/11/1916	05/11/1916
War Diary	Front Line In Front Of Le Sars		05/11/1916	07/11/1916
War Diary	Support Trenches Between Le Sars & Martin Puich		07/11/1916	07/11/1916
War Diary	Martin Puich		08/11/1916	10/11/1916
War Diary	Bazentin-Le-Petit Wood		11/11/1916	15/11/1916
War Diary	In Support Martin Puich		16/11/1916	18/11/1916
War Diary	Front Line Infront Of Le Sars		18/11/1916	21/11/1916
War Diary	Peake Wood Central Camp		21/11/1916	25/11/1916
War Diary	Front Line In Front Of Le Sars (Left Sector)		26/11/1916	30/11/1916
War Diary	Scots Redoubt Camp South		30/11/1916	30/11/1916
Map	Trench Map			
Map	Map			
Heading	145th Brigade 48th Division 1/4th Battalion Oxford & Bucks Light Infantry December 1916			
War Diary	Scotts Redoubt		01/12/1916	04/12/1916
War Diary	Middle Wood Camp		05/12/1916	08/12/1916
War Diary	Shelter Wood Camp North		09/12/1916	11/12/1916
War Diary	Front Line In Front Of Le Sars (Left Sector)		12/12/1916	12/12/1916
War Diary	Front Line In Front Of Le Sars		13/12/1916	13/12/1916
War Diary	Scotts Redoubt South		14/12/1916	14/12/1916

War Diary	D Camp Becourt	15/12/1916	27/12/1916
War Diary	Camp At Bresle	28/12/1916	31/12/1916
Heading	War Diary Of The 1/4th Battn. Oxfordshire & Buckinghamshire Light Infantry (145th Inf Bde 48th Div) For January 1917		
War Diary	Camp At Bresle	01/01/1917	09/01/1917
War Diary	Cerisy-Buleux Billets	10/01/1917	27/01/1917
War Diary	Cerisy-Buleux	28/01/1917	29/01/1917
War Diary	Hamel	30/01/1917	31/01/1917
Heading	War Diary Of The 1/4th Battn Oxfordshire & Buckinghamshire Light Infantry (145 Inf Bde 48th Div) For February 1917		
War Diary	Hamel Huts	01/02/1917	03/02/1917
War Diary	Marly Camp Huts	04/02/1917	07/02/1917
War Diary	Sophie Trench Herbecourt	08/02/1917	09/02/1917
War Diary	Front Line Opposite La Maisonnette	09/02/1917	13/02/1917
War Diary	Brigade Support 1500X E Of Flaucourt	14/02/1917	16/02/1917
War Diary	Brigade Support E. Of Flaucourt	17/02/1917	17/02/1917
War Diary	Camp 56 Cappy	18/02/1917	24/02/1917
War Diary	Brigade Support ? E of ?court	25/02/1917	25/02/1917
War Diary	Front Line Opposite La Maisonnette	25/02/1917	27/02/1917
War Diary	Brigade Reserve Sophie Trench Herbecourt	28/02/1917	28/02/1917
Heading	War Diary Of 1/4th Oxfordshire & Buckinghamshire L.I. From 1st March To 31st March 1917 Vol 24		
Heading	War Diary Of The 1/4 Batt Oxfordshire & Buckinghamshire Light Infantry (145 Inf Bde 48th Div) For March 1917 Vol XXIII		
War Diary	Brigade Reserve Sophie Trench Herbecourt	01/03/1917	01/03/1917
War Diary	Front Line Opposite La Maisonnette	02/03/1917	03/03/1917
War Diary	Sophie Tr. Herbecourt	04/03/1917	06/03/1917
War Diary	Marly Camp Huts	07/03/1917	07/03/1917
War Diary	Sophie Tr. Herbecourt	08/03/1917	11/03/1917
War Diary	Front Line Opposite La Maisonnette	12/03/1917	13/03/1917
War Diary	Camp 56 Cappy	14/03/1917	20/03/1917
War Diary	Peronne	20/03/1917	21/03/1917
War Diary	Cartigny	22/03/1917	25/03/1917
War Diary	Tincourt	25/03/1917	26/03/1917
War Diary	Hamel	26/03/1917	27/03/1917
War Diary	Tincourt	27/03/1917	29/03/1917
War Diary	Marquaix	29/03/1917	31/03/1917
Map	Map		
War Diary		16/03/1917	16/03/1917
War Diary	Roisel	26/03/1917	26/03/1917
Miscellaneous	Active Operations Of 1/4 Inf & Bucks Lt		
Heading	War Diary Of The 1/4 Bn Oxfordshire & Buckinghamshire Light Inf (145 Inf Bde-48th Div) For April 1917 XXIV		
War Diary	Marquaix	01/04/1917	02/04/1917
War Diary	Villers Faucon	03/04/1917	06/04/1917
War Diary	Camp K 5	07/04/1917	13/04/1917
War Diary	Outpost Line In Front Of Ronssoy	14/04/1917	15/04/1917
War Diary	Camp S To Emilie	16/04/1917	17/04/1917
War Diary	Outpost Line In Front Of Ronssoy	18/04/1917	19/04/1917
War Diary	Hamel	20/04/1917	25/04/1917
War Diary	In Support Positions About F.27	26/04/1917	27/04/1917
War Diary	In Outpost Line About Gillemont Farm	28/04/1917	30/04/1917

Heading	War Diary Of The 1/4 Bn Oxfordshire And Buckinghamshire Light Infty (145th Inf Bde-48th Div) For May 1917 XXV		
War Diary	Hamel	01/05/1917	01/05/1917
War Diary	Camp At Doingt	02/05/1917	11/05/1917
War Diary	Combles Area	12/05/1917	12/05/1917
War Diary	Beaulencourt	13/05/1917	14/05/1917
War Diary	Support Position About Hermies	14/05/1917	18/05/1917
War Diary	Outpost Line N.E. Of Hermies	19/05/1917	25/05/1917
War Diary	Beaumetz	25/05/1917	31/05/1917
Map	France		
Miscellaneous	Glossary		
Heading	War Diary Of The 1/4 Bn Oxfordshire & Buckinghamshire Light Infty (145 Inf Bde-48th Div) For June 1917 XXVI		
War Diary	Outpost Line East Of Demicourt	01/06/1917	03/06/1917
War Diary	Camp In Velu Wood	04/06/1917	05/06/1917
War Diary	Camp At O.6.b.9.9	06/06/1917	08/06/1917
War Diary	Outpost Line East Of Demicourt	09/06/1917	15/06/1917
War Diary	J.20.c.8.7	16/06/1917	21/06/1917
War Diary	Outpost Line NE Of Demicourt	22/06/1917	27/06/1917
War Diary	Camp O 6b	28/06/1917	30/06/1917
Miscellaneous	1/4th Batt Oxf & Bucks Lt Infantry Operation Order No. 104	12/06/1917	12/06/1917
Heading	War Diary Of 1/4th Bn Oxfordshire & Buckinghamshire Light Infty Volume XXVII From 1st July 1917 To 31st July 1917		
War Diary	Outpost Line N.E. Of Demicourt	01/07/1917	03/07/1917
War Diary	Bihucourt	04/07/1917	05/07/1917
War Diary	Bailleulmont	06/07/1917	22/07/1917
War Diary	Houterque	22/07/1917	30/07/1917
War Diary	Camp 3/4 Mile W Of St Jan Ter Biezen	30/07/1917	31/07/1917
Heading	War Diary Of The 1/4 Bn Oxfordshire & Buckinghamshire Lt. Infy (145 Inf. Bde-48 Div) August 1917 XXVII		
War Diary	Camp Y St. Jan Ter Biezen	01/08/1917	04/08/1917
War Diary	Dambre Camp	04/08/1917	05/08/1917
War Diary	Steenbeek Kitcheners Wood	05/08/1917	07/08/1917
War Diary	O.G.1	08/08/1917	08/08/1917
War Diary	Dambre Camp	08/08/1917	15/08/1917
War Diary	Alberta Farm	15/08/1917	15/08/1917
War Diary	Steenbeek	16/08/1917	16/08/1917
War Diary	Mon Du Hibou	16/08/1917	17/08/1917
War Diary	Dambre Camp	18/08/1917	26/08/1917
War Diary	Canal D'Yser	26/08/1917	27/08/1917
War Diary	The Triangle	27/08/1917	27/08/1917
War Diary	Spring Field	27/08/1917	28/08/1917
War Diary	Vancouver	28/08/1917	29/08/1917
War Diary	Dambre Camp	29/08/1917	29/08/1917
War Diary	Road Camp	30/08/1917	30/08/1917
War Diary	St. Jans Ter Biezen	30/08/1917	31/08/1917
Heading	War Diary 1/4th Bn. Oxford & Bucks Lt. Infty September 1917 Vol XXX		
War Diary	Road Camp	01/09/1917	01/09/1917
War Diary	St. Jans Ter Biezen	02/09/1917	07/09/1917
War Diary	Road Camp	08/09/1917	16/09/1917

War Diary	Bonningues	16/09/1917	22/09/1917
War Diary	Licques	23/09/1917	23/09/1917
War Diary	Estmont Ouestmont	24/09/1917	25/09/1917
War Diary	Reigersburg	25/09/1917	26/09/1917
War Diary	St. Julien Front Mon Du Hibou	27/09/1917	28/09/1917
War Diary	Hubnerquebec Farm Bavaroise House	28/09/1917	29/09/1917
War Diary	The Triangle Forward or East rear Or West	30/09/1917	30/09/1917
War Diary	Cheddar Villa	30/09/1917	30/09/1917
Heading	1/4 Bn Oxfordshire & Buckinghamshire Light Infantry October 1917		
War Diary	Cheddar Villa	01/10/1917	02/10/1917
War Diary	Reigersburg Camp	02/10/1917	04/10/1917
War Diary	Cheddar Villa	04/10/1917	04/10/1917
War Diary	Arbre	04/10/1917	04/10/1917
War Diary	Cheddar Villa	05/10/1917	08/10/1917
War Diary	Dambre Camp	08/10/1917	11/10/1917
War Diary	Road Camp	12/10/1917	14/10/1917
War Diary	Ligny St. Flochel	15/10/1917	15/10/1917
War Diary	Caucourt	15/10/1917	18/10/1917
War Diary	Villers-Au-Bois	18/10/1917	31/10/1917

1/4 Batt
Ox ʌ Bucks
Light Infantry

April 1915 — Oct 1917

48TH DIVISION
145TH INFY BDE

1-4TH BN OXF & BUCKS LT INFY.
APR 1915-~~JAN 1919~~

1917 OCT

TO ITALY

145th Inf.Bde.
48th Div.

Battn. disembarked
Boulogne from
England 30.3.15.

1/4th BATTN. THE OXFORDSHIRE & BUCKINGHAMSHIRE
LIGHT INFANTRY.

M A R C H

(27.3.15 to 3.4.15)

1 9 1 5

Jan '19

Confidential

War Diary

of

1/4th Batt. Oxford. & Bucks. Light Infantry

from 27th March, 1915 to 31st March, 1915.

Army Form C. 2118.

WAR DIARY
or
INTELLIGENCE SUMMARY
(Erase heading not required.)

Instructions regarding War Diaries and Intelligence Summaries are contained in F. S. Regs., Part II. and the Staff Manual respectively. Title pages will be prepared in manuscript.

Hour, Date, Place	Summary of Events and Information	Remarks and references to Appendices
March 27th WRITTLE	Orders received BM S/2. that Transport 2 officers 84 other ranks to entrain for Embarkation at 6.35 a.m. March 28th. Orders received S.M.D No M/88(A) The Battalion would entrain at CHELMSFORD in two detachments, first at 6.35 p.m. Second at 7.5 p.m. March 29th for Embarkation	
March 28th WRITTLE	Transport paraded at 3.45 A.M. under Lt. Irving and entrained at CHELMSFORD at 6.35 A.M.	
March 29th WRITTLE	Batt. entrained as above Embarked on S.S ONWARD at Folkestone disembarked at BOULOGNE, went into Rest Camp - Marched to PONT de BRIQUES Station at 11/15 entrained for ST OMER 13.15 detrained. Transport was at same train Marched CASSEL 18.50. STEENVOORD 6½ JCB Billeted in Farms.	
April 2nd STEENVOORD	Batt. was part of Brigade inspected by Sir HORACE SMITH DORRIEN.	
April 3rd STEENVOORD	Orders received that the Brigade would move tomorrow Sunday 4th inst in vicinity of FLÊTRE and MERRIS. Two Supply waggons two Bris. war 4 horses, 2 waggon mess 1 Cuplant mess transferred to divisional train	

1247 W 3299 200,000 (E) 8/14 J.B.C. & A. Forms/C. 2118/11.

P.H. Whalley Lt. Col. Comg. H. Bn. Bucks R. Regt.

145th Inf.Bde.
48th Div.

**1/4th BATTN. THE OXFORDSHIRE & BUCKINGHAMSHIRE
LIGHT INFANTRY.**

A P R I L

1 9 1 5

Confidential

War Diary
of
1/4 Battalion. Oxfordshire & Buckinghamshire
Light Infantry

From 1st April 1915 To 30th April 1915

(Volume   )

Army Form C. 2118.

WAR DIARY
or
INTELLIGENCE SUMMARY

(Erase heading not required.)

Instructions regarding War Diaries and Intelligence Summaries are contained in F. S. Regs., Part II. and the Staff Manual respectively. Title pages will be prepared in manuscript.

Hour, Date, Place	Summary of Events and Information	Remarks and references to Appendices

1247 W 3299 200,000 (E) 8/14 J.B.C. & A. Forms/C. 2118/11.

Army Form C. 2118.

WAR DIARY
or
INTELLIGENCE SUMMARY

(Erase heading not required.)

Instructions regarding War Diaries and Intelligence Summaries are contained in F.S. Regs., Part II. and the Staff Manual respectively. Title pages will be prepared in manuscript.

Hour, Date, Place	Summary of Events and Information	Remarks and references to Appendices
April 1st STEENVOORDE.	Fine. Companies on outpost of Courtmans Farm and their Sen.	
	Musketry and Bayonet fighting.	JnB
April 2nd	Bath on part of Brigade witnessed by Sir H. SMITH	JnB
	DORRIEN	
April 3rd	Orders received that the Brigade would move Sunday April 4th	
	Letter in the vicinity of FLÊTRE and MERRIS.	
	70 Supply wagons with horses and Drivers 2 beggars have arrived	
	attached to A.S.C. S.M.D. Train.	
	Fine all day but bright.	JnB

WAR DIARY
or
INTELLIGENCE SUMMARY

(Erase heading not required.)

Army Form C. 2118.

Instructions regarding War Diaries and Intelligence Summaries are contained in F.S. Regs., Part II. and the Staff Manual respectively. Title pages will be prepared in manuscript.

Hour, Date, Place	Summary of Events and Information	Remarks and references to Appendices
April 4th STEENVOORDE	Marched off at 1.40 p.m. followed by 5th Gloucesters via EECKE CAESTRE. FLETRE and billeted in farms beyond MOOLENACKER. Distance 8 miles, arrived about 4.45 p.m. Received Brigade instructions as to Billeting and other how to to be noted.	JaB
April 5th MOOLENACKER	Wet morning — and became worse — Inspection and marching in ground.	JaB
April 6th	Orders received the Brigade would move tomorrow and billet East of BAILLEUL. Fine morning. Company training. Continued having 2nd Reserve Machine Gun Section and sample fusebun.	JaB
April 7th "	Fine morning. Showground. Pte 2733 Pte WEST and 2736 Pte TURNER attached to H.L. SMD. in duty. Paraded at 2 p.m. from a Brigade column march the to heat of BAILLEUL marched via BAILLEUL to Parish of MOEPPEWAL hidden our men by Staff. Coy 11th Bgde Brigade and to BLUG at OOSTHOVE FARM sheet 36. Sheet B BELGIUM. FRANCE Batts all Battalion Hdqrs march booms	JaB

WAR DIARY or INTELLIGENCE SUMMARY

Army Form C. 2118.

Hour, Date, Place	Summary of Events and Information	Remarks and references to Appendices
April 7th (continued)	Stormy and cold. Got out into the trench by 7 p.m.	
	The Battalion is to be attached to Rifle Brigade and London Rifle Brigade for instruction in trench work	
	RIFLE BRIGADE for instruction in trench work	
	Officers & each section Commander and each platoon for instructions for	
	work for next 4 days	J.W.B.
April 8th OOSTHOVE FM	Squally and windy showers with the new sun.	
	A Coy in support in PLOEGSTEERT WOOD at 8.15 a.m	
	Remaining Companies being instructed in the present	
	A Coy went into trenches attached to East LANCASHIRE Regt.	
	D Coy. night work in PLOEGSTEERT WOOD. M.G. Section went into trenches also	
	A few shells fell near the Battalion Billets.	
	Became fine and cold. No important action occurred.	J.W.B
April 9th OOSTHOVE F.M	Fine morning. Nothing happened during the night.	

Army Form C. 2118.

WAR DIARY
or
INTELLIGENCE SUMMARY

(Erase heading not required.)

Instructions regarding War Diaries and Intelligence Summaries are contained in F. S. Regs., Part II. and the Staff Manual respectively. Title pages will be prepared in manuscript.

Hour, Date, Place	Summary of Events and Information	Remarks and references to Appendices
April 9th continued	B Coy afternoon tactics in the wood. Paraded at 11.45 a.m. Church Pde	
	Very heavy rain. A thunder storm. Church up.	
April 10th OOSTHOVE Fm	B Coy delivered A Coy in trenches	
	Instruction continued. C & D Coys went into trenches & D 10 R	
	with the LONDON RIFLE BRIGADE. Few casualties	
	Other Coys with a few shells about 500 yards away.	V.B.
April 11th "	Instruction continued. Orders received that the Regiment would	No 2610 Pte J.H.R. WHITE
		killed.
	move tomorrow. Very fine day. Several aeroplanes over.	J.A.B
	1 man C Coy killed by Sniper.	
April 12th " OOSTHOVE Fm	Paraded at 8.45 a.m. & marched to field below Brigade Starting Point	
	T of RABOT. Marched via STEENWERCKE Station and STEENWERCKE	

Army Form C. 2118.

WAR DIARY
or
INTELLIGENCE SUMMARY

(Erase heading not required.)

Instructions regarding War Diaries and Intelligence Summaries are contained in F. S. Regs., Part II. and the Staff Manual respectively. Title pages will be prepared in manuscript.

Hour, Date, Place	Summary of Events and Information	Remarks and references to Appendices
April 12th (Unfinished)	5.45 Found own beats 1km S of BAILLEUL Station.	7 men sent home b/fast up communication with own units Sgt Robson Cpl Prior with Cpl Palmer Pte Bacon Dickinson Bayley and McVeagh
	Later h/n march. Battalion company altogether. Fine …	
April 13th Billet 14 pm	Company in two Company Companies two Officers per	No 2882 Pte White D Coy Hospital gun-shot hand.
S of BAILLEUL Station	Company had two Sergeants … Ration but to instructed …	
	On board the march Col Padden not one cut both	
	Wiltshires to B Coy. for Bitumen than them	
	Fine not town	AR
April 14th	Not present … not … in the — Carpenters in the	
	Company Commanders Wiltshires … Boots throwing Corporal	
	Adm hunted this Bugle bold Yate the tucker of	

1247 W 3299 200,000 (E) 8/14 J.B.C. & A. Forms/C. 2118/II.

WAR DIARY
or
INTELLIGENCE SUMMARY

(Erase heading not required.)

Army Form C. 2118.

Hour, Date, Place	Summary of Events and Information	Remarks and references to Appendices
April 14 (continued)	11th Infy. Brigade. The battalion to be in Reserve at NIEPPE and to be there at 5 p.m.	
April 15th	Marched via STEENWERCKE to NIEPPE and billeted in that place	J.A.B.
	and PONT de NIEPPE. Transport near ROMARIN. Fine	J.S.L.
April 16. NIEPPE	Majors OVEY and J. Officer and 2 N.C.Os per Company	
	attached to ARGYLL and SUTHERLAND HIGHLANDERS	Capt. Hatton and 3 men to hospital
	to get acquainted with trenches and cut in gullies	
April 17. NIEPPE	Marched to ROMARIN arrived at 10.30 a.m. Marched on	
	to PIGGERY. T 24 d. shes 28. Two Platoons at 6 p.m.	
	took trench held by 5th Gloucester A & B Companies at 7.30 p.m.	One man to hospital

WAR DIARY
or
INTELLIGENCE SUMMARY

(Erase heading not required.)

Army Form C. 2118.

Instructions regarding War Diaries and Intelligence Summaries are contained in F. S. Regs., Part II. and the Staff Manual respectively. Title pages will be prepared in manuscript.

Hour, Date, Place	Summary of Events and Information	Remarks and references to Appendices
April 17th Caestre	Left HYDE PARK Corner and took over trenches T.7. ARGYLL and SUTHERLAND HIGHLANDERS on left of 5th Gloucesters. The left section of S.M.I.B. The G.O.C. S.M.D. Resumes command of Division at 12 M.N. The Division holding line from RIVER WARNAVE to MESSINES – WULVERGHEM road – The GLOUCESTER & WORCESTER Brigade right sector. S.M.I.B. Centre sector – WARWICK Brigade left sector. The trenches were taken over by 9.17 p.m.	
April 18th PROWSE POINT Section	The Battalion took over 2 machine guns from Royal BERKS. The section held by the Battalion was the PROWSE corner section. Artillery activity down towards the unknown world. Be believed by Royal Berks tomorrow and take up Support line being held by Bucks Battalion. With some improved communication trenches and making more dug outs & other shelters. Fine but warm.	1 man to Hospital

1247 W 3299 200,000 (E) 8/14 J.B.C. & A. Forms/C. 2118/11.

Army Form C. 2118.

Instructions regarding War Diaries and Intelligence Summaries are contained in F. S. Regs., Part II. and the Staff Manual respectively. Title pages will be prepared in manuscript.

WAR DIARY
or
INTELLIGENCE SUMMARY

(Erase heading not required.)

Hour, Date, Place	Summary of Events and Information	Remarks and references to Appendices
April 19 PLOWE Pt Sector PLUGSTEERT	Relieving 1 Hant with return Moving by ½ to half bright	No 3222 Pr Scott wounded
	Relieved by 1st ROYAL BERKS. Battalion moved to	
	Support and 2 Companies to huts at HUNTERSTON, 2 Companies in PLUGSTEERT. No casualties on marches where it	
	at about 3.30 A.M. heavy rifle fire and shrapnel fire at	
	night.	J.B.
April 20th PLUGSTEERT	Battalion at fatigues from 8 A.m. and whole Battalion	2 men strapped
	at night. Warm and fine.	Capt Hadden returned
April 21st "	Finding fatigues by day on Second line, by night on first line	Jd B.
April 22nd "	do same.	J.B.
April 23rd "	The Regt relieved 1st Roy BERKS in PROWSE POINT SECTION of trenches. B Coy OXFORD Trench. D Coy ARMAGH and SUTHERLAND Trenches, HQ. RENFORDS Farm of (C.O.)	J.B.

I247 W 3299 200,000 (E) 8/14 J.B.C. & A. Forms/C. 2118/11.

WAR DIARY
or
INTELLIGENCE SUMMARY

(Erase heading not required.)

Army Form C. 2118.

Hour, Date, Place	Summary of Events and Information	Remarks and references to Appendices
	In BERKSHIRE trench 2/Lt CRABBE's Platoon & C Coy in support in PARK AVENUE Dug out. A Coy and Head Quarters at DISTILLERY & Platoons C Coy GRANDE MUNIQUE FARM. Nothing to report. Very much mud and dirt.	JwB.
April 21st PROWSE Pt Section	All quiet. Went round relieving parties. Lt L. EDMUNDS Platoon took over trenches and then relief front S of PROWSE Pt from GLOSTER Regt. We took over whole Platoon beneath with BERKSHIRE Trench. Arrangements met with Lt Col F.W. SCHOFIELD and been informed O.C. No 8 Infantry Dept at HAVRE Major R.L. OVEY assumed Command of Battalion.	
April 22 PROWSE Pt SECTION	Lt Col SCHOFIELD left. All quiet. The section has been extended on the RIGHT and Un Platoon C Coy took over New Trench known as GROUSE BUTT. Nothing to report	

WAR DIARY
or
INTELLIGENCE SUMMARY

(Erase heading not required.)

Army Form C. 2118.

Instructions regarding War Diaries and Intelligence Summaries are contained in F. S. Regs., Part II. and the Staff Manual respectively. Title pages will be prepared in manuscript.

Hour, Date, Place	Summary of Events and Information	Remarks and references to Appendices
April 26th PROWSE Pt Section	A prisoner taken reported that enemy trenches have been relieved by fresh troops. Nothing to report.	JMB
April 27th PROWSE Pt Section	Bat'n relieved by Royal Berks and moved to ROMARIN	
	1 billet and into Companies & Lunches. Quiet day.	Nos 9107 Pt STRONG killed
ROMARIN	9 p.m. "A" "C" men B Coy went to OXFORD TRENCH	
	Remainder remained in ROMARIN. "A" Coy was held by M Burgess had been out on fatigues are returning & fatigues were held by	
	8" WORCESTER REGT from billets of BULLS Bat to GERMAN farm. "A" & "C" Coys were holding the line. One Company of	
	HUNTERSTON SOUTH and one Company in PLOGSTEERT	AB
	A & C Coys. Head Quarter RIFLE HOUSE. D Coy in	
April 28 ROMARIN	Bat'n left their position in reserve in LA HUTTE	
DUMMERT	Hut at HUNTERSTON SOUTH. B Coy in PLOGSTEERT. huts at HUNTERSTON	

WAR DIARY
or
INTELLIGENCE SUMMARY

Army Form C. 2118.

Hour, Date, Place	Summary of Events and Information	Remarks and references to Appendices
April 28 (Continued)	No BRUNOS seen. War thus divided into 3 Sections. Right Section BIRDCAGE Section. Centre Section ST YVES Section. Left Section PRONE R.E. Section. Very hot day — men very tired.	
April 29 PLUGSTEERTWOOD	Artillery & sniped 2 men wounded one by rifle R.E. men from a house near C/R. The uniform a sort of horse shoe. Vide MAP 26 I.	M 1777 - R.E. at POINT no 1441 see WATSON report. See MAP I PLOEGSTEERT WOOD.
April 30	Signed many spies about. So felt how. Boot Maurice no damage done — nothing seen during night.	

R L Oven Major
Comdg 1st Bat. R. Innisk Dragoons

145th Inf.Bde.
48th Div.

1/4th BATT. THE OXFORDSHIRE & BUCKINGHAMSHIRE
LIGHT INFANTRY.

M A Y

1 9 1 5

CONFIDENTIAL.

War Diary
of
1/4th Batt. Oxf. and Bucks. Light. Infantry.

from 1st May 1915.   To. 31st May 1915.

(Volume)

Army Form C. 2118.

WAR DIARY
or
INTELLIGENCE SUMMARY

(Erase heading not required.)

Instructions regarding War Diaries and Intelligence Summaries are contained in F. S. Regs., Part II. and the Staff Manual respectively. Title pages will be prepared in manuscript.

Hour, Date, Place	Summary of Events and Information	Remarks and references to Appendices

1247 W 3299 200,000 (E) 8/14 J.B.C. & A. Forms/C. 2118/11.

Army Form C. 2118.

WAR DIARY
or
INTELLIGENCE SUMMARY

(Erase heading not required.)

Instructions regarding War Diaries and Intelligence Summaries are contained in F.S. Regs, Part II. and the Staff Manual respectively. Title pages will be prepared in manuscript.

Hour, Date, Place	Summary of Events and Information	Remarks and references to Appendices
May 15th PLUGSTREET WOOD 2.50 p.m.	Very little fine day. It seems that the ESSEX Officer was injured about 2 am sent to see if their sentries posts were correct and in their excitement that a D of Officer was in a car which he to help the fire but stopped it shortly when they were firing. Shots today had not been fired to... about 66 shots came up & the wood which turned my men to RIFLE PROOF information received that Captain DUG-OUT overhead apertures Examiner in tacking Exewater Area. Sail their no Officer very quiet day. About 6.70 h slept sent Hood Lieutenant from our Coy to see were N.C.O. arrive & born in the Provost Marshall in... I dug out sent 2 Corporals on Report centre to have 2 men Brandenlers. B and D Coys relieved A & C. Coys in headquarters. A lot of shooting going on all night on both sides	
May 5th "	Fine but colder - very quiet day. Informer received 2 civilians of Army were sent forward. WARNETON. The two... in Bizet ordered to occupy the tell... in a motor.	

WAR DIARY
or
INTELLIGENCE SUMMARY

(Erase heading not required.)

Army Form C. 2118.

Instructions regarding War Diaries and Intelligence Summaries are contained in F. S. Regs., Part II. and the Staff Manual respectively. Title pages will be prepared in manuscript.

Hour, Date, Place	Summary of Events and Information	Remarks and references to Appendices
May 3rd (Continued)	A quiet day try to the Station. A quieter night though NB	NB
May 4. PLUGSTREET WOOD.	A quiet day. Wood was visited by few who were in. Enemy increased the accuracy of their flight. Shell were received in the evening when a return was made. Trench Mortar from St Yvon VAB.	Lt G.L. Rees returned for duty from 5 weeks permission.
May 5th. PLUGSTEERT WOOD	Wet morning. Very pit. Few th. Messines 7.03, ?? and Rifle Grenades from 7035. Few th. morning replied in 7A. Stock Bombs and Rifle Grenades sent to Little b'thrs. 8a men in 8a to normal. Relief was in by normal day as the enemy relief. Others were in duties were experienced in part of Australia ?? Equipment. ?? A + C 1015 relieved B + D in the trenches. B + C PLUG ST	Wright Kelly wounded by shrapnel & Rifle Grenade.
May 6th	D to HUNTERSTON SOUTH. Normal day. a few shells round RIFLE HOUSE. Band 9 toys on fatigue in the morning - very close and sultry. A nice form of ?? ??.	No 4320 Corp. Timms wounded in the leg.
May 7th	Very close and stuffy. a normal day in the trenches.	
May 8th	Cooler. Other items at H.P.Q. Plug Street ?? ?? ?? ?? ?? ?? ?? a Abnormal day.	No 273 Lspr Dawson killed in ?? ?? No 2580 Pte Looking ?? ??

Army Form C. 2118.

WAR DIARY
or
INTELLIGENCE SUMMARY

(Erase heading not required.)

Instructions regarding War Diaries and Intelligence Summaries are contained in F. S. Regs., Part II. and the Staff Manual respectively. Title pages will be prepared in manuscript.

Hour, Date, Place	Summary of Events and Information	Remarks and references to Appendices
May 9th PLUGSTEERT WOOD	A quiet night – nothing to report in morning except— A first rumour in all gun fire – will return to be taken by Pattison Ave. Two machine guns put out of action in the bank in square U.23 a.o. U.23 a.o. U.16. U.17 also burst of rifle sought to bear on this square.	
8 a.m.	Rapid rifle grenade and mortar fire accompanied by bursts of rifle and Machine Gun fire opened—	
9.15	Other received that in addition to above 3 more bursts of Infantry will Machine gun fire were to bear on the LA DOUVE VILLE — PONT ROUGE road and bridge over river LYS.	
10.30	3 minutes burst of rapid infantry fire. Enemy replied with rifle grenades 2 men A Co. wounded. Mud shower often covered	
11.30	Artillery opened slow fire all along the Divisional line	
1 pm	Machine Gun fire on enemy's dugout and communication trenches.	No 1811 Pte Partridge killed No 1853 Pte Beasley wounded
3.30 pm – 4.30 pm	Trench mortar & Rifle grenade Fire. Enemy replied with Rifle grenades shell burst and set on fire two communication trench.	

1247 W 3299 200,000 (E) 8/14 J.B.C. & A. Forms/C. 2118/11.

WAR DIARY
or
INTELLIGENCE SUMMARY

(Erase heading not required.)

Army Form C. 2118.

Instructions regarding War Diaries and Intelligence Summaries are contained in F. S. Regs., Part II. and the Staff Manual respectively. Title pages will be prepared in manuscript.

Hour, Date, Place	Summary of Events and Information	Remarks and references to Appendices
May 9th (Continued) 5 p.m.	The Cpt. Nethermore and Pte. Senior went up into telephone line from their lost in Shaw and Members them under return hot rifle fire are fire.	No 2468 Pte Elmer wounded enquiry of Rifle fire
6 p.m.	Slow fire and looking fire all along the line very noisy —	No 2660 Pte Lytton wounded fire at his trench
7.30	Passed Wing R to the right Branch of firing line over the [illegible]	
	The fire in the trenches to our fire still posting severe & heavy/showers rifle fire from the lines at a range of about 30 yds. No casualties. the PLUGSTEERT & ST ELOI road forming a portion of the at KAYERSKY TOWN SOUTH	
May 10th PLUGSTEERT WOOD		
May 11th PLUGSTEERT WOOD	Very hot. No col Dutton & Major wounded we move from trenches at 8 pm to be relieved & great pleasure the relieving Platoons moved up given is on the 3rd Worcesters & their Conversation in German	Pte J.M. Dale wounded
May 12th	known from two Apostles from Col. J 30 a.m. hence more Moves in the W to 30 Trenches on the R of 8.30 p.m. from another Post	Capt. E. J. Dutton DSO & Lt. W. M. S. Carpenter & his unit connected on the 3rd Wilts

WAR DIARY or INTELLIGENCE SUMMARY

Army Form C. 2118.

Hour, Date, Place	Summary of Events and Information	Remarks and references to Appendices
May 13th PLUGSTREET WOOD	German started at 4.20 a.m. a bombardment with rifle grenades and a few shrapnel chiefly on the 5th GLOSTERS on our left. accompanied by machine gun on a rifle fire lasted about 2.5 minutes. We have had a very quiet day. Snipers busy on our support trenches. 4 Suffolks wounded. 4 Suffolks (Simpson) & 1 R.B. Sand Bags wounded. 10 German telegrams received from Trench No 58 - 70 looks probable from this that an appreciation of the work carried out yesterday morning by trench mortars & our work against it will cause them to work up. The character of this fire has fallen considerably & they have probably spun their enemy ahead also. Will settle enemy of his during the day & be deceitful cannon in a few days.	Lt Cpl Sudgate Pte MECROFT wounded & evacuated
May 14th PLUGSTREET WOOD	A very quiet night but very wet. Showers of a sort 3 p.m. Showers 9 P.M. a very rainy condition. A quiet day. Relief carried out. B Co to Camp. Rest D Co to Huts.	
May 15	A quiet day. dull and wet. Nothing to record. A quiet day.	
May 16	Army training of 1st Army Order Asn to all that Snipers are to be particularly active today. Every man to rub little belly a few little guts & our first let loose during the War. No 51 Trench left with Rifle Grenades. Several actual fell in enemy's trench.	No 4/6 HOPCRAFT death wounded

Army Form C. 2118.

WAR DIARY
or
INTELLIGENCE SUMMARY

(Erase heading not required.)

Instructions regarding War Diaries and Intelligence Summaries are contained in F. S. Regs., Part II. and the Staff Manual respectively. Title pages will be prepared in manuscript.

Hour, Date, Place	Summary of Events and Information	Remarks and references to Appendices
May 17. PLUGSTEERT WOOD	A very quiet day. —	
May 18	" Reliefs carried out	
May 19	Was a very interesting. Nothing to report	
May 20	Fine Anything to report.	
May 21 "	—	
May 22 "	A + C Coys relieved B + D. Very quiet day.	
May 26 "	Field Ambulance [illegible] RINB under w/ 8.30am 150 shells proceeded by 5 min also [illegible] fire from machines from fire from [illegible] on trenches. Enemy reply with shrapnel about [illegible] C'Coys [illegible] fire ½ hour shells [illegible] over it all at time Black battery fire ½ hour bigger. [illegible] they have been opened.	No 2604 Pte SHARRATT C [illegible] killed
11.15pm	German Trench Mortar (SPYDES Section) who opened 2 rifle, No 32 Trench (C Coy) took it up and fire a lot of Ammunition. No damage to Either Side.	No 2706 L/Corp BROWN # [illegible] wounded in L.[illegible]

WAR DIARY
or
INTELLIGENCE SUMMARY

(Erase heading not required.)

Army Form C. 2118.

Hour, Date, Place	Summary of Events and Information	Remarks and references to Appendices
May 24th PLUGSTEERT WOOD	A very hot day. Quiet 2nd Lt G REENWELL rejoined from HAVRE	
May 25 "	Nothing to report.	
May 26 "	Very hot, nothing to report - Coys relieved B and D to huts.	
May 27 "	Very hot quiet day. Jus men wounded in GERMAN HO by bomb from trench mortar. One man in 32 Trench wounded by a ricochet from our Trench periscope. One Man in shop billet in Suffield line. One man in D Coy killed by stray bullet in Support line.	No 8220 Pte EARL B. Coy (since died) No 2944 Pte BROOM B. Coy No 2663 Pte TAYLOR D. Coy No 1760 Pte BUTLER A. D. Coy killed 2nd Lt Herman Hodge to hosp Pte Lupton wounded in latrines Pte Lee wounded in support line
May 28 "	Nothing to report - Very hot, quiet day, the wind Southey.	
May 29 "	Very foggy in H[illegible] few enemy [illegible] at Head Quarters. He showed some Starshels bombs apparently very carefully. After they exploded 69 witnessed. Left Head and reported. Head Quarters moved back to hut of HUNTEROTON.	
May 30 "	Very hot & Quiet day. L/A Coys relieved D & B. Taylor of Hut 12. Pte G Jilich Plt [illegible] Very warm Tank attached to HUNTERS AVENUE. Colder. Nothing to report. Tallow on hour to relief at Dressing Station of a Indian Coy wounded by O S gun extracted at H[illegible]	
May 31 "		

145th Inf.Bde.
48th Div.

1/4th BATTN. THE OXFORDSHIRE & BUCKINGHAMSHIRE LIGHT INFANTRY.

J U N E

1 9 1 5

Attached:

Map.

CONFIDENTIAL

WAR DIARY
of
1/4th Batt. Oxfordshire & Buckinghamshire Light Infantry

from 1 June 1915 to 30 June 1915

(Volume " ")

Army Form C. 2118.

WAR DIARY
or
INTELLIGENCE SUMMARY

(Erase heading not required.)

Instructions regarding War Diaries and Intelligence Summaries are contained in F. S. Regs., Part II. and the Staff Manual respectively. Title pages will be prepared in manuscript.

Hour, Date, Place	Summary of Events and Information	Remarks and references to Appendices

1247 W 3299—200,000 (E) S/14 J.B.C. & A. Forms/C. 2118/11.

WAR DIARY
or
INTELLIGENCE SUMMARY

(Erase heading not required.)

Army Form C. 2118.

Hour, Date, Place	Summary of Events and Information	Remarks and references to Appendices
June 1st PLUGSTEERT WOOD.	Nothing to report. Fine Hot	
June 2nd	Nothing to report. Rain receved that only two Platoons will occupy the Subsidiary line at night	3 men in C Coy wounded
June 3rd	Hot and close. Had to rain. A good deal of shelling on A+B sides. One man in B Coy slightly wounded with a piece shell. B+D Coys Relieved A+C.	1 man in B Coy wounded.
June 4th	Very hot. Nothing to report.	
June 5th	Very hot. Information received that in two or three days R.E. Mining officer reported German to mining very close to our men under Bird cage. And that it might be necessary to fire our mine at any time. We found a satisfactory & laying 5 tons of gun powder from ESSEX FARM to mine head. Several orders received during the night as to procedure when mine was fired - All men in Subsidiary line had to sleep in their both boots as much noise as possible was to be made in consequence in own and further Artillery was up to make an attack to discourage Enemy that was prearranged.	

WAR DIARY or INTELLIGENCE SUMMARY

Army Form C. 2118.

Hour, Date, Place	Summary of Events and Information	Remarks and References to Appendices
June 6th PLUGSTEERT WOOD		
2.11 a.m.	Information received mine wouldn't be exploded till 7 a.m.	
9.40 a.m.	Information received mine to be exploded at 10.10 a.m.	One man slightly wounded in Subsidiary line
10.15 a.m.	Mine exploded. Enemy replied with rifle grenades & machine guns	
10.25	Enemy started firing shrapnel and high explosive on support line & Coys. report no damage done to our parapets, and that ELGER HOUSE and about 30 yds German parapet destroyed. Enemy started shelling of PLUGSTEERT wood west of it.	
11 a.m.	Intermittent shelling for rest of day. Enemy very active with rifles and machine guns all day. Information received that the Divisional troops to Right of Battalion & troops to N.E. of NIEPPE turn out and return when.	
June 7th PLUGSTEERT WOOD	Orders received for move to Billets in PONT DE NIEPPE. No 32 French to hand over to BUCKS Battalion. and 31 Turn to and half and turn to 4th GLOSTERS. Relief started at	145 Inf.Bt. Brigade order No.16
3.30 p.m.	Battalion reached to billets. Last Company at 9 p.m.	

Army Form C. 2118.

WAR DIARY
or
INTELLIGENCE SUMMARY.
(Erase heading not required.)

Instructions regarding War Diaries and Intelligence Summaries are contained in F. S. Regs., Part II. and the Staff Manual respectively. Title pages will be prepared in manuscript.

Hour, Date, Place	Summary of Events and Information	Remarks and References to Appendices
June 7th continued 11 PM	Enemy shelled Sutherboy line with Black Maria from direction of MESSINES about to shake our line and falling on Cathway about 4 feet from A Coy's sentry. A very hot day in deed.	
June 8. PONT de NIEPPE	Very hot. baths and inspection	
June 10th PONT de NIEPPE	Very hot in deed. Inspection and anti-aircraft instruction by Mar Gen R FANSHAWE. CB DSO.	
June 11th	Moved to take our trenches from 5th Roy BERWICK REGT. Trenches 36-40 and 61-63. in charge the old PROWSE POINT section. A Coy	
	on the extreme D Coy on the left Been shown in at ASH HOUSE.	
	A,B,C Coys relieved in afternoon. Distribution in sketch II	Sketch II.
June 12th ASH HOUSE	Enemy retired during the whole of very active Sniping on the	
	early morning also afternoon rapid fire for a time in trenches where C + D Coys. Shelled in afternoon and a sniper of afger WHITE	
	HOPE. been head sentry	
June 13th "	Shelling casualties all day B Coy had two W.C HOPE in them	Enemy Dlm wounded
	killed and one chipped wounded 6 times	Sharpnel fire
[June 14]:	Enemy blew up a mine on our left about 24 Trench	

Forms/C. 2118/11.

Army Form C. 2118.

WAR DIARY
or
INTELLIGENCE SUMMARY.
(Erase heading not required.)

Instructions regarding War Diaries and Intelligence Summaries are contained in F. S. Regs., Part II. and the Staff Manual respectively. Title pages will be prepared in manuscript.

Hour, Date, Place	Summary of Events and Information	Remarks and References to Appendices
June 14 Continued	About 2.10 a.m. Very heavy rifle fire and a good deal of artillery fire died out to be in what turned out to be enemy shelled along our line heavily. 5.1. Royal Berks on Company attacked by infantry. Repulsed by 1/4 Royal Berks & Queens May a few later a 1/2 le 63 and 1/2 trench 62. B. Coy killing Rest. Completed A.D. MISFH. D & B Coys. our RE rifles & behalf. See above conference of the Bn. from Gibraltar line trenches to relieve 4 R & S Downs. FARM We & Pleas. Run ASH House with a shell or Hyde Park & Grange R. in dug outs with a Section of contrary LA 44175 to dug Trench held down being. K.L. AL.L. Ph.	
June 15 WHITE LODGE	Nothing to report.	
June 15	Relieving relief. Pte Snook B'y Helen by shop shell in Salisbury line.	

Army Form C. 2118.

WAR DIARY
or
INTELLIGENCE SUMMARY.
(Erase heading not required.)

Instructions regarding War Diaries and Intelligence Summaries are contained in F. S. Regs., Part II. and the Staff Manual respectively. Title pages will be prepared in manuscript.

Hour, Date, Place	Summary of Events and Information	Remarks and References to Appendices
June 18th WHITE LODGE	Very wet. Battn to report & good of shelling in trench line	1 man D. Coy. killed
June 19 -	Heavy shelling and rifle in PLOEGSTEERT WOOD at Stand to. time cover. Battn relieved by 8th WORCESTERS. Brigade moved to billets and huts in a farm between ROMARIN and Rivers the Rot in billets between ROMARIN and NEUVE EGLISE.	1 man D. Coy wounded.
June 20th Antoinette	Very hot and fine. Battalion furnish attack from trench to trench at PETIT PONT 2am in the afternoon.	100 officers proceeded on leave.
June 21st "	Very hot. Usual instructions other breakfast. Company drill in the morning.	

(9 29 6) W 2794 100,000 8/14 H W V Forms/C. 2118/11.

Army Form C. 2118.

WAR DIARY
or
INTELLIGENCE SUMMARY.
(Erase heading not required.)

Instructions regarding War Diaries and Intelligence Summaries are contained in F. S. Regs., Part II. and the Staff Manual respectively. Title pages will be prepared in manuscript.

Hour, Date, Place	Summary of Events and Information	Remarks and References to Appendices
June 22nd Hutures Is.	Very hot indeed. Visual inspections and respirator drill before breakfast. Company drill and Guard mounting practice in morning. Cricket match at ROMARIN v R.A.M.C. 1/4 Oxfordshire 94. R.A.M.C. 47.	
June 23rd "	Much cooler and rain in the morning, peas and hot in the afternoon. Visual inspections and Company drill. An order came in from the Brigade in the evening that the Battalion would be inspected on the following night and would proceed to BAILLEUL. A further order later that the Battalion should be ready to turn out at half an hours notice without transport all that night and the following day.	

Army Form C. 2118.

WAR DIARY
or
INTELLIGENCE SUMMARY.
(Erase heading not required.)

Instructions regarding War Diaries and Intelligence Summaries are contained in F.S. Regs., Part II. and the Staff Manual respectively. Title pages will be prepared in manuscript.

Hour, Date, Place	Summary of Events and Information	Remarks and References to Appendices
June 24th Hutwerets.	Very hot and fine. Brigade order about radiers to turn out concealed. Battalion to reach starting point for BAILLEUL at 9.30 p.m. where the Brigade is to concentrate and proceed as such to billets at BAILLEUL	
June 26th BAILLEUL	Marched in brigade to VIEUX BERQUIN arriving at about midnight.	
June 26th VIEUX BERQUIN	Marched at 8.30 a.m. to billets in vicinity of GONNEHEM via MERVILLE & ROBECQ distance about 15 miles. Arrived at 3.30 a.m. 27th 7 men fell out.	
June 27: GONNEHEM	Marched at 6.30 a.m. to ALOUAGNE distance about 4 miles. Thunder storm during day. Lost march & the Division now forms part of IV Corps. 1st Army.	
June 28: ALOUAGNE	Such day - had unexpectedly American Sergeant's inspection of rifles.	

Army Form C. 2118.

WAR DIARY
or
INTELLIGENCE SUMMARY.
(Erase heading not required.)

Instructions regarding War Diaries and Intelligence Summaries are contained in F. S. Regs., Part II. and the Staff Manual respectively. Title pages will be prepared in manuscript.

Hour, Date, Place	Summary of Events and Information	Remarks and References to Appendices
June 28th to July 30th	Remained at ALLOUAGNE. The Division being in Corps Reserve.	

J. A. Tulloch Capt. & A.D.
1/4 R.S.F. Brig. M.G.O.

145th Inf.Bde.
48th Div.

1/4th BATTN. THE OXFORDSHIRE & BUCKINGHAMSHIRE
LIGHT INFANTRY.

J U L Y

1 9 1 5

WAR DIARY
or
INTELLIGENCE SUMMARY.
(Erase heading not required.)

Army Form C. 2118.

Instructions regarding War Diaries and Intelligence Summaries are contained in F. S. Regs., Part II. and the Staff Manual respectively. Title pages will be prepared in manuscript.

Hour, Date, Place	Summary of Events and Information	Remarks and References to Appendices
July 1st ALLOUAGNE	Remained in Corps Reserve. Training and resting.	
July 12" "	Orders received to move to NOEUX LES MINES 10am/1pm.	
	2nd Line transport from 14 & 27 Battns to move out.	
	V.P. Vyner here before in a Reserve dump/motor	2 men died of injuries.
	and on man killed.	
July 13 NOEUX LES MINES	Orders taken over. Another "cancelled" and information that Brigade would remain at NOEUX-LES-MINES three nights	
	and be employed digging trenches on Second line	
	Battalion in Bivouac. damp day. Much rain	
	moved bivouac, two companies going to billets.	
July 14 "		
July 15 "	very heavy rain. very wet night.	
July 16 "	Brigade moved at 9 p.m. to AMES. very wet night	
Jul 17 AMES	No Teams about 15 miles arrived at 3.30 a.m. 8 hours	
	filled. a heavy march as many men had been on working	
	parks the night before. and also in training. Information	
	received that the Brigade would be have tomorrow.	

WAR DIARY or INTELLIGENCE SUMMARY

Army Form C. 2118.

Hour, Date, Place	Summary of Events and Information	Remarks and References to Appendices
July 18. AMES.	Battalion entrained at BERGUETTE Station enclosure 7th held very hot march. Left BERGUETTE at 4 p.m. arrived at DOULLENS at 9 p.m. detrained & had tea & a little bivouac at TERRAMESNIL the train about 6 miles. Information later received that Division was formed part of VII Corps, 3rd Army. The Corps consisting of 4th, 48th and a new Division, and this is what takes over line down from the French.	
July 19. TERRAMESNIL	Marched at 4 p.m. to Bivouac at COIGNEUX Château about 8 miles. Very hot indeed.	
July 20. COIGNEUX	Officers went to trenches Trenches near HÉBUTERNE. Battalion marched at 7.30 p.m. to 1 a.m. over trenches from 91st Territorial Infantry at HÉBUTERNE all from Company in Reserve. Trenches quite different to what we have occupied before being trenches not trenchworks. All 4 Coys in the line holding them our support a Maye of dugout communications trenches. Very quiet all internment by 11 p.m.	Map No. 3

Army Form C. 2118.

WAR DIARY
or
INTELLIGENCE SUMMARY.
(Erase heading not required.)

Hour, Date, Place	Summary of Events and Information	Remarks and References to Appendices
July 21st HEBUTERNE	A quiet day. Very hot. Company learnt geography of trenches. Transport moved to THIEVRES. Billets Bivouac relieved the French at one night.	
July 22nd "	A quiet night. One man in C. Coy wounded & one man killed in trench BOUCHET in the early morning, a shell came into village and behind Coys kitchen, a quiet night, very wet.	1 man killed C. Coy. 1 " wounded
July 23rd "	Enemy shelled communication trench behind C. Coy at 9 a.m. Quiet all day. Occasional showers. Trenches very wet and greasy. A quiet night.	
July 24th "	Dry - A quiet morning. Enemy shelled communication trench behind Trench BUCKET at about 11 a.m. About 4 p.m. heavy trench shelling along the line and near communicating trenches. Relieved by 4 Royal BERKS and moved into billets in HEBUTERNE.	1 man wounded B. Coy.
July 25th	Working parties in HEBUTERNE.	
July 26th "	A Coy furnished two companies with the Bedfords under Capt. OWEN.	

Army Form C. 2118.

WAR DIARY
or
INTELLIGENCE SUMMARY.
(Erase heading not required.)

Instructions regarding War Diaries and Intelligence Summaries are contained in F. S. Regs, Part II. and the Staff Manual respectively. Title pages will be prepared in manuscript.

Hour, Date, Place	Summary of Events and Information	Remarks and References to Appendices
July 27 HEBUTERNE	Working parties in HEBUTERNE met 2 Lt. JUDSON and RICHARDSON joined	
July 28 "	Battalion relieved 4th ROYAL BERKS in trenches B2 southern allotted 3 companies in the front line and one	
"	Company in reserve. Two of Batt. Head Quarters. Two	
July 29 "	A quiet day in trenches, remained silent	
July 30 "	Suspension allowed the Brigade to form the garrison of HEBUTERNE, with 2 battalion in trenches one is HEBUTERNE Sec in SAILLY. We handed over trenches B2A7 to the right of	1 man (?) killed
"	the line to E/144th Brigade and took over trenches the garrison of trench BRIAIRE also JENA and GUDIN from 5th GLOSTERS having only two companies in the trenches and two in local reserve. A log in the village	See map 3.
"	B. Coy in dug outs near head quarters	
July 31 "	A good deal of shelling. French in line left.	Ja B
		Ja Baker (Capt A) 1/4 OBJ?S with Hhalf

Forms/C. 2118/11.

```
                                                        145th Inf.Bde.
                                                        48th Div.
```

1/4th BATTN. THE OXFORDSHIRE & BUCKINGHAMSHIRE LIGHT INFANTRY.

A U G U S T

1 9 1 5

Attached:
    Fighting Strengths.

Army Form C. 2118.

WAR DIARY
or
INTELLIGENCE SUMMARY.
(Erase heading not required.)

Instructions regarding War Diaries and Intelligence Summaries are contained in F. S. Regs., Part II. and the Staff Manual respectively. Title pages will be prepared in manuscript.

Hour, Date, Place	Summary of Events and Information	Remarks and References to Appendices
Aug 1st HEBUTERNE	Information received Battalion would remain 8 days in trenches. A good deal of shelling both morning and afternoon. Information received that the French report important movements of enemy South west from LENS. A + B Coys relieved C + D. A quiet night. A Coy sent out patrol which met a German Patrol which when our patrol infiltrated that our patrol opened fire.	1 man C Coy wounded
Aug 2.	A quiet day. Enemy fired a few shells in the morning otherwise very quiet our battery Registering all day may have had something to do with it. A tremendous Thunder storm in the afternoon Trenches in an awful mess after Quiet night but very wet.	
Aug 3.	Heavy shower all day. Hour's to hand over see four Aug. O.C. in the Butts field to R.A. about how our others the two are lying.	
Aug 4.	A hot but then two in an awful state. A quiet day	

WAR DIARY
or
INTELLIGENCE SUMMARY.
(Erase heading not required.)

Army Form C. 2118.

Hour, Date, Place	Summary of Events and Information	Remarks and References to Appendices
Aug 5. HERVILERS	Fine a good drying day. Relieved by 6 Royal BERKS. a good deal of shelling in afternoon. 2nd Buchan and in artillery of village. 1 man P.L. G. wounded in Bucham shell in nature. He finished his job and went to his Platoon Commander and said "I think they have hit me". He then collapsed having been cut from his knee, as we have been out.	P. LOVEDAY attached
Aug 6. SAILLY	A wet morning. Heavy in festivities. A Coy had to the. A rather dirty village. went to W of channery up. was Shells into village in afternoon 3 of which did not explode. They were French Shells about 4.6 inch, supposed to some of from factories French at ANNOBERGE.	
Aug 7. "	wet	
Aug 8. "	Fine. 16 shells into village. 3 duds. Machine gun section attacked	

WAR DIARY
or
INTELLIGENCE SUMMARY

(Erase heading not required.)

Army Form C. 2118.

Instructions regarding War Diaries and Intelligence Summaries are contained in F. S. Regs., Part II. and the Staff Manual respectively. Title pages will be prepared in manuscript.

Hour, Date, Place	Summary of Events and Information	Remarks and references to Appendices
Aug 12th SAILLY.	Remained in SAILLY working parties in communication trenches but no our hardly any. Roads near hospital and Dieron Sportsman saloon café.	
Aug 13th "	Returned to Regt BERLES hamlet C&D to their own A&B to their homes	
Aug 14th HEBUTERNE Sector J.	Fine a good deal of shelling of ints.	
Aug 15th "	Stormy and rather wet. a quiet day. Exchanged our him to Trench MORANT.	See map.
Aug 16th "	Fine a lot of shelling - 4 men wounded. McBeath up our it from Boy School	
Aug 17th "	A good deal of shelling on D Coys trenches paraded in MORANT 1 man D by our men at Sand 5 knocked in. A & B coys trenches C & D very heavy in morant	
Aug 18th "	a normal day, number of M of waters very wet morning	
Aug 19th "	Dying day. Show day. Shopping up in the trenches. Div at HQ gulley hump day being rather rather above. Commanding off in bed of leave.	
Aug 20th "	Dying day. normal day in trenches hearing shelling rather	

WAR DIARY
or
INTELLIGENCE SUMMARY

(Erase heading not required.)

Army Form C. 2118.

Hour, Date, Place	Summary of Events and Information	Remarks and references to Appendices
Aug 21st HETBUTERNE	Normal day. Enemy shelled village and trenches slightly during day. Two platoons started to gain experience of taking Battalion trenches by night. BERKS and BROWN into village - and DOWNS out. BRIDGES punished taken. Men shelled slightly into trench and then brown out. Fine in rested pastime area.	
Aug 22nd		
Aug 23rd	Sillery to r tents tr morning. Regns rearranged trenches. Fine from a tactical. View from a tactical.	
Aug 24 - Aug 30	Batt. took over trenches to Accordion to Puisieux Colleu no 2.9. The 5th Gloster from trenches 31 & 24. Re trench 4.	I have C.Coy trenches in position two. VaB
Aug 31st	Quiet day. Enemy without a reference Batt relieved 5th GLOSTERS. Three companies A.C.& D in trenches. A coy 24-28. C coy 29.30. D coy 31 & 32. A fine day and great night. Trenches require a remainder amount of work.	I.H.Balfour (Lieut & Adjt)

Parade State. (Fighting Strength.)

Compy.	Officers	Other Ranks	Grenade Sch.	Bitter Hosh. School	Machine Gun	Signallers	Pioneers	Stretcher Bearers	Sanitary Squad	Sergt Cook	Cooks	Cavy. Qr. Corpls	Orderlies	Butcher	Orderly Room	Police	Armourer	Transport	Grooms	Officers Servants	Officers Mess	Post Corporal	Shoemakers Shop	Leave	Machine Gun Fighting Course	Total
H.Q.			1		44	22	9	16	7	1	1	1	6	1	3	2	1	37	10	4	2	1	3	3		175
A.	6	153									4	1								2				3		163
B.	6	145	1	2		3					4	1								2				1		159
C.	5	145		2							4	1								2						154
D.	5	155									4	1								2					1	163
	5	598	2	4	44	26	9	16	7	1	17	5	6	1	3	2	1	37	10	12	2	1	3	7	1	814

31-6-15

Parade State. (Fighting Strength.)

Compy.	Officers	Other Ranks	Grenade School	Batt Hospital	Machine Gun	Signallers	Pioneer	Stretcher Bearers	Sanitary Squad	Sergt Cook	Cooks	Coy Or Hr Sergt	Orderlies	Batman	Ordly Room	Police	Armourer	Transport	Grooms	Officers Servants	Officers Mess	Pack Mule	Shoemakers Shop	Leave Officer	Leave Other Ranks	Total
H.Q.	4		1	1	43	20	10	15	8	1	1	1	6※	1	2	2	1	38	11	4	1	1	2		8	177
A.	4	136	9	2							4	1								2					6	160
B.	5	133	9	1		2					4	1								2					3	155
C.	4	135	11	1							4	1								2					4	158
D.	4	146	8	3							4	1								2					3	167
Total.	17	550	38	8	43	22	10	15	8	1	17	5	6	1	2	2	1	38	11	12	1	1	2		24	817

21st Aug:

※: 4 Coy Orderlies
2 h.O. Orderlies

S.J Pearce S.y.

J. Watson a. Lieut & Adj.

145th Inf.Bde.
48th Div.

1/4th BATTN. THE OXFORDSHIRE & BUCKINGHAMSHIRE
LIGHT INFANTRY.

S E P T E M B E R

1 9 1 5

Attached:

Fighting Strengths.

CONFIDENTIAL

WAR DIARY

of

1/4th Batt. Oxf. & Bucks Light Infantry.

from 1 Sept. 1915 to 30 Sept. 1915.

WAR DIARY
or
INTELLIGENCE SUMMARY

(Erase heading not required.)

Army Form C. 2118.

Hour, Date, Place	Summary of Events and Information	Remarks and references to Appendices
Sept 1st Believe G. JHS BUTERNE	A fine morning. Enemy Artillery rather more active. Started back in afternoon. Machine gun & rifle fire fairly quiet.	
Sept 2nd	C Coy with Royal WARWICKS for about 2 days time in a 48 hours tour of trenches. A great many casualties. Rather rather quiet in afternoon etc.	
Sept 3rd	Orders received as rearrangement of time. The Bryant Machine Guns. The Batt. front with 7th WORCESTERS & 6th Bryant. A wet day. Passed in C & D Coys trenches fell in.	
Sept 4th	A quiet day. C Coy 11th WARWICKS went out. Our C Coy taken over their line. The Brigade Machine Guns first engaged from 9.30 to 10.30pm. 10th Scouts that reached 30 x 31 were shelled by enemy. No damage done but 7 swan shells fell in trenches 3.10 p.	
Sept 5th	Battalion relieved by 7th WORCESTERS. Trenches out at 2.35. Has 6 Mr 8th WORCESTERS at 10 am. Enemy rather active during morning.	

WAR DIARY
INTELLIGENCE SUMMARY

Army Form C. 2118.

Hour, Date, Place	Summary of Events and Information	Remarks and references to Appendices
Sept 5th G. Sexton Lt BUTE RNR	Battalion relieved & known 2 and 3 P.M. by 7th WORCESTERS and marched to COURCELETTES for a rest. Spent that particular in billets by 7 A.M.	
Sept 17th	In billets in COURCELETTES and spent the day resting and cleaning up. Heavy rain fell.	
Sept 16th ""	Bn to move via BUS - SLEDGE R.- TUTING - BUS Road & march via the Army Commander at BUS and were met. the Genl that he was satisfied.	
Sept 17	Battalion relieved 7th WORCESTERS in trenches Sector G on the left Bn on the right. B on head enemy A in reserve.	
Sept 18	Fairly quiet day. Enemy dropped two little Willies in to Trenches 31. 32. Sent out wounded 1 officer and 3 men of P.C. Shropshires to the attached for instruction. June	
Sept 19	Quiet day. June Six 5.9" shells fell between Tr. Bn saps and Bouquet No casualties close.	

WAR DIARY or INTELLIGENCE SUMMARY

Army Form C. 2118.

(Erase heading not required.)

Instructions regarding War Diaries and Intelligence Summaries are contained in F. S. Regs., Part II. and the Staff Manual respectively. Title pages will be prepared in manuscript.

Hour, Date, Place	Summary of Events and Information	Remarks and references to Appendices
Sept 20.	Quiet day. Fine.	
Sept 21.	Our guns shelled enemy's trenches. Little retaliation on Tr 31 & 32. No damage. Fine.	
Sept 22.	Our guns shelled PUISIEUX and GOMMECOURT. Enemy retaliated on HEBUTERNE. 2 R.A.M.C. stretcher wounded.	
24.	War cutting by our guns and enemy's trenches heavily shelled. 2 Platoons of 6th ROYAL SUSSEX relieved two of ours in fire trenches. 6 men wounded of ours in Tr 32. our subsequently chief in hospital. Enemy slightly damaged our trenches. Raining in afternoon but fine in evening.	
25.	War cutting carried on intermittently day and night by our guns with good much effect. Enemy retaliated on our trenches. No damage. Small of their shells failed to explode. Cold but fine	

1247 W 3299 200,000 (E) 8/14 J.B.C. & A. Forms/C. 2118/11.

WAR DIARY
or
INTELLIGENCE SUMMARY

(Erase heading not required.)

Army Form C. 2118.

Hour, Date, Place	Summary of Events and Information	Remarks and references to Appendices
Sept 26.	Heavy shelling on 6/R tps in morning. Much quieter in afternoon. Orders received from Brigade that in an attack on [Moltke?] did [Sussex?] Regiment that in the event of failure, take and hold trenches first purposed [illegible] No [path?] cut through wire [illegible] encounters. No pati[?] impass to the first [enemy?] line as yet but hopes to [illegible] some time. My guns evidently searching some times. Orders received that attack is indefinitely postponed. Sussex platoons returned by ones and twos [illegible] [Evening?] and working parties. No [illegible] either side. Raining heavily. Trenches in a filthy state and took tent up for [Lack?] of transport.	
Sept 27.		
28.	Still cold and raining. Sent out a patrol at [night?] to [recce?] H.Q. line [illegible] get [information?] re building in front that [illegible] it [not?] in an to "get into" [illegible] at [illegible]. Patrol [reports?] that [illegible] was [illegible] looking on [illegible] [illegible] a [illegible] passage [illegible] tent lying on a	

Army Form C. 2118.

WAR DIARY
or
INTELLIGENCE SUMMARY
(Erase heading not required.)

Instructions regarding War Diaries and Intelligence Summaries are contained in F. S. Regs., Part II. and the Staff Manual respectively. Title pages will be prepared in manuscript.

Hour, Date, Place	Summary of Events and Information	Remarks and references to Appendices
Sept 28.	Hill Garrison. Our patrol bombed and fired at by enemy. GLOSTERS lost an officer and 2 men whilst on a similar patrol. News that FRENCH to SOUTH & ENGLISH to NORTH are making some progress.	
Sept 29.	Enemy searched for M.G. positions with 30 milies on Tr 31 & 32. No damage. Battalion relieved by 7ᵈ WORCESTERS and proceeded to old billets in COURCELLES.	
30. COURCELLES	Cold but fine. Day spent in general clearing up.	

M. Musgrove. Lieut
Actg Adjt

PARADE STATE. (Fighting Strength.)

Compy.	Officers	Other Ranks	Grenade School	Billet Hospital	Machine Gun	Signallers	Pioneer	Stretcher Bearers	Sanitary Squad	Sergt. Cook	Cook	Coy. Q.r Sergt.	Orderlies	Batmen	Ordly. Room	Police	Shoemaker	Armourer	Transport	Grooms	Signal Officers Mess	Post Office	Leave	H. of Course	Total
H.Qrs			1	—	44	22	9	16	8	1	1	1	6	1	3	2	3	1	37	10	4	2	1	2		175
A.	6	151		1		3					4	1									2		2			161
B.	6	145	1								4	1									2		3			159
C.	4	146		2							4	1									2		1			156
D.	4	152		2							4	1									2		2	1	1	162
Total	20	594	2	5	44	25	9	16	8	1	17	5	6	1	3	2	3	1	37	10	12	2	8	1	1	813

In the Field

Saturday 4th Sept. 1916.

E.J. Pearce
2 i/c

Sgt absent

Major & Adjt

1st Dof-B Bucks Lt. Luffy.

P.T.O.

Other Officers on Strength.

Lt. Col. W. F. B. R. Dugmore D.S.O.
Major & Adjt. J. A. Ballard.
Major R. L. Ovey.   @ Grenade School.
Major R. R. S. Bowell.
Major & Q.M. A. A. Bridgewater.
Lieut. A. K. Gibson.   Transport Officer.
Lieut. H. A. Wilsdon   Machine Gun Officer.
Capt. J. M. Treble.   on Leave.
Capt. P. Pickford   — do —
Lieut. M. C. Cooper,   Machine Gun Course.

Parade State (Fighting Strength)

Company	Officers	Other Ranks	French Scout Rifles	Hotchkiss gun	Signallers	Pioneers	Stretcher Bearers Squad	Sgt Cook	Cooks	Coy Qr Mr Sgt	Orderlies	Batmen	Bd. Room	Police	Armourer	Transport drivers	Grooms	Officers Servants	Off. Mess	Shoemakers	Lathrine Sanit. Servants	Leave	Total
H.Qrs	4	148	1	1	44	22	9	16	8	1	1		6	1	3	2	1	34	10	3	2	1	3	5	175
A.	6	148	2			3				1	4	1				2			2					4	161
B.	4	139	1	5						1	4	1				2			2					4	155
C.	3	138								1	4	1		1		2			2				3		154
D.	5	143	2							1	4	1		1		2			2			1	3		158
Total	22	569	2	11	44	25	9	16	8	1	17	5	6	1	3	4	1	34	10	11	2	1	3	19	803

In the Field.

Saturday 11th Sept 1915.

Major & Adjt.

P. T. O.

Other Officers:

Major R.L. Oxley.   Brigade Bomb School
Lieut A.K. Gibson.   Transport Officer
Lieut R.Q. Weldon   On Leave
Capt. G.K. Rose   On Leave
Lieut B.B. Brooks   On Leave
Lieut H.W Edmunds   On Leave
Lieut H.C. Cooper   Machine Gun Course.

Parade State (Fighting Strength).

Company	Officer	Other Ranks	Ghurkha School	Biller-Headqtr	Machine Gun	Signallers	Pioneers	Stretcher Bearer	Stretcher Squad	Sergt Cook	Cooks	Coy Q'mr Sergt	Orderlies	Butler	Orderly Room Peon	Armourer	Standard	Gunns	Officers Servants	Officer boys	Post Office	Shoemaker	H. Qtrs School	Barber Shd	Leave	Total
H.Q	4		9		44	22	9	16	8	1	1	1	6*	1	3	2	1	30	11	5	2	1	3	*	2	3	172
A	6	142	9	2							4	1								2						4	155
B	4	130	9	1		3					4	1								2						3	144
C	13	129	8	2							4	1								2				1		4	142
D	5	132	7	2							4	1								2						4	146
Total	29	533	33	7	44	25	9	16	8	1	17	5	6	1	3	2	1	30	11	13	2	1	3	1	2	18	792

In the field.

Saturday 18th Septr 1915.

× {2 med. orderlies
{4 Coy Orderlies

J. H. Griswood.
Lieut. Actg. Adjt.
1/4 Bn of Buchos ct Infty.

P.T.O.

Other Officers

Major Grey. R.L. - Brigade Grenadier School
Capt. Fortescue C.C. - Hospital
Lieut Griffin. J.E. - Base
Lieut Gibson. A.K. - Transport Officer

4 on Leave.

Parade State (Fighting Strength)

Company	Officers	Other Ranks	Parade Sheet	Batt. Headqts.	Machine Gun Section	Signallers	Pioneers	Battn. Stretcher Bearers	Sanitary Squad	Sergt. Cook	Cooks	Coy Q.M. Sgt.	Orderlies	Butchers	Ord. Room	Police	Armourer	Transport	Grooms	Officers Servants	Stretcher Bearers Red Cross	Machine Gun Emerg.	Total
Hd.Qrs.	5	-	-	-	44	22	9	2	16	8	1	1	*6	1	3	2	1	40	11	2	5	3		179
A.	6	146	6										1							2				160
B.	6	134	9			3							1							2				154
C.	4	128	7	1									1							2				144
D.	5	134	2	1									1							2		1		146
	26	542	24	2	44	25	9	2	16	8	1	1	10	1	3	2	1	40	11	2	5	3	1	783

Saturday 25th Sept. 1915. J.H. Girouard. Lieut. & Adjutant.

* Fitness of Officers orderlies & Coy Orderlies.

4/6 Offrs & 16 nch + H. Duffy.

P.T.O.

Other Officers

Major R.L. Every @ Brigade Bomb School
Capt. E.C. Anderson in Hospital
Lieut. Gibson A.K. Transport Officer
Lieut. J.C. Griffin @ Base.

145th Inf.Bde.
48th Div.

1/4th BATTN. THE OXFORDSHIRE & BUCKINGHAMSHIRE
LIGHT INFANTRY.

OCTOBER & NOVEMBER

(1.10.15 - 1.12.15)
1 9 1 5

Attached:

Fighting Strengths.

Army Form C. 2118.

WAR DIARY
or
INTELLIGENCE SUMMARY
(Erase heading not required.)

Instructions regarding War Diaries and Intelligence Summaries are contained in F. S. Regs., Part II. and the Staff Manual respectively. Title pages will be prepared in manuscript.

Hour, Date, Place	Summary of Events and Information	Remarks and references to Appendices
Sept 1st to Oct 1st – 4th COURCELLES	In Rest Billets. Working parties employed on Corps Line. Returned and not rested.	
– 5th	ROUTE March. Bus & Lorry – Bus returned Battn.	
8th Sec MIRGON	Brigade Rural McClintock gave a lecture Guard A Coy attached. General quite pleased.	Quissy lost of 25 other ranks arrived and return to strength.
– 9th	The memorising. Van we. Practice alarm carried out satisfactorily. Verbal discussion was in.	
– 11th	Battalion relieved 7 WORCESTERS in trenches. New scheme of dispositions – vide scheme attached. B & C Coys in the trench. A & D in supt. Hqrs East of rd. to trench. New Baths Hqrs to be made. June.	Refr discussions G Saks
Mer Tranches 12th	Tour of trench duty 6-6 to 8 days instead of 4-2. Divisions fairly quiet. Men dealing w shelter – Several suddenly anxious to enter this and warm. Work started on ries. l'officer & men on Wednesday sthose R3 on Tuesday.	

WAR DIARY or INTELLIGENCE SUMMARY

Army Form C. 2118.

(Erase heading not required.)

Hour, Date, Place	Summary of Events and Information	Remarks and references to Appendices
In the Trenches. Ot- a Henin	"D" Company 10th Royal Irish Rifles attached for instruction. Two Platoons in trenches, one two Platoons in HEBUTERNS. Rest of platoons any 24 hours. Enemy dropped 20 Little Willies on and around Tr. 30, 31, 32. One was Rein forced or penetrated shrapnel & pt KITCHEN. "B" Co. in afternoon. Assisted under Capt ROSE went out to dig and collect a sniper who was in no mans land. Unfortunately sniper wasn't mortal. If wounded but her. Heard between 9 pm & 12 midnight. and rain away. Raining.	#2111 KITCHEN C.J. Injury
13	Quiet in morning. Enemy party, quiet. Our guns registered on several points in German 2nd line trenches forcing men to burst. Wind in N.W. 7 a.m. 1 mr. shell. two of which failed to burst. Four Rifle Grenades dropped on 1st Barricade 12.15 midnight. No damage done. Quiet all day.	
14.	Quiet but cloudy. Enemy dropped 12 Little Willies on Tr. 30, 31, 32, and six Rifle Grenades all of which did No damage. We retaliated with three no of which dropped right into enemy's trench. Three MINENWERFERS	

WAR DIARY
or
INTELLIGENCE SUMMARY

Army Form C. 2118.

(Erase heading not required.)

Hour, Date, Place	Summary of Events and Information	Remarks and references to Appendices
In the Trenches. Oct 14th (cont)	He dropped over our trenches. Enemy's machine guns very active at about 6 p.m. He retaliated and our front line was thin. We got very warry as we held the trenches but quite clear during daytime. Generally positive enemy round in the morning and seemed quite pleased with work generally.	
15th	Very quiet until 10 a.m. Shelling my quiet in the morning and quiet afternoon. We had a few strong Bursts from a certain amount of success. About 6.15 p.m. enemy suddenly but a stream of Little Willies and one or two heavier shells into and round T.81.32 probably looking for our sub gun emplacement. No damage done. Our howitzer slowly crept to look of material. A railway truck but from FONQUEVILLERS through HEBUTERNE down to VERCINGETORIX turning especially active with machine guns but seemed to be all evenings but so far has shewed little or no concern.	

WAR DIARY or INTELLIGENCE SUMMARY

Army Form C. 2118.

Hour, Date, Place	Summary of Events and Information	Remarks and references to Appendices
In the Trenches Oct 15th G. SECTION	Very misty again in morning. Patrol of ours went out and reconnoitred up in front of our trenches under cover of mist. Saw a German in long grass and fired at him as it was too light to try and catch him. German was seen to drop. Evening very quiet in morning. In afternoon our guns fired on their 2nd line trenches. Trenches made very good practice. We find six bombs at enemy with excellent results, and 3 Trench Mortars also with comminute. Enemy retaliated with a number of shells of various calibres doing no damage. First much action in the evening but and always very quiet. B Coy to G Royal Irish Rifles came in as a Coy for instruction for the last time. 2nd Lieut FORTESCUE attached for SNIPING COURSE under Capt HESKETH PRICHARD. Begins to-mono. A German machine guns active in evening.	

WAR DIARY
or
INTELLIGENCE SUMMARY

(Erase heading not required.)

Army Form C. 2118.

Hour, Date, Place	Summary of Events and Information	Remarks and references to Appendices
In the Trenches Oct 7th G Section	Still very misty in morning. Wish for several rounds to get out [illegible] and to find at [illegible] The enemy [illegible] to [illegible] from Enemy sides of wire. A scout sent to [illegible] no sign of enemy first or [illegible] no enemy first or enemy supply line [illegible] [illegible] 1 rifle fairly quiet day on the whole MR HARDIE's company [illegible] [illegible] RMR 2 RMR Bns Buried 6 enemy in [illegible] [illegible] In the morning burned [illegible] a number of [illegible] on our front found also dead a sniper [illegible] of ammunition [illegible] an officer and several [illegible] of [illegible] [illegible] [illegible] to our [illegible] [illegible] [illegible] [illegible] NOTE: FLYING CORPS [illegible] and [illegible] [illegible] was forestalled [illegible] at 3.15 p.m. This [illegible] by the Germans who suddenly opened a heavy bombardment on our front trenches on the [illegible] 31 Coming in for 20 mts out of their walls. Bombardment slacked from 1.30 h.m and went on to about 4.30 to 5 heads [illegible] used 82 guns	

WAR DIARY
or
INTELLIGENCE SUMMARY

(Erase heading not required.)

Army Form C. 2118.

Hour, Date, Place	Summary of Events and Information	Remarks and references to Appendices
In the Trenches Oct [?] G Sector 18 Batt[?]	of which 12 men in Tryto had no response. It 31 was smashed almost that out most the a Bangalore torpedo at his dug out practically smashed. Casualties 1 Captain, 1 Cpl and 1 man in 11:30. Our men recovered dismantled rifle had to taken out. Had sent [?] in am roll [?] covering all prisons and outposts most up and had our trenches in case of an attack wiring put out 6 MINENWERFERS of ammo 6 pm observer may by this guard. Our men which on patrol reported having 6 such as were as possible in the windows of R.E. shed by the several and no attempt to [?] Supported by 7th WORCESTERS and moved back to COURCELLES to take up at 61 [?] Bath in billets 6.23 p.m.	✶ CAPTAIN TREISE [?] Cpl RIDDLES [?] PTE TIMMS C [?]

19.

WAR DIARY
or
INTELLIGENCE SUMMARY

Army Form C. 2118.

Hour, Date, Place	Summary of Events and Information	Remarks and references to Appendices
COURCELLES Oct 20th	Back in billets. General cleaning up. Baths for B & C Coys. Cold moist.	
21st	Baths A & D Coys. C.O.& in Arras. Corps Comr. Misty m? increase in afternoon.	
22nd	Rode round inspecting outposts B.H.Q. (W)ELLINGTON R 26 c - A 26 c5 - c9. B.H.Q. near all and Guard Room Q 31 b 3 4 E. On the way for Coy Combat some night. Beautifully fine. Still frost. Horses stay Coys huts. Gas respirators morning 30 mins in tear gas	
23rd		
24th	SUNDAY. Church parade 11.30 am in school Bring of Coy's other Cold rather cell Relief observed. Refund cold	

WAR DIARY or INTELLIGENCE SUMMARY

Army Form C. 2118.

(Erase heading not required.)

Hour, Date, Place	Summary of Events and Information	Remarks and references to Appendices
COURCELLES. Oct 26th	Very cold and wet all day. Batt'n chosen to represent 48th Div at Ceremonial parade. Marched to ACHEUX at 11.15 am and inspected by H.M. THE KING GEORGE V and PRESIDENT POINCARE. Parade consisted of 10th,14th,3rd & 4th Div. Bn history and old Battn men such as 48th and 27th Divs. Men cheered in overcoats and looked very smart and smart my speech in spite of wearing old Battn marches back and arrived at billets at 8 p.m.	
27th	Battn relieved 7th WORCESTERS in L. Section Trenches. A and D Coys in front lines. C. Batt'n Resv. B Res Resn. D Coy of 10th Batt'n ROYAL WELSH ANZ FUSILIERS attached for instruction for 7 days.	
G SECTION. 28th	Very cold and pouring in to rain. Bombardment of enemys trenches as laid down carried out to make hostile front very quiet. At 9 p.m. their front about	

Army Form C. 2118.

WAR DIARY
or
INTELLIGENCE SUMMARY

(Erase heading not required.)

Instructions regarding War Diaries and Intelligence Summaries are contained in F.S. Regs., Part II. and the Staff Manual respectively. Title pages will be prepared in manuscript.

Hour, Date, Place	Summary of Events and Information	Remarks and references to Appendices
G SECTION. Oct. 28th 1917	shell bursts small pieces on our trucks. About no damage. Our field guns retaliated and stopped any further firing on their part. Trucks in a terrible state and infans beds & gear & gas. Men all fed & from the rain during the night. Rain all clear during night.	
-29th	Cold but duty fine. Embarkment completed & all actions on sidings fast and 'second line' trucks commencing at 8:10 am and lasting for about an hour. Bombs made very good shooting and lots of timber and stores were seen to fly into the air. Several very near our batteries and a few 5.9 shells around trucks—mostly on Tr St. no damage done and no casualties.	See attached sketch for particulars S.

1247 W 3299 200,000 (E) 8/14 J.B.C. & A. Forms/C. 2118/11.

WAR DIARY or INTELLIGENCE SUMMARY

Army Form C. 2118.

(Erase heading not required.)

Hour, Date, Place	Summary of Events and Information	Remarks and references to Appendices
G. Section. Oct. 30th	Rather warmer. Smell [enemy] guns shelled PUISIEUX in afternoon. Quiet morning. General FANSHAWE and GEN. LAMBTON visited our trenches in the morning. Work on trenches generally progressing but JEAN BART is a very difficult task as all the sides are beginning to fall in with the wet weather.	
Oct. 31st	Very cold and raw. Enemy shelled most of the day. A certain amount of shelling on both sides intermittently during the morning and afternoon. Trenches in a terrible state of mud and wet. Enemy fairly quiet during the day time.	
Nov. 1st	Very wet. Raining all day long. Enemy very quiet in the morning. Also our artillery. A few shells just now on of our working parties in JEAN BART during the morning, otherwise all quiet. Pte Allen B Coy tried by F.G.C.M a charge of Drunkenness Acquitted when on active service	

WAR DIARY
or
INTELLIGENCE SUMMARY

(Erase heading not required.)

Army Form C. 2118.

Hour, Date, Place	Summary of Events and Information	Remarks and references to Appendices
In the Trenches G. Section. Nov 2. HEBUTERNE	Pouring with rain all day. Men wet through & lying in a terrible state. Men in Trenches very tired. Enemy very quiet.	
In the Trenches G. Section Nov 3 HEBUTERNE	Still raining. Trenches getting worse. Enemy still quiet.	
Bihucourt Nov 4	Battalion relieved by 4th Worcesters. Returned to Hd. Quarters at COURCELLES. Enemy shelled communication line. No casualties.	
COURCELLES Nov 5	Day spent by men cleaning up selves, clothes & equipment. Went to baths at BAILLY.	
Bihucourt Nov 6	Two companies at work on Corps line. Weather getting colder. Major Ballard (Adjutant) left for England to take up duties & Command of Service Bn Rifles.	

Army Form C. 2118.

WAR DIARY
or
INTELLIGENCE SUMMARY

(Erase heading not required.)

Instructions regarding War Diaries and Intelligence Summaries are contained in F. S. Regs., Part II. and the Staff Manual respectively. Title pages will be prepared in manuscript.

Hour, Date, Place	Summary of Events and Information	Remarks and references to Appendices
COURCELLES Nov 8th	Battalion Route Marches	
Also Nov 9, 10, 11	Weather bad. Used working parties on Corps Line.	
Nov 12	Battalion relieved 7th Worcesters in G Section Trenches. B & C Coys in firing line, A Coy Batt Reserve, D Coy Brigade Reserve. Relief had some shell fire took place. Some heavy shelling in trenches. All dug outs flooded & leaking. Sections impassable.	
In the Trenches G Section 13 HEBUTERNE	Enemy very quiet all day. Evidently employed in repairing trenches. Kept two platoons working day & night on JEAN BART clearing communication trench which had fallen in and become impassable.	

Army Form C. 2118.

WAR DIARY
or
INTELLIGENCE SUMMARY

(Erase heading not required.)

Instructions regarding War Diaries and Intelligence Summaries are contained in F. S. Regs., Part II. and the Staff Manual respectively. Title pages will be prepared in manuscript.

Hour, Date, Place	Summary of Events and Information	Remarks and references to Appendices
In the Trenches G Section HEBUTERNE Nov 14	Weather fine but colder. Getting trenches in better condition. Enemy put over several rifle villies and a few heavier shells in trenches 30 + 31, during morning. Practically no damage done. Enemys machine guns very active on parts of trenches in morning.	
Ditto Nov 15.	Much colder. Snow fell in early morning. Winter weather fine and clear. Our Artillery and Enemy's fairly active. Snowing very quiet all day. Continued clearing trenches.	
Ditto Nov 16	Very wintry weather. Another fall of snow during night. D Coy R.C Irish Rifles 13th Battn came in for instruction. Little shelling during day. Otherwise everything very peaceful.	

1247 W 3299 200,000 (E) 8/14 J.B.C. & A.   Forms/C. 2118/11.

Army Form C. 2118.

WAR DIARY
or
INTELLIGENCE SUMMARY

(Erase heading not required.)

Instructions regarding War Diaries and Intelligence Summaries are contained in F. S. Regs., Part II. and the Staff Manual respectively. Title pages will be prepared in manuscript.

Hour, Date, Place	Summary of Events and Information	Remarks and references to Appendices
In the Trenches G Section HEBUTERNE Nov 17	Went fort during night. Enemy very quiet. All quieter was quite reporting morning. Trenches working day & night & no to have shafts	
both Nov 18	Few shells over during the day into VERCINGETORIX and LA CARRIERE doing no damage. One man wounded R.I.R.3 wounded by bullet in thigh. Enemy's minnen destroying Penelope.	
both Nov 19	Usual amount of shelling, both cleaning out and revetting trenches still continues unceasingly. Relieved by 7th Worcesters	
both Nov 20	Place in morning inspected of arrangement by me in consequence of a bombardment by me to Brown (in our right) when trenches however never came off. Returned to the Chateau CourceLLES	

1247 W 3299 200,000 (E) 8/14 J.B.C. & A. Forms/C. 2118/11.

Army Form C. 2118.

WAR DIARY
or
INTELLIGENCE SUMMARY
(Erase heading not required.)

Instructions regarding War Diaries and Intelligence Summaries are contained in F. S. Regs., Part II. and the Staff Manual respectively. Title pages will be prepared in manuscript.

Hour, Date, Place	Summary of Events and Information	Remarks and references to Appendices
COURCELLES Nov 21	Day spent supplying men and cleaning up after the antics' trenches ?? we have put them in the trenches.	
Billets Nov 22 to 26	Usual working parties each day on Corps Line. Weather fine & frosty. Usual Route march on 25th.	
Nov 27	Lt Col DUGMORE D.S.O. went to 2nd S.M. Field Ambulance at LOUVENCOURT.	
28	Battalion relieved 7th Worcesters in G Section Trenches day previous to days here frosts but 2 nights. Some important tether over as before. Major R.L. OVEY assumed command from Bike School to take over command of Battn. D Coy 20th tomorrow MANCHESTER Regt attached for instruction.	

Army Form C. 2118.

WAR DIARY
or
INTELLIGENCE SUMMARY
(Erase heading not required.)

Instructions regarding War Diaries and Intelligence Summaries are contained in F. S. Regs., Part II. and the Staff Manual respectively. Title pages will be prepared in manuscript.

Hour, Date, Place	Summary of Events and Information	Remarks and references to Appendices
In the Trenches G Section HEBUTERNE Nov 29	Thaw set in during night and rain began to fall in early morning also a continuance practically the whole day. Trenches in a hopeless condition 3 to 4 feet of water in some parts. Trench walls and surrounds falling in making trench impassable in places. Enemy fairly quiet. All available men working day & night clearing, pumping, baling &c.	
Nov 30	Trenches getting worse in spite of all our work. Day quiet & weather finer.	
Dec 1	Trench walls falling in everywhere and filling with water. Communication trenches impassable in some places. Enemy seen working on their trenches. A few shells over otherwise our front quiet.	

J.E. Pitt Major
1/4 Oxf & Bucks L.I.

CONFIDENTIAL

WAR DIARY
of
14th Batt Onf L Bucks Lt Infy.

from 1/10/15 to 1/12/15

PARADE STATE (Fighting Strength)

Company	Officers	Rank & File	School	Machine Gun Section	Signallers	Stretcher Bearers	Sanitary Squad	Reg Cook	Cooks	Coolie Q.M. Sgt	Orderlies	Butcher	Barber	Police	Armourer	Transport	Grooms	Officers Servants	Post Off	Tailor	Stretcher Bearers	Machine Gun Class	On Leave	Total
H.Q.	6			44	24	9	16	8	1		1	i 6	1	3	2	1	41	10	4	2	1	2			179
A.	3	120	10							4	1														135
B.	4	115	8							4	1														128
C.	4	120	9							4	1												1		135
D.	4	119	7							4	1														131
Total	21	474	34	44	24	9	16	8	1	16	5	6	1	3	2	1	41	10	4	2	1	3	1		708

In the field.

24th Nov. 1915.

J.E. Grigg Lieut. & Adjt-
1/4th 18th Bn Off B ucks Lt Infty

Includes 1 Officer 28th Indian Cavalry Attached for Instruction.

Parade State (Fighting Strength)

Coy	Officers	Other Ranks	Butcher-Hook	Machine Gun Section	Signallers	Pioneers	Stretcher Bearers	Brigade Sanitary Squad	Regt. Cook	Cooks	Coy Q.M. Staff	Athletic	Butler	Orderly Room	R.S.M.	Armourer	Transport	Grooms	Officers Servants	Officers horses	Bat O/C	Transport	Gunnery Store	Barbers	Ambulance Gun Centre	Total
H.Q.	5		2	43	22	9	16	2	3		2	3	1	3	2	1	17		2	3		3				179
A	5	134	1							4	1								2				12			157
B	6	131			2					4	1				1				2				11			152
C	4	120	2							4	1								2				12			142
D	5	121	4							4	1								3				9			142
Total	25	509	9	43	24	9	16	8	1	16	5	6	1	3	4	1	39	11	13	2	1	3	41			772

In the field.

2nd Oct. 1915.

J. Whinsworth
Lieut. & Adjt

4th Bn. O & B Lt Inf.

P.T.O.

Other Officers.

Major R. L. Osey. To Grenade School
Lieut. R. Fortescue. under instruction at Grenade School
Lieut. A. K. Gibson Transport
Capt. C. C. Fortescue. hosp.
Lieut. L. E. Griffin at the Base
Major J. O. Summerhayes. Med. Officer.

Parade State (Fighting Strength)

Coys.	Officers	Other Ranks	Pioneers L.Sgt	Batt. Machine Gun Section	Signallers	Pioneers	Stretcher Bearers	Sanitary Squad Cook	Cooks	Batt. HQ & Sgt	Orderlies	Butler	Hdy Menu	Police	Sanitary	Transport	Grooms	Officers Servants	Batt O/R	Stretcher	Barber	Tailor	Washing ?	Total
H.Q.	5			2	44	20	9	16	8	1	1	6	1	3	2	1	38	11	5	2	1	3	2	1	178
A.	5	136	7	1		2				4	1				1				2						151
B.	6	138	2	-						4	1			1					2						150
C.	4	134	5	2						4	1			1					2						152
D.	5	131	1	3						4	1								2	1					143
Total	25	542	15	8	44	22	9	16	8	17	5	6	1	3	4	1	38	11	13	2	1	3	2	1	174

In the field

9th Oct 1915.

x. (2 had Officers Orderlies
(4 Coy Orderlies.

1/4th OK? L..?

M...?

Lieut Coly Adjt

P.T.O

Other Officers

Major R. L. Otey.   t. Grenade School
Capt. E.C. Fortescue   Hospital
Lieut A.K. Gibson   Transport Officer
Lieut. J.E. Griffin   at the Base
Lieut T.R. Fortescue   Under instruction at Grenade School.

Major J.O. Summerhayes.   Medical Officer

Parade State (Fighting Strength)

Company	Officers	Other Ranks	Parade Sheet	Billet-Host	Machine Gun Section	Signallers	Pioneers	Shoeing Smiths	Saddlery Squad & regt. bch.	Cooks	Hy.A. Cyclists	Orderlies	Butcher	Orderly Room	Police	Armourer	Transport	Grooms	Servants Officers	Off. Mess	Bat Mn	Shoemakers	Barber	Machine Gun Course	Leave	Tailor	Total
H.Q.	4				4 3	17	7	16	8	1	1	6	1	3	2	1	39	10	4	2	2 1	3	2		4	1	173
A.	6	134	8	1						4	-								2						2		157
B.	5	126	9			3				4	1								2						2		152
C.	4	132	9			1				4	1								2						2		155
D.	4	114	8	1		1				4	1								2			1		1	2		139
Total	23	509	34	2	4 3	22	7	16	8	17	4	6	1	3	2	1	39	10	12	2	2 1	3	2	1	12	1	759

Saturday 16th Oct 1915
In the field.

Winstone Lieut Adj.
1/4th Oxf & Bucks Lt. Infty.

P.T.O.

Other Officers.

Major R. L. Otey.   O/C to Bde Grenadier School.
Capt Fortescue C.S.   In Hospital.
Lieut J. E. Griffin.   At Base.
Lieut A + Gibson   Transport Officer.
Lieut B. B. Brookes.   Under Instruction at Grenade School.

Officers on Leave.

Major A. A Bridgewater.
Lieut W. C. Cooper.

Parade State (Fighting Strength)

Company	Officers	Other Ranks	Grenade School	Machine Gun Section	Signallers	Pioneers	Stretcher Bearers	Sanitary Squad	Cook	Cook's Mate	Coy. Q.M. Sgt	Orderlies	Batmen	Ord. Room	Police	Armourer	Transport	Grooms	Officers Servants	Off. Mess	Tailors	Shoemakers	Machine Gun Class	Pioneers	Total
H.Q.	6			42	23	8	16	8	1		1	1	6	1	3	2	1	40	11	5	2	1	1	3		176
A	5	126	10							4	1															141
B	5	115	11							4	1															131
C	3	125	9							4	1													1		140
D	4	125	10							4	1															140
Total	23	491	40	42	23	8	16	8	1	17	5	6	1	3	2	1	40	11	5	2	1	1	3			728

In the field.

20th Nov. 1915.

9 Sgn.
Lieut. Adjg. Appr.
1/4th 13th Off. R. Bucks. B. Infty.

Includes 1 Officer 26th Cavalry attached for Instruction.

PARADE STATE (Fighting Strength)

Company	Officers	Rank & File	Grenade School	Machine Gun Section	Squadron	Pioneers	Stable Squad	Sanitary Squad	Sergt Cook	Cooks	County & H'Sergh	Orderlies	Butler	Bath Room	Police	Armourer	Transport	Grooms	Officer Servants	Officers Mess	Tailor	Shoemaker	Machine Gun Class	~~Instructor~~	~~At base~~	Total
H.Q.	6			43	24	9	16	8	1	1	1	5*	1	3	2	1	40	9	5	2	1	1	3			176
A.	4	123	12							4	1															140
B.	4	119	12							4	1															136
C.	3	125	10							4	1															140
D.	2	123	10							4	1															138
Total	19	490	42	43	24	9	16	8	1	19	5	5*	1	3	2	1	40	9	5	2	1	1	3			730

In the Field

13th Nov. 1915

J.E. Cripps — Lieut: Actg. Adjt.
1/4th 13th Bn of Bucks Lt. Infty.

Men on leave not included in fighting strength. Vide D.R.O.

Parade State (Fighting Strength)

Company	Officers	Other Ranks	Parade School	Machine Gun Section	Squadron	Pioneers	Shuklin	Sanitary Squad	Serg Cook	Cooks	Coy Or. Sergt	Orderlies	Butler Body Room	Police	Drummer	Transport	Grooms	Officer Servants	Officers Mess	Batmen/Tailors	Shoemakers	Machine Gun or Lance	Total
H.Q.	6			43	24	8	16	8		1	1	5	1	3	2	1	39	9	6	2	1	3	5	199
A	4	141	2							4	1												7	155
B	5	128	1							4	1												6	145
C	5	133	-							4	1												7	145
D	3	134	-							4	1												7	146
Total	23	536	3	43	24	8	16	8	1	17	5	5	1	3	2	1	39	9	6	2	1	3	32	765

In the Field

6th Nov: 1915

2 Sgt ― Lieut a/Adjt

1/4th Bn O. of B. seeks S. Augt B

Parade State (Fighting Strength)

Coys	Officers	Other Ranks	Grenade Seloos	Machine Gun Sekn	Signallers	Pioneers	Stretcher Bearers	Sudden Squad	Bright-ist	Cooks	By Night	Orderlies	Butcher	Baykeen	Police	Armourer	Transport	Grooms	Mess Servants	Officers Servants	Tailors	Shoemakers	In Civil Em/on Leave	Total
H.Q.	6			41	23	8	16	8	1	1	1	5	1	3	2	1	40	10	5	2	1	3	5	178
A	5	135	12							4	1												2	154
B	4	129	11							4	1												3	148
C	3	137	10							4	1												4	156
D	4	123	10							4	1												1	140
Total	22	524	43	41	23	8	16	8	1	17	5	5	1	3	2	1	40	10	5	2	1	3	15	777

In the field.

30th Oct 1915

J Ryan
Lieut & Adjt.

1/4.45th Off of Bucks L. Infty

Parade State (Fighting Strength)

Company	Officers	Other Ranks	General Service	Instructors Gun Section	Signallers	Farriers	Saddler Reserve	Saddlery Squad	Sing-cook	Cook	Coy Q.M. Sgt	Mobilies	Butler	Sick Room	Police	Drivers	Transport	Gunners Officers Servants	Officers Servants	Post Off Asst	Tailors	Shoeing Smiths	L. Gun Class Lance	Total
H.Q.	6		42	22	9	15	8	1	1	1	6	1	3	2	1	39	10	5	2	1	1	3	4	177
A.	5	139	1							4	1												4	149
B.	6	136	1	3						4	1												3	148
C.	3	136	1							4	1												4	146
D.	4	124	-							4	1												3	132
Total	24	535	3	42	25	9	15	8	1	17	5	6	1	3	2	1	39	10	5	2	1	1	3	18 - 752

In the field.

Oct- 23rd 1915.

J E Cush

1/4th 6th Of/JB Bucks - Lt. Infy.

In Lieut: O/Adji

145th Inf.Bde.
48th Div.

1/4th BATTN. THE OXFORDSHIRE & BUCKINGHAMSHIRE LIGHT INFANTRY.

D E C E M B E R

(2.12.15 to 31.12.15)
1 9 1 5

Attached:

Fighting Strengths.

WAR DIARY
or
INTELLIGENCE SUMMARY

Army Form C. 2118.

Hour, Date, Place	Summary of Events and Information	Remarks and references to Appendices
In the Trenches G Sector HEBUTERNE Sec 2.	Rain fell again during night the trench being communicating (1/4th Oxford Bucks L.I. Infty) were. The task before us in keeping the trenches in repair appears impossible. Trenches are flooded, walls falling in, & in some places the dug-outs communications & some of the front almost knee another falls in. Barring the company who left then sunk into haven and had to be dug out. In spite of this—although the men are dog tired, their cheerfulness is wonderful. Following the day Passed quickly as had our working Parties carried on unmolested.	1 Unit
6th Dec 3	Conditions getting rapidly worse. We are absolutely unable to cope with the work. As 6 am this morning a dug-out collapsed in PAPIN killing 4 men and injuring 2 of B Coy. Several other dug-outs have also collapsed but (Cont overleaf)	4 men killed

WAR DIARY
or
INTELLIGENCE SUMMARY

(Erase heading not required.)

Army Form C. 2118.

Hour, Date, Place	Summary of Events and Information	Remarks and references to Appendices
In the Trenches G Section HEBUTERNE Dec 3 (continued)	fortunately there were out at the time so we meant have had several more casualties. Our Artillery carried out a programme in the afternoon to which we had some reply, but fortunately no damage done. Communications blocked in several places. The men are obliged to move in the open in daylight, so often all one might just as well be shot as be drowned in "slush" in trenches alive.	
B/the Dec 4	There was view fell, he some annoyed that goes on, hardly a day out on the trenches habitable. We have had two complete companies in HEBUTERNE village. Enemys machine guns more active and his usual amount of shelling, otherwise we were not much worried.	

Army Form C. 2118.

WAR DIARY
or
INTELLIGENCE SUMMARY
(Erase heading not required.)

Hour, Date, Place	Summary of Events and Information	Remarks and references to Appendices
In the Trenches G Section HEBUTERNE Dec 5.	At last a fine clear morning. The usual Sunday artillery shoots on both sides, using up reserve of weeks "ration", with little or no effect. Much work on trenches. Able to make some headway in clearing communication.	
6th Dec 6	Another wet day. Communication to fire trench impassable by day. The two forward Platoons of "D" Coy. HEBUTERNE at 5 pm. The Battalion came back into billets at COURCELLES. The last relieved "D" Coy. did not arrive yet back to billets till 3-30 am.	Relieved by 7th WORCESTERS.

WAR DIARY
or
INTELLIGENCE SUMMARY

(Erase heading not required.)

Army Form C. 2118.

Hour, Date, Place	Summary of Events and Information	Remarks and references to Appendices
Billets COURCELLES Dec 7	Men washing and cleaning up. Went baths at SAILLY. Enemy artillery dropped some shells on COLINCAMPS Rd close to village, mostly "duds"	
Billets Dec 8	Between 8-30 and 9am Enemy put between 20 and 30 5.9 shells into COURCELLES. The change show, nearly half the shells were "duds".	
Billets Dec 9, 10	Usual working parties in Corps line. Weather showery.	
Billets Dec 11	Billets. Opening cement on Richer Well which has been driven in village.	

Army Form C. 2118.

WAR DIARY
or
INTELLIGENCE SUMMARY

(Erase heading not required.)

Instructions regarding War Diaries and Intelligence Summaries are contained in F. S. Regs., Part II. and the Staff Manual respectively. Title pages will be prepared in manuscript.

Hour, Date, Place	Summary of Events and Information	Remarks and references to Appendices
Billets COURCELLES Dec 12 & 13	Usual working parties on Corps line. Weather fine and colder.	
Billets Dec 14	Battalion moved up to relieve 7th WORCESTERS in G Section. Relief of front trenches was night support impossible in daylight as the Communication trenches are impassable. Front Companies of trenches were reinforced ie. WORCESTERS had moved into new Headquarters in VERCINGETORIX (see map 4) One dugout at present available which shall only for H'qrs mess, Orderly Room, Signal Station, Adjutants dug-out. Weather fine and frosty. Enemy quiet. Relief carried out without casualty. Brig General DONE took over command of 145th Bde vice Brig General McCLINTOCH to Hospital. D.S.O.	7th WORCESTERS.

WAR DIARY
or
INTELLIGENCE SUMMARY

(Erase heading not required.)

Army Form C. 2118.

Hour, Date, Place	Summary of Events and Information	Remarks and references to Appendices
In Trenches HEBUTERNE G Section Dec 15	Communication trenches mostly beyond recovery VERCINGETORIX only, we open. Lyn? to clean VILLARS. Carried on making out and laying wires for volunteer numbers. Rain fell in evening. Enemy quiet. In consequence of receipt of letter from W.O. letter M.O.I # 01/27 October 1915, we understand that we are holding the night sector of the advanced front. On our right we have the 4th Division. The 5th Florkers, of our Brigade, on our left. (ref Mops 5)	
See 16	Fine morning, but foggy all day; mist able to move about on top. Rain fell heavily during night. Clearing and appearing wire possible. Enemy quiet.	Major Rimmer to Hospital.

Army Form C. 2118.

WAR DIARY
or
INTELLIGENCE SUMMARY
(Erase heading not required.)

Instructions regarding War Diaries and Intelligence Summaries are contained in F. S. Regs., Part II. and the Staff Manual respectively. Title pages will be prepared in manuscript.

Hour, Date, Place	Summary of Events and Information	Remarks and references to Appendices
In the Trenches HEBUTERNE G Section Dec 17	Weather again foggy all day, but fine. Proposed bombardment by artillery postponed. Quiet day. Nothing to report.	
" 18	Weather still foggy. D Coy 18th Bn LIVERPOOL Regt came in for instruction, one platoon attached to each company of ours. Day quiet.	
" 19	Fine clear morning, several aeroplanes, ours and Boche, up. Heavi Sunday artillery activity. Draft of 25 O.R. arrived from POPERINGHE	
" 20	Quiet day, nothing to report. Rifles down during day.	
" 21	Artillery bombardment by our guns, as per programme. Hun nothing to report.	Bombardment G 21/12/15

WAR DIARY
or
INTELLIGENCE SUMMARY

(Erase heading not required.)

Army Form C. 2118.

Hour, Date, Place	Summary of Events and Information	Remarks and references to Appendices
In the Trenches HEBUTERNE G Section Dec 22	Relieved by 7th WORCESTERS as usual. Battalion went back into billets at COURCELLES. No 1 Platoon arrived in billets at 9 p.m. No casualties.	
Billets COURCELLES Dec 23	Men cleaning up. Band inspection by Quartermaster and Medical Officer. Buses at SAILLY.	
Dec 24	Route march arranged for today cancelled. All men received in billets and had their clothes disinfected by the Irish machine. Concert in evening, carols and Christmas Band.	

WAR DIARY
or
INTELLIGENCE SUMMARY

Army Form C. 2118.

Hour, Date, Place	Summary of Events and Information	Remarks and references to Appendices
Billets COURCELLES Dec 25.	Christmas Day. The Battalion was excused from all fatigues. In morning was spent playing Regimental football and a C Coy. and the M.G. Section in the front. Plenty but no spirits. M.G. Section won. All the men had an excellent Christmas dinner, the day passed without any hostile feeling from the Boche.	
" 26	Moved Corps Line Fatigues.	
" 27	Have received that we are to relieve 7 WORCESTERS tomorrow. Men changed to six days which worked 1 expect.	
" 28	Relieved 7 WORCESTERS in C Sector. During the morning several German aeroplanes flew over our lines. Numerous heard but	

WAR DIARY or INTELLIGENCE SUMMARY

Army Form C. 2118.

Hour, Date, Place	Summary of Events and Information	Remarks and references to Appendices
Bieurs COURCELLES Dec 28 (Cont)	Bombs were dropped at SAILLY and COUIN by him. The aeroplane evidently spotted host relief was taking place, as hay 5 killed. No names and particulars during our relief, but still no damage. Relief complete by 7 p.m.; no casualties. New system adopted of sending 2 Companies forming the trench garrison, support for them than 2 Companies supplying these town working parties, reserves and reliefs. At 10 p.m., Lieut DOYNE and 1 man who have gone out to inspect the wire, were reported missing. The men returned but reported that he had missed Lt DOYNE. Another patrol was sent out. Capt JONES immediately went out and returned some two hours later with the officer's body, when they found in a shell-hole. It had evidently been killed by a bullet from German machine gun, where has opened fire on the spot where he was found.	LT DOYNE A. Coy killed. Paullant manner shot through the head.

Army Form C. 2118.

WAR DIARY
or
INTELLIGENCE SUMMARY

(Erase heading not required.)

Instructions regarding War Diaries and Intelligence Summaries are contained in F.S. Regs., Part II. and the Staff Manual respectively. Title pages will be prepared in manuscript.

Hour, Date, Place	Summary of Events and Information	Remarks and references to Appendices
In the Trenches HEBUTERNE G Section Dec 29	Enemy Artillery very active all day, responding to by ours. Enemy aeroplanes flying over our lines in morning and afternoon. Enemy machine guns and snipers more active than otherwise nothing to report.	1 man A Coy badly wounded by Shell in trench 32. (died from wounds 30/12/15)
Dec 30	Quiet day nothing to report. Weather quite fine and colder.	
Dec 31	Artillery bombardment as per programme (J 31st Dec 1915) Carried out. Enemy replied considerably in trenches 31. 6 casualties in our own. Continued intermittently Shelling from both sides all day. At 10.55 pm Germans opened rapid rifle and machine gun fire and put up a lot of flares + rockets from soon afterwards. It was probably done just to mark the New Year, The Germans have been firing guns, I have 5 minutes in advance of ours.	3 Men A Coy Killed 3 " A Coy Wounded 1 man D Coy Wounded

Rovey Major Commdg
1/4th O/B Bucks Bt. Inf Bg

Confidential.

War Diary of

1/4th Battalion Oxfordshire and Buckinghamshire Light Infantry.

from 1st December 1915 to 31st December 1915.

Volume IX.

Parade State (Fighting Strength)

Company	Officers	Other Ranks	General Service	Cooks	Sgt Cook	Sy Drill Sgt	Orderlies	Pioneers	Shoemakers	Tailor	Officers Mess	Officers Servants	Transport	Farrier	Mechanic	Signaller	Drummer	Signallers	Machine Gun	Butcher	Saddler	Lewis Gun to Infantry	Indians
H.Q.	6				1	1	6	4	3	1	2	5	35	11	2	3		25	1	1	6		8
A	3	110	9	4			1					3											37
B	4	101	9	4			1					4											35
C	4	120	7	4			1					4										1	38
D	4	106	7	4			1					4											23
Total	21	437	32	16	1	1	10	4	3	1	2	20	35	11	2	3		25	1	16	8	1	677

In the Field 9/12/15   Lieut 9/12/15

1st Off. Bucks to Infty

19th Dec 1915

Parade State (Fighting Strength)

Comp.	Officers	Other Ranks	Hospital Sgts.	Coy. Sgt. Majors	Sgt. Cook	Coy. Q.M. Sgts.	Bicycles	Pioneers	Shoemakers	Tailors	Officers horses	Ammunition	Transport	Grooms	Police	Red Cross	Armourer	Signallers	Machine Gun Section	Butcher	Butcher Asstnt. Scouts Cooks	Butcher Saddler		Total
H.Q.	5				1		* 6	4	3	2	2	5	39	10	2	2	1	23	41	1	15	8	1	169
A.	3.	109	9	4		1	1					3												125
B.	5.	105	9	4		1	1					5												125
C.	3.	121	7	4		1	1					3										1		137
D.	5.	109	8	4		1	1					5												128
Total	21	443	33	16	1	4	10	7	3	2	2	21	39	10	2	3	1	23	41	1	15	8	1	687

In the Field

11th Dec 1915

X { C. Head Orderlies.
    2 u Batsn Orderlies.

Ypres Lieut/Adjt.
1/4th D. of Wcks. Lt. Infty.

Parade State (Fighting Strength)

Coys.	Officers	Other Ranks	Grenade Sect.	Lewis Gun	Sgt Cook	Coy Off Sgt	Orderlies	Runners	Shoemakers	Tailors	Officers Mess Orderlies	Officers Servants	Transport	Grooms	Police	Old Rooms	Sig. Sec. Machine Gun Sect.	Batln. Stretcher Bearers Sect.	Batln. Sig. Sect. Stretcher Bearers	Total
HQ	6	115	9	4	1		6	8	3	2	2	3	40	11	2	3	23	42	1	14	8	1	242
A	4		9	4		1	1					4									94
B	5	113	9	4		1	1					5									137
C	2	132	9	4		1	1					2									152
D	4	119	9	4		1	1					4									134
Total	21	479	32	16	1	4	10	8	3	2	2	18	40	11	2	3	23	42	1	14	8	1	719

25th Dec 1916 6105 hrs

In the Field —   + { 2 Med. Orderlies
                    { 4 Batln. Orderlies

J.R. Girk
Lieut & Adjt
1/4 ... Rifles

145th Brigade.

48th Division.

1/4th BATTALION

OXFORD & BUCKS LIGHT INFANTRY

JANUARY 1 9 1 6

Appendix attached :- Strength Return.

WAR DIARY
or
INTELLIGENCE SUMMARY

(Erase heading not required.)

Army Form C. 2118.

Instructions regarding War Diaries and Intelligence Summaries are contained in F. S. Regs., Part II. and the Staff Manual respectively. Title pages will be prepared in manuscript.

1916

Hour, Date, Place	Summary of Events and Information	Remarks and references to Appendices
In the Trenches HEBUTERNE G Section Jan 1/16	Quiet day. Nothing to report. Weather showery.	Arrived 1/4th Ox & Bucks W 31/14
Jan 2	Unusual amount of artillery activity on both sides. Weather showery all day.	1 man D Coy Wounded
Jan 3	Artillery very active during the early part of the afternoon, on W.E. ridge. Battalion relieved by 1/4 Wheelers returned to usual billets at Couvrelles. Two companies proceeded	
— 4	Usual inspection carried out. to Sailly for baths.	
— 5.	2 Companies on fatigue on Corps line; all other available men practiced in Tube helmet drill, wire heaving & section conduct. Weather very bad.	
— 6	Usual fatigue on corps line & heald making. No occur no end to be seen	

WAR DIARY
or
INTELLIGENCE SUMMARY

Army Form C. 2118.

Hour, Date, Place	Summary of Events and Information	Remarks and references to Appendices
Cincelle Jan 7. 1916	Usual fatigues in Corps line. Concert given by the Battalion in the School of Instruction. The Divisional Band played during the afternoon. A British aeroplane was forced to descend behind our lines, way from Cincelle after a fight with two German planes; his engine had suffered, partially damaged by bullets from the German aeroplane, which shot at the aeroplane, which shot at the German lines. The aeroplane was attempted by landing badly, but the airman was not hurt. He had landed at the Mens.	
" Jan 8th	Company drill & musketry out into schools, also a lecture on First Aid was given by the M.O. during the morning. The Battalion played the Divisional Supply Column in the competition for the Trenchard Ancaster Cup & was defeated by a few bullets & the	

WAR DIARY or INTELLIGENCE SUMMARY

Army Form C. 2118.

Hour, Date, Place	Summary of Events and Information	Remarks and references to Appendices
COURCELLES Jan 8th (continued)	learn by 6 goals to 1. Our men had on B. Players together once before. A Cinematograph show was given by the D.S. Column in the School of Instruction at 5.15 & 7. Both performances were well attended & much appreciated.	
HEBUTERNE Jan 9th	Relieved the 7th Warwicks in the RMK Section trenches as before. Quite a bright cold day. The fresh water has had a way much the trenches. Untouched by artillery over head throughout the day our own neck. North of our section. Quiet on both sides.	
" 10th		
" 11th	A large number of rifle grenades were fired at trenches on the right sector - and all night there a few minenwerfers. Our artillery replied on the front & support lines.	Lt. G. Howe. slightly wounded
" 12.15	Nothing of importance on positions. A shell fell in one of the billets in Hebuterne & exploded	1 man killed 4 wounded

Forms/C. 2118/W.

WAR DIARY
or
INTELLIGENCE SUMMARY

(Erase heading not required.)

Army Form C. 2118.

Hour, Date, Place	Summary of Events and Information	Remarks and references to Appendices
HEBUTERNE Jan 12th 1916	inside the upper room of the Mairie. Bombs the remainder or men may thence only if the wooden roof of yard below. Silence not broken.	
Jan 13th	Organised bombardment by our artillery all along the Corps line. Very heavy wind & raining at times. There was no reply from the Germans other than rifle grenades and too much manoeuvre on the right Sector. There are becoming a decided nuisance.	
Jan 14th	Arrangements have been made with the Bay artillery & Field gun, Stokes or gun of each used on unexpected bursts of every kind over Hun support & communication. The intended retaliation on the march to artillery camp in this direction. Quiet night.	1 O.R. Rank slightly wounded
Jan 15th	In the early hours of the morning, there was a lively rapid rifle & machine gun fire on the left Sector. The 7th WORCESTERS relieved the Battalion in G Section. Moved down to reserve billets at COURCELLES	

WAR DIARY
or
INTELLIGENCE SUMMARY

(Erase heading not required.)

Army Form C. 2118.

Hour, Date, Place	Summary of Events and Information	Remarks and references to Appendices
Billets COURCELLES Jan 16	Received orders that the Battn would take over K Section next turn from the 6th GLOSTERS. The BUCKS Battn who now held this section while our Brigade is in to take over an old trenches in G Section from the 7th WORCESTERS. Day spent cleaning up.	
Jan 17, 18, 19 & 20	Morning & indents to report. Company and section training carried out daily.	
Jan 21.	The Battn relieved 6th GLOSTERS in K Section. The relief was completed without casualty by 2.30pm. A Coy on the right, B Coy on the left. C Coy in Local Reserve in Village. D Coy in Brigade Reserve in KEEP. On our right are the 4th ROYAL BERKS (our own Bde) and on our left the 14. 3 Bde (Warwicks)	

Army Form C. 2118.

WAR DIARY
or
INTELLIGENCE SUMMARY

(Erase heading not required.)

Instructions regarding War Diaries and Intelligence Summaries are contained in F. S. Regs., Part II. and the Staff Manual respectively. Title pages will be prepared in manuscript.

Hour, Date, Place	Summary of Events and Information	Remarks and references to Appendices
In the Trenches K. Section HEBUTERNE Jan 22.	Our artillery carried out a pre-arranged bombardment to which the enemy made some reply. Otherwise quiet day.	
23	Enemy put over 5 minenwerfer into the CALVAIRE about 3-30 pm and a few small shells doing no damage. In the morning 9 enemy aeroplanes	
24	passed over HEBUTERNE circling on a bombing expedition. Artillery active on both sides. Weather bright and fine.	

1247 W 3299 200,000 (E) 8/14 J.B.C. & A. Forms/C. 2118/11.

WAR DIARY
or
INTELLIGENCE SUMMARY

(Erase heading not required.)

Army Form C. 2118.

Hour, Date, Place	Summary of Events and Information	Remarks and references to Appendices
In the Trenches IK Section HEBUTERNE Jan 25.	At about 2 am enemy started a heavy bombardment with various shells on our manoeuvres, on the WARWICKS on our left. This continued for nearly an hour, and caused some alarm. The enemy seemed to have sent a small party across + got into the WARWICK front line wiring. Some unexploded bombs behind their trenches among the damage on enemy trenches. Our artillery replied vigorously and by about 2.50 am all was quiet again.	
26.	Quiet day, nothing to report.	

WAR DIARY or INTELLIGENCE SUMMARY

Army Form C. 2118.

Hour, Date, Place	Summary of Events and Information	Remarks and references to Appendices
In the Trenches K. Section HEBUTERNE Jan 27.	Day quiet nothing to report. Battalion relieved by 6th GLOSTERS and moved back into reserve and billets at COURCELLES. In the evening about 6-30 pm we had a GAS alarm which however was afterwards found to be false.	
Billets COURCELLES. Jan 28.	Day spent in name cleaning up. 2 more GAS alarms at 6-30 am and 8-30 am. These alarms also appear to have no real cause for trepidation.	
" Jan 29.	Yet another GAS alarm at 7 am also false, although since then the alarm has come from different parts of the line. Everybody now fed up with these "GAS alarms", this being the fourth in about 36 hours.	

WAR DIARY
or
INTELLIGENCE SUMMARY

(Erase heading not required.)

Army Form C. 2118.

Hour, Date, Place	Summary of Events and Information	Remarks and references to Appendices
Billets COURCELLES Jan 30	6 Officers and 390 men on Corps Line fatigue. Remainder of Battalion went to route march.	
" Jan 31	In the morning the Battalion, less A Coy, were practiced in field work. 2 Officers and 100 men of A Coy on Corps Line fatigue. Battalion to move to SAILLY.	

Roney Major
Commdg 1/4th D+B of Bucks Bn Infantry

Parade State (fighting strength)

Comp.	Officers	Other Ranks	Grenade School	Machine Gun Section	Battalion Bombers	Sanitary Section	Pioneers	Cyclists	Cooks & Ch. Sts.	Orderlies	Butcher	Tailors	Shoemakers	Btl. Res.	Police	Transferred	Officers Servants	Officers mess	L.G. Office	Sgt Englnr	Lewis Battery	Pat O/C	Total
H.Q	6	—	—	40	21	13	8	8	4	*5	1	2	2	3	2	2 36 10	2	4	1	1		1	160
A.	4	115	2						4	1								1	1		1		124
B.	5	120	3						4	1								1			1		130
C.	3	131	2						4	1											2		141
D.	4	115	3						4	1													124
Total	22	481	10	40	21	13	8	8	16	10	1	2	2	3	2	2 36 10	2	4	1	1	4	1	679

In the Field.

1st Jan. 1916

x: {2 med Orderlies
    3 Bath Orderlies

J.C. Capp—Lieut A/Adjt.

1/4 Bn Oxf & Bucks Lt Infty

Parade State (Fighting Strength.)

Coy.	Officers	Other Ranks	French School	Machine Gun Section	Signallers	Stretcher Bearer Section	Pioneers	Police	Orderly Room	Butchers	Coy Q.M. Sgt	Orderlies	Officers Mess	Officers servants	Shoemakers	Tailors	Pat Chk Sgt Bugler	Transport	Grooms	Batman	Cook	Total
H.Q.	6			40	15	8	9	2	3	–	1	6*	2	5	3	1	1	1	34	9			154
A.	4	109	4					1			1	1				1						4	121
B.	4	114	5								1	1										4	125
C.	4	127	3								1	1				1					1	4	138
D.	4	109	3								1	1										4	118
Total	22	459	15	40	21	15	8	9	3	–	4	10	2	5	3	2	1	1	34	9	1	16	681

In the field.
8th Jan 1916.

B J P Simpson

J S Cuff
Lt Col Offg. O.C. 6/13 Bucks Bn. R. Inf. Fus.

* { 2 Medical Orderlies
   { 4 Batt'n Orderlies

Parade State (Fighting Strength)

Coy	Officers	Other Ranks	Signallers	Machine Gun Section	Stretcher Bearers	Pioneers	Police	Sanitary Section Cyclists	Orderlies	Tailors	Shoemakers	Bd. Room	Transport	Grooms	Officers Mess	Officers servants	Bugler	For the ...	Critical	Butcher	Cooks	Light Railway	Barber	Total
H.Q.	5		16	24	15	8	2	8		6		3	3	30	11	2	5	1						135
A.	5	121	4			1		1	1	1											4			134
B.	5	118	4			1		1	1	1											4			128
C.	5	120	3			1			1	1									1		4	2		134
D.	5	119	4			1		1	1	1											4			129
Total	27	478	15	16	24	15	8	3	8	4	10	2	3	3	30	11	2	5	1	1	16	3	1	660

In the Field
15th Jany 1916.

1/14th & 16th Oct 15 weeks to July 15.
In East Africa

Parade State (Fighting Strength)

Coy	Officers	Rank & File	Privates Sick	Signallers	Stretcher Bearers	Pioneers	Coy O.R.-Sgts	Boy Cooks	Orderlies	Police	Butcher	Tailors	Shoemakers	Odd Jobs	Transport	Grooms	Officers Servants	Post Office	Sgt Bought	L.G. Clerk	Total
H.Q.	6		24	15	8	8				6	3	1	1	3	3	29	10	2	5	7	131
A	5	134	4				1	4		1	1		1								146
B	4	130	4				1	4		1	1		1								140
C	4	133	3				1	4		1	1		1					1			144
D	5	119	3				1	4		1	1										128
Total	24	516	14	24	15	8	4	16	10	4	1	2	3	3	29	10	2	5	1	1	277

In the field
22nd Jany 1916

Parade State (Fighting Strength)

Coys.	Officers	Other Ranks	Rank & File School	Signallers	Shields Bearers	Sanitary Section	Pioneers	Coy Q.M.Sgts	Coy Cooks	Batmen	Police	Butchers	Tailors	Shoemakers	Ord Room	Transport	Grooms	Officers Servants	Officers Mess	Pat O/s	Sgt Bugler	O/r Clerk	Total
H.Q.	6	-	-	23	14	8	8	1	1	6	3	1	-	3	3	28	10	2	5	1	1	1	116
A	5	131	4	-	-	-	-	1	4	1	-	-	-	-	-	-	-	-	-	-	-	-	143
B	4	130	4	-	-	-	-	1	4	1	-	-	-	-	-	-	-	-	-	-	-	-	140
C	4	132	3	-	-	-	-	1	4	1	-	1	-	-	-	-	-	-	-	-	-	143
D	5	137	4	-	-	-	-	1	4	1	-	-	-	-	-	-	-	-	-	-	-	-	147
Total	24	530	15	23	14	8	8	4	16	10	4	1	2	3	3	28	10	2	5	1	1	1	689

In the field
29th Jany 1916
E/S.m.

J.S. Pipe
Lieut & Adjt

1/4th Bn D/of B Wales Rgt Infy

145th Brigade.

48th Division.

1/4th BATTALION

OXFORD & BUCKS LIGHT INFANTRY

FEBRUARY 1 9 1 6

Army Form C. 2118.

WAR DIARY
or
INTELLIGENCE SUMMARY

(Erase heading not required.)

Instructions regarding War Diaries and Intelligence Summaries are contained in F. S. Regs., Part II. and the Staff Manual respectively. Title pages will be prepared in manuscript.

Hour, Date, Place	Summary of Events and Information	Remarks and references to Appendices
Billets COURCELLES Feb 1/16.	Baths at SAILLY in morning and football matches in afternoon.	Units 1/4th Oxf & Bucks & Buffs.
Bill'ts Feb 2.	The Battalion relieved the 6th GLOSTERS in K section as before. We are told that the whole Brigade will be in the trenches for 30 days	Ref Map 6
In the Trenches HEBUTERNE K Section Feb 3	Quiet day, nothing to record. Major R.L. Bury D.S.O. Commanding the Battn. gazetted Lt Colonel (temp.)	
Bill'ts Feb 4. " Feb 5	Enemy exceedingly quiet, it is believed that we have now in of any rate different troops opposite to us	

1247 W 3299 200,000 (E) 8/14 J.B.C. & A. Forms/C. 2118/11.

Army Form C. 2118.

WAR DIARY
or
INTELLIGENCE SUMMARY

(Erase heading not required.)

Instructions regarding War Diaries and Intelligence Summaries are contained in F. S. Regs., Part II. and the Staff Manual respectively. Title pages will be prepared in manuscript.

Hour, Date, Place	Summary of Events and Information	Remarks and references to Appendices
In the Trenches HEBUTERNE K section Feb 6	Enemy put over several trench mortar bombs and some 30 shells during day. Situation normal.	
Ditto Feb 7	Enemy again put over several trench mortar bombs and quite a lot of 77mm and some 5.9 shells, doing no damage. Our trench mortar battery was in action during afternoon with good results.	
Ditto Feb 8	Practically all day from 9 am to 5 pm the enemy bombarded the trenches and upper end of village with 77mm 5.9 and larger size shells. Very little damage was done, considering the number of shells put over. The KEEP was most damaged than anything else.	3 O.R. wounded.

Army Form C. 2118.

WAR DIARY
or
INTELLIGENCE SUMMARY

(Erase heading not required.)

Instructions regarding War Diaries and Intelligence Summaries are contained in F. S. Regs., Part II. and the Staff Manual respectively. Title pages will be prepared in manuscript.

Hour, Date, Place	Summary of Events and Information	Remarks and references to Appendices
In the Trenches HEBUTERNE 1K Section Feb 9.	Again all day, the enemy's artillery fire was fairly intense. Some 3000 shells of various sizes must have fallen on the trenches and in the Village. The damage done was unimportant. The enemy have evidently moved up more guns on to our front. This village is going a very unhealthy place to live in.	
Trenches HQ. Hébuterne Feb 10. Feb	Another day of heavy shelling. The time the shelling was less incessant, but there were several bursts of very intense fire. No casualties were caused, & but very little damage either to the village or to the trenches. One fuse which was dug up yesterday proved to be of Belgian manufacture, bearing the letters (EP)	

Army Form C. 2118.

WAR DIARY
or
INTELLIGENCE SUMMARY

(Erase heading not required.)

Instructions regarding War Diaries and Intelligence Summaries are contained in F. S. Regs., Part II. and the Staff Manual respectively. Title pages will be prepared in manuscript.

Hour, Date, Place	Summary of Events and Information	Remarks and references to Appendices
In the Trenches HEBUTERNE K Section Feb 11th	Hostile artillery again active on the same lines as yesterday. About one o'clock a shell hit the roof of the Gateway into Headquarters, where Sergt Major PEARCE and Captain GRIFFIN happened to be standing. A piece of the shell entered the Sergeant Major's head, and he died immediately afterwards without recovering consciousness, and Captain GRIFFIN received severe wounds high on right arm, and on right thigh. During the afternoon a 5.9 Howitzer shell burst into a large dug out behind TRENCH 10 [MACDONALD] where over twenty men of a working party had taken shelter, fortunately only one man was injured, by a falling timber.	Capt. P.E. GRIFFIN Acting Adjutant wounded Right arm & thigh Sergt Major E.J. PEARCE killed 1 O.R. Wounded
Ditto Feb 12th.	Enemy artillery less active today, though there was still more activity than the normal. Our artillery shelled a spot were work was in progress, & the work stopped.	

1247 W 3259 200,000 (E) 8/11 J.B.C. & A. Forms/C. 2118/11.

WAR DIARY
or
INTELLIGENCE SUMMARY
(Erase heading not required.)

Army Form C. 2118.

Hour, Date, Place	Summary of Events and Information	Remarks and references to Appendices
In the Trenches HEBUTERNE K Sector Feb 13th	Hostile artillery not so active today; during the morning enemy sent a number of shells from a low trajectory gun; a part of this shell fell on a dud, and the first burst with heavy explosion about 40 feet in the air near Post Chapel around ALESIA FRIEND & CHAVEZ. Afternoon quiet except for a few rifle shots.	
Do. Feb 14th	Our Artillery carried out a combined bombardment at various times during the day; paying particular attention to GOMMECOURT WOOD. Enemy unusually quiet all day, did ~~not reply~~ to our guns.	
Feb 15th	Heavy rain during night 12/13 consequently trenches became very muddy; fall of water, heavy.	
Do.	TO M M Y(9) commenced to (?) tower, keeping especially bad. Worked on it all day. Hostile Artillery quiet; quiet day all round.	

WAR DIARY or INTELLIGENCE SUMMARY

Army Form C. 2118.

Hour, Date, Place	Summary of Events and Information	Remarks and references to Appendices
On the Trenches HEBUTERNE LEFT SECTION Feb 16th	Enemy extraordinarily quiet all day; our guns fired a little at different times. Rained heavily all last night & all the morning; consequently trenches were in a bad state; much improved by the end of the day; often working day & night at pumps &c.	
Do. Feb 17th	At 10.15 a.m a H.2 ment shells entered BUCQUOY HOUSE which was empty at the time; damage was slight; otherwise enemy was quiet all day. Weather fine; consequently the state of the trenches must improved.	
Do. ReSector Feb 18th	At 1.30 a.m. till 2.10 a.m Enemy shelled Warwicks on our left very heavily; caused some alarm. Our guns replied vigorously; all was quiet again by 3 a.m; at 3.30 a.m our guns shelled hostile communication lines for about ½ an hour. Rained all day; pumping & clearing all day.	
Do. Feb 19th	A quiet day; nothing of interest occurred; weather finer; state of trenches much improved. Enemy bombarded the 12th Infantry Bde on our right during the afternoon; aeroplanes active during the early part of the night; several were heard going & kent over our own trenches between 10 & 11 p.m.	

Forms/C. 2118/11.

WAR DIARY or INTELLIGENCE SUMMARY

Army Form C. 2118.

Hour, Date, Place	Summary of Events and Information	Remarks and references to Appendices
Sable Trenches HEBUTERNE. K Section Feb 20?	Great preparations made for a patrol to the Z ledge for purpose of knowing a casualene the men to be held out all day watching enemy movements. It was anticipated that enemy were topping the mine as about two companies fell not into the trench of interest received was the fire considerable aerial activity.	
40 Feb 21	Enemy quiet on our front, then artillery was active on our left. In evening a patrol of 2 officers + 30 men went out & 2 large patrols (6) went out for the Germans till 9 p.m.; no hostile patrol arrived	
40 22	Enemy quiet during the day, then to reply to our the tank between our lines / front to the BERCs at about 5 p.m. 20 shells came over at 11.30 pm 143 Bde relieved by 140 Bde on Gomme court enemy refused with heavy machine gun + shells various casualties on our WARWICKS, our patrol were out on patrols again. Weather cold with a little snow.	
40 23	Snowed mostly all day. Enemy very quiet, about 5.5 pm fell men shell of BPAT at about 3 km. A man white waving a shovel killed one shell was through the roof of No. 9 the shelter was unoccupied. Fairly quiet night, one patrol would certainly have killed from	

Army Form C. 2118.

WAR DIARY
or
INTELLIGENCE SUMMARY
(Erase heading not required.)

Instructions regarding War Diaries and Intelligence Summaries are contained in F. S. Regs, Part II. and the Staff Manual respectively. Title pages will be prepared in manuscript.

Hour, Date, Place	Summary of Events and Information	Remarks and references to Appendices
In the Trenches HEBUTERNE. 10 Section A.9.2.c.9	Rather quiet day. Enemy more active than usual, but no shells. Enemy aircraft ? field guns & trench mortars fired fairly a few rounds early in the morning. Our own guns retaliated & put 4 hundred shells over.	
Ditto 25th	Enemy lost about 15 to 20 shells round about the CALVAIRE in the morning, & damage our own. About 6 inches of snow hindered operations considerably.	
Ditto 26th	Snow still remains. Trenches kept clear of it in spite of a thaw starting the 26th, but 3 lbs of men. Both sides very quiet - nothing of interest occurred at night.	
Ditto 27th	Enemy artillery rather more active. Strong; except for a few small shells by CALVAIRE & the GOMMECOURT Rd, they left us alone. Hoping more, the bomb 5/GLOSTERS on night (Sat). A slight thaw in morning, trenches at bit softer, mud again. Enemy pulled up round.	
Ditto 28th	Hostile artillery more active. In the afternoon 4 2 cm shells round CALVAIRE. In afternoon 25 rifle gun about the CALVAIRE nothing. Our men slightly during after their trenches are getting on to stay as the 2nd is more but at present all are passable.	I.O.R. slightly wounded

WAR DIARY or INTELLIGENCE SUMMARY

(Erase heading not required.)

Army Form C. 2118.

Hour, Date, Place	Summary of Events and Information	Remarks and references to Appendices
In the Trenches HEBUTERNE. K Section Feb 2.9—	Rain storm making trenches very bad, all offficers full of water in My huridug, but all are passable. Our 6 in Howitzers were to bombard enemy Y Sap at 10.30 but postponed & eventry to 3.15. they Observation Balloon being up, at 3.15 they did good work on Y SAP. enemy replied on 143 Bde on our left. at 9am enemy aeroplane dropped 2 bombs W of PPPIN. Some aeroplane activity all the morning	

RS Shako 2/Lt
R/A/G
Capt Combe

RPA Dyke 2/Lt
A/Adj
1/5 OXf & Bucks LT Infy

Feby. 5th 1916

Parade State.

	Officers		Signallers	Rifles	Officers Mess	Machine Gunners	Cooks(?)	Bandsmen(?)	Batmen	Jackets	Sanitary Sq.	Stretcher Bearers	Pioneers	Transport	Grooms	Total
H.Q.	4		20	3	6	4	2	7	3	3		16	10	35	8	117
A. Coy.	4	139									2					141
B. Coy.	4	140									2					142
C. Coy.	5	141									2					143
D. Coy.	3	147									2					149
Totals	20	567	20	3	6	4	2	7	3	3	8	16	10	35	8	692

RS Blake
2nd Lieut.
Acting Adjutant.
1/4th Queen's Oxford & Bucks Lt Infy.

H.G.	6	20	2	6	3	2	7	3	2		16	8	35	6	110
A.	3	138													140
B.	4	146								2					148
C.	4	136								2					138
D.	5	147								2					149
	22	697	20	2	6	3	2	7	3	2	8	16	8	35	6	685

28 Flake

Feby 19/19.

Parade State.

	Officers										Total
H.Q.	6	22	3	6	3	2	7	3	2	16 10 41 8	123
A Coy	4	135				2					137
B Coy	4	144				2					146
C Coy	5	138				2					140
D Coy	4	145				2					147
Total	23	562	22	3	6	3	2	7	3	2 8 16 10 41 8	693

1st Shake
2nd Lieut.
at 1st Regiment
1st Reserve Bat'n Parachute Inf.

Feby 26th 1916

Parade State

	Officers	Strength	Police	Officers Mess	B.M. Staff	Orderly Room	Fatigue	Defaulters	Tailor	Shoemaker	Shoulder Braces	Prisoners	Transport	Grooms	Total
H. Qrs.	6		22	3	6	4	2	7	3	2		16	10	42	8	125
A. Coy.	4	183									2				185
B. Coy.	4	178									2				180
C. Coy.	5	173									2				175
D. Coy.	3	172									2				177
Total	22	709	22	3	6	4	2	7	3	2	8	16	10	42	8	842

R. S. Shake
2nd Lieut,
Acting Adjutant
1/4th Batn Oxford & Bucks Lt Inf

145th Brigade.

48th Division.

1/4th BATTALION

OXFORD & BUCKS LIGHT INFANTRY

MARCH 1 9 1 6

WAR DIARY
or
INTELLIGENCE SUMMARY

(Erase heading not required.)

Army Form C. 2118.

Hour, Date, Place	Summary of Events and Information	Remarks and references to Appendices
In the Trenches HEBUTERNE K Section 1st March	A quiet day; one machine gun fired intermittently from 2.30 - 6 pm. Trenches slightly improved but still rather muddy, worked on them all day & night.	
Do. 2nd March	Another quiet day; improving day and night continuously all trenches as now either except EBLIE. Lt Col R.L. OVEY DSO returns from leave and took over command of the Battn. from Capt CAMBERRE.	
Do. 3rd March	Another fine & clear day; trenches much improved; snow started at about 9 pm & continued all night making the trenches very bad again.	
Do. 4th March	Snowed all day; bowl thawed at the same time consequently trenches full of water & falling in; from a military point of view a miserable day. Both sides fighting the elements.	
Do. 5th March	Some aeroplane activity but not of interest. Enemy threw a few shells into SAILLY. 24 77mm shells fell around our right fire and support trenches and ricochetted and landed on the Medical Room; it passed through the roof & lay unexploded on the ceiling. Altogether 11 out of the 24 shells failed to explode. Weather rather fine; trenches improved but made under in some parts.	

1247 W 3299 200,000 (E) 8/14 J.B.C. & A. Forms/C. 2118/11.

Army Form C. 2118

WAR DIARY
or
INTELLIGENCE SUMMARY
(Erase heading not required.)

Instructions regarding War Diaries and Intelligence Summaries are contained in F.S. Regs., Part II. and the Staff Manual respectively. Title Pages will be prepared in manuscript.

Place	Date 1916	Hour	Summary of Events and Information	Remarks and references to Appendices
Tranchee HEBUTERNE N Section	MAR. 6	/	Enemy put a few shells into the village, Hostile machine guns fired into the village at intervals; 2 u 77mm. shells fell near left Coy trench H.Q. doing no damage. All fell near left Coy. village at intervals; 2 u 77mm. shells fell in the vicinity of our trenches. Several failing to explode, no damage done. Weather fine, condition of trenches improved.	
do.	7	/	A quiet day as far as hostilities were concerned. A new communication trench started from CALVAIRE ST. & FT 2, parallel to CHAVEZ ST. which is in a [ ] state of impassability, nothing of interest to record.	
do.	8	/	Hostile artillery active; it seemed almost as if enemy had started a stafe on the village again; 3 u 2 shells fell near H.Q. one entered the roof of the Orderly Room & bursted on the ceiling; the damage was remarkably slight, the most serious being the displacement of the tiles on the roof. Most of the shells went into the further end of the village. Western generally fine, some aerial activity, the long stay in the trenches is beginning to tell on the men, the sick lists grown longer every day, but they are sticking it well.	
do.	9	/	Hostile artillery fairly active; a few shells fell in the village doing no damage; at about 8.30 enemy started sending over one shell every 20 minutes [ ] to the same spot, near CHAVEZ ST. this went on for about 2 hours. Hand machine gun fire into village at intervals.	
do.	10	/	Nothing to record.	

WAR DIARY
or
INTELLIGENCE SUMMARY

(Erase heading not required.)

Army Form C. 2118

Instructions regarding War Diaries and Intelligence Summaries are contained in F. S. Regs., Part II. and the Staff Manual respectively. Title Pages will be prepared in manuscript.

Place	Date	Hour	Summary of Events and Information	Remarks and references to Appendices
In the trenches HEBUTERNE IC Sector	Jan 11	/	Hostile artillery active; several shells (77mm) fell round about FONQUEVILLERS RP. No damage done; one left for the nothing of interest occurred. 2nd Lieuts. G.M. PRIERRE, G.M. RAWLINSON & T.D. HUGHES joined the Batt. for duty.	A.H. POWELL
Do	12	/	Our machine guns had a strafe at night, enemy did not reply. A quiet day.	
Do	13	/	Great change in the weather. Perfectly fine sunny day. Considerable aeroplane activity. One of our aeroplanes was brought down near SERRE. C & D Coys relieved A & B in the fire trench.	
Do	14	/	Another very fine day. Many aeroplanes up. 7 German observation balloons could be seen from our fire trench. Fairly quiet day.	
Do	15	/	Fairly quiet day. The enemy fired several salvoes into the village, some the boom in the late afternoon.	
Do	16	/	Ditto. Several salvoes into the village in the morning. 2 men in D Coy hit by shrapnel, one of them being able to return to duty. The nose of a shell came through the window into the Orderly Room.	4921 Pte COX F. 1574 Bugler SMITH E.
Do	17	/	Fairly quiet morning. A certain amount of shelling in the afternoon. 1 man in C Coy injured.	

WAR DIARY
or
INTELLIGENCE SUMMARY

(Erase heading not required.)

Army Form C. 2118

Place	Date	Hour	Summary of Events and Information	Remarks and references to Appendices
In the Trenches HEBUTERNE K.3.1.tr.	March 18th	3 A.M.	2 Lt E.E. SMITH arrived with a draft of 27 O.R. A good deal of shelling all day, especially round trenches 8 & 9. The enemy seem to be using their 15 cm trench mortars more freely than usual. It is also believed that they have brought up one or two new batteries. It appears that they have one or two guns of 3.6 inch calibre. The Battn has been lucky to escape without a casualty, as there were several direct hits on the Right Coy Fire Trench.	
Do	19th	2 A.M.	An intense bombardment opened on our right in Q sectr & further S. The Battn on our right was also shelled fairly considerably. A good many shells fell near ALESIA STREET where a direct hit was obtained on the Signallers dugout. Maurice Wood also fired upon the CALVAIRE. & Shrapnel was put over the Francais and FONQUEVILLERS road. The Battn stood to & manned the alarm posts in very good style. The gas alarm was passed along the Battn, probably owing to the heavy laughrymatory shells thrown here as there was no wind. The bombardment died down about 3 A.M. Details lacking, but it appears that though the enemy's artillery fire caused several casualties in the platoons holding the front line, & succeeded in entering the trenches hdly 1/6 GLOSTERS, they were unable to carry off a prisoner & probably lost heavily from our barrage. They lift one prisoner behind our wire. Otherwise quiet day.	
Do	20th		Nothing particular to report.	

WAR DIARY
INTELLIGENCE SUMMARY

Army Form C. 2118

Place	Date	Hour	Summary of Events and Information	Remarks and references to Appendices
In the trenches HEBUTERNE K. Sect.	March 21st		At midday today, a change being taken over by a Company of the 5th Royal Sussex, having Batt. H.Q. in the Keep. Our disposition now became 1 Coy in Fire trench, 1 in Batt. Reserve in Keep, and one at BAYENCOURT resting; this position filled unfortunately by D, C, B, A, Coys. This is the first time that we have had a Company "out" since the beginning of February. A draft of 63 OR arrived about 5 P.M.	
Do	22nd		Fairly quiet day. 2 officers and 8 NCOs of the 18th W. Yorkshire Regt attached to the Battalion for four days.	2382 Pte BUTT. H. Coy wounded.
Do	23rd		About 12.30 AM raids on the enemy trenches were attempted by two battalions of the Warwick Brigade on our left, and by the 5th GLOSTERS on our right. Both the 5th WARWICKS and the 5th GLOSTERS were unable to get through the wire as sufficient time had not been allotted in the pre-arranged scheme. The 8th WARWICKS however succeeded in getting in and taking a prisoner. The Battalion was ordered to stand to from 12.15 till about 2.30 AM. About 2.5 AM there was a very severe burst of enemy artillery fire, solely along the FONQUE-VILLERS ROAD. As the men had been ordered to stand down, they had left their cellars and some casualties were caused.	2399 L/cpl WAKE A.T. B/cy killed. 2344 Pte Baugh R. B/cy Wounded. 2146 Pte BAKER G. D/cy wounded.
Do	24th		Bad weather again. Snow in the early morning. A draft of 32 OR arrived in the afternoon.	

WAR DIARY
or
INTELLIGENCE SUMMARY
(Erase heading not required.)

Army Form C. 2118

Place	Date	Hour	Summary of Events and Information	Remarks and references to Appendices
In the trenches HEBUTERNE K Sec. En	March 25th	/	Relief day. C Coy to Fire trench. D Coy to rest at BAYENCOURT. A Coy in Batt. Reserve. B Coy remain in KEEP.	1. O.R. wounded 1259 Pte Walton J.
Do	26th	/	Fairly Quiet day. Weather improved again. Another Quiet day. A man in B Coy hit in the head by a stray bullet near the pond.	
Do	27th	/	2nd Lieut F.E. Jones joined the Battalion. 2 officers & 8 O.R. of the 13th York & Lancaster Regt attached to the Battalion for five days for instruction. A Quiet day, but a good deal of rain in the afternoon.	
Do	28th	/	Nothing particular to record.	
Do	29th	/	Relief day. B Coy to Fire trench. C Coy to rest at Bayencourt. D Coy to KEEP. A Coy remaining in Batt. Reserve. One of the attached NCOs of the 13th York & Lancs Regt slightly wounded by shrapnel in the shoulder.	1. O.R. (attached) wounded.
Do	30th	/	A very large body of enemy been marching into BUCQUOY from the N. This body of troops reported by some to be cavalry manoeuvring. Enemy relief suspected.	
Do	31st	/	Weather very fine, & hot. Much activity except in the air. One of our aeroplanes fired & descended near the Bois Du BIEZ. Strong patrols sent out to Z hedge & May Bush.	

Rovey Lt. Col. Comdg. 1/4 Batt. Oxf. & Bucks L.I.

145th Brigade.

48th Division.

1/4th BATTALION

OXFORD & BUCKS. LIGHT INFANTRY

APRIL 1916

WAR DIARY or INTELLIGENCE SUMMARY

Army Form C. 2118

Place	Date	Hour	Summary of Events and Information	Remarks and references to Appendices
In the trenches HEBUTERNE K Sect.	April 1st		Glorious Weather. A good deal of aerial activity, but otherwise a fairly Quiet day.	
	2nd		A new system of holding the Brigade front introduced. The extreme right of the Brigade is G Section, was taken over by the 144 Bde. The remainder of the Bde line to be held in future by two Battalions. One Battalion hold frontages to the right by the addition of trenches K 10.3 & K 10.5 inclusive. [part of HOCHE. BATAILLE. IENA. QUDIN. MORAND] The portion of our line now become our Right Coy. Whatman organises on B Coy. becomes our Centre Coy. The left Coy. being still held by the 5th Roy Sussex. Relief completed by Noon A & R right the trench. D & Centre front trench C. in Battalion Reserve. B to KEEP. 1/5 GLOSTERS on our Right. Still very fine, a fairly quiet. Another longp patrol sent out at night but no enemy encountered. 1. O R Wounded	207 Pte BUCKLE.? A Coy Bullet wound in
	3rd		Several shells on our Right Coy trenches including some 15 cm HE shrapnel. One of these severely wounded two Sergts in A Coy. Two men also in A Coy received slight bullet wounds. A patrol from D Coy under 2Lt E.E. SMITH reconnoitred enemy saps at K A c 95.10 and K A c 6.3. The patrol reported both saps unoccupied.	52 Sgt EVANS 1677 — HINTON 1735 Pte WELLH P 3556 — PERRIN J All A Coy. wounded

1875 Wt. W593/826 1,000,000 4/15 J.B.C. & A. A.D.S.S./Forms/C. 2118.

Army Form C. 2118

WAR DIARY
or
INTELLIGENCE SUMMARY
(Erase heading not required.)

Instructions regarding War Diaries and Intelligence Summaries are contained in F.S. Regs., Part II. and the Staff Manual respectively. Title Pages will be prepared in manuscript.

Place	Date	Hour	Summary of Events and Information	Remarks and references to Appendices
In the trenches HEBUTERNE K Sector	April 4th	/	Fine Weather still holding. 1/5 GLOSTERS on our right relieved by the 1/4 Royal BERKS. Fairly quiet day. No moon & night very dark, & in consequence there was a cessation in patrolling which has been very energetically carried out for the last week or so.	
Do	5th	/	Fairly quiet day. The minenwerfer in GOMMECOURT PARK, which had not fired for some considerable time, reappeared in the German 2nd line trench on the side of the Wood facing us, & fired on the trenches on our left held by the 5th Royal Sussex. The light trench mortar, which has worried us lately in February, also reappeared and fires a few rounds on our trenches near the GOMMECOURT Rd and further South.	
Do	6th	/	About 9 PM an intense local bombardment started well away to the South owing to the distance, it was not necessary for the Battalion to stand to. It was afterwards discovered that the tunnel road had been attempted against the 31st Division. Only about few shells fell near head MARCOURT. [K.10.6]	
Do	7th	/	About 40-50 shells chiefly 10.5 & 15 cm Hows. fell on our front trenches between 11 & 1.30 PM. Two or three direct hits but no casualties.	
Do	8th	/	The Battalion was relieved in the trenches by the 1/Bucks BATTN. The relief	

Army Form C. 2118

WAR DIARY
or
INTELLIGENCE SUMMARY
(Erase heading not required.)

Place	Date	Hour	Summary of Events and Information	Remarks and references to Appendices
Whilets. BAYENCOURT	April 8 (continued)		WAS carried out in the morning & was completed by 11 AM. Coys marched via IENA across track to SAILLY & thence to BAYENCOURT where the billets & the Bricks Barn were taken over. Arrived at 1 PM. Mens billets rather crowded, but with time to make the necessary improvements, the village could be made fairly comfortable. A Draft of 20 OR arrived.	Killed: L/Cpl R Patt A Coy Wounded: Ptes Lovy Day Simmonds Lloyd Bishop Smilely Young Selander
Do.	9.		Quiet rested all day, preparatory to going out on fatigue all night. The 145" Bde dug a new trench about 600 yds in front of the present front line from K16B80 to K10D34. 4 Offrs & 45 Other Ranks did work & Bucks x 4 Berks provided covering parts. Work started about 6 pm & last party returned at about 4.30 am on 9th. A-D Coys found wiring parties. B & C dug & built barricade across PUISEUX Road, the work was beautifully done with a total of 30 casualties in the Brigade of which one suffered 1 killed OR killed 7 OR wounded. HQ GOC 48" Division congratulated the Bde on the excellence of the work & granted cash. Rolls one other done.	
Do.	10		Men rested all the morning; football soon the inter. of the platoon _____ _____ gave a private performance in the _____ SBRNLLM	
Do.	11		Companies carried out Kit inspection & nothing more seen by A.M. C & D Coys marched to SAILLY. ORPHULS gave a fine rate performance in the evening. very wet in afternoon	
Do.	12		Rained all day; quite impossible training our Company was arranged.	
Do.	13		Very wet; proposed inter-coml football.	

WAR DIARY
or
INTELLIGENCE SUMMARY

(Erase heading not required.)

Instructions regarding War Diaries and Intelligence Summaries are contained in F. S. Regs., Part II. and the Staff Manual respectively. Title Pages will be prepared in manuscript.

Place	Date	Hour	Summary of Events and Information	Remarks and references to Appendices
Sn Billek BAYENCOURT	14	—	Bakrs went for route march. G.O.C. 48th Division met the Batt⁹⁸ reinforced his pleasure at the smart turn out & good marching of the men. In the evening a concert took place & was very much loved that the Batt⁹⁸ own quite a number of men. Graffity 20 O.R. arrived.	
Do	15	—	Company training in morning, football & Div¹ Band in afternoon. Vades performed in evening. Sergt S. SMITH of B Coy greeted West and brothers to Coy in command. Capt COMBERE to English to resume medical studies. Capt HADDEN Frenches	
h. tranles HEBUTERNE K Sector	16	—	the Batt⁹⁸ relieved the 1/Bucks in the Sector. B & C Companies in the Batt⁸ Relief complete by 10:45 am the Bivoua having been relieved 10:45. took over trenches adjoining those of the 1st & 3rd Bde. We can + Frenches K·104 (Batailles) to K.32. (Bracet) left inclusive.	
Do	17	—	A guiet wet day. at 4 pm Gloucester Batt¹ started a strafe, enemy replied with about 9 MINNIES, doing but slight damage. More shots sent up by 12 midnight.	
Do	18	—	A continuance of wet weather. Our leave party returns today having treveled two days to Caly. Reason unknown. The enemy shelled the new French Eof Hebuterne between 9 & 11 PM. Our artillery retaliated. The enemy put 50-60 How. shells into our Frenches.	
Do	19	—	Another wet day. Practically the only work that can be done is to keep on cleaning up and repairing the trenches. One man wounded in CAZATRE by a trench Mortar shell which was hit into dugout.	22·30 Pte HARRIS C.S. B. Coy wounded

WAR DIARY or INTELLIGENCE SUMMARY

Army Form C. 2118

Place	Date	Hour	Summary of Events and Information	Remarks and references to Appendices
Hebuterne K Sector	April 20th		Company relief. A relieved C on Right. D relieves B on left. C to Batt. Reserve. B to KEEP. 1/4 Royal Berks relieved 1/5 Glosters on our right. Still bad weather. One N.C.O. in B Coy hit. Bullet wound in arm.	Cpl HALEY. P. B Coy wounded.
Do	April 21st		Good Friday. Still horrible weather. The 1/Berks Batt who took over from the Batt last time, took over C Sector on the Right of the Brigade front. 3 Batt of the Brigade thus being in the line instead of 2.	
Do	April 22nd		Another wet day. A certain amount of artillery activity. About 3.45 P.M. A Coy had a post knocked out at a place called A.2 Hunter 24.H. 5 men wounded, two of them seriously. A transport man hit by shrapnel on the KEEP. A good deal of night shelling on the night 22/23rd on H. Batt on our right. The enemy evidently determined to have their revenge for the big French days on the 9th.	2290 Pte WEBB, F.J. 2772 Pte SURRIDGE, A. 3515 Pte BARNES, W. 5264 Pte PARKER, W. 4755 Pte UNDERWOOD, A. All A Coy wounded. Pte MARTIN, L. 1425 B Coy wounded.
Do	April 23rd		Great improvement in the weather. A good deal of artillery activity on both sides. Culminating in a very nasty & intense on slaught by the enemy about 4.15 P.M. especially on our left Coy. Trench K.3.2 [BATAK?] was very fully knocked in by [Calvaire?]. 4 men in it were not killed but shell & the men improved, but they were able to be got made their way out.	

WAR DIARY or INTELLIGENCE SUMMARY

Army Form C. 2118

(Erase heading not required.)

Place	Date	Hour	Summary of Events and Information	Remarks and references to Appendices
In trenches HEBUTERNE K 5 c.6	April 24th		Splendid weather. 11 AM Minenwerfer on our left Coy. threw mortars again & fire on trench round SOMMERSET Road, knocking two K.9.1. (MARBOT) about. Batten hastily. About midnight this burst of very intense enemy artillery fire on the Battalion or our right & further on our right trenches.	
Do	25th		Battalion relieved in the trenches by the 1/6 GLOSTERS. Companies relieved by about 11 am and marched via IENA Communication Trench & SAILLY to HUTS previously occupied at BAYENCOURT. A & H. 1/4 WORCESTERS manned BAYENCOURT & did not leave till 3 P.M. The Batt'n had to bivouac in the orchards etc for dinners. Owing to the fine weather this was no hardship. Performance nightly. Enemy started shelling the 60 pounder battery in the SAILLY - BAYENCOURT road, & between 110 5.9" How shells in about an hour. One hit scored direct hit on a limber full of cartridges which created a flame about 20 ft. high. Quite day for Battalion. Usual inspections. In the afternoon C.O. Adjt. & 2 Coy Commanders attended G.O.C.'s intended conference in neighbourhood of COIGN. An officers mess whist stated. Still splendid weather. Performance by the CURIOS in the Evening. Divisional Band played in the village from 2.30 - 4 P.M.	
In Huts BAYENCOURT	26th	5 pm		

WAR DIARY or INTELLIGENCE SUMMARY

Army Form C. 2118

(Erase heading not required.)

Place	Date	Hour	Summary of Events and Information	Remarks and references to Appendices
In Billets BAYENCOURT.	April 27th.	/	Another very fine warm day. B Coy provided a fatigue party of 100 men for burying cattle at SAILLY. Other Companies carried out Company training. Coy Scouts started training under 2/Lt KING. The valley just E. of COIGNEUX was used as a miniature range. About 50 men inoculated by M.O. A very good performance by the "ORPHULS" in the Evening.	
Do	April 28th	/	Perfect weather. A B & part of C Coy to Baths at SAILLY. Company training carried on as before. Men as yesterday, inoculated and Baths. A draft of 1 officer & 30 O.R. arrived @ 8.30 P.M. The officer being CAPT. E.C. FORTESCUE, who assumed the Bath after about 7 months absence, & who took over command of D Coy.	
Do	April 29th	/	Very hot day. Whilst having the Battalion took was a fielding with the 1/5 GLOSTERS, starting N. of SAILLY and working down the valley towards COUIN & SOUASTRE by S. We owe here a N side of Valley. The movement was not very successfully carried out, doubtless owing to the Batta. being somewhat stale after such a long spell in the trenches. 6 P.M. A performance by the VARIETIES. This was cut short at 7 P.M. by an order from the Bde. that all men were to be in billets by 7 P.M. as it was reported that the enemy's artillery has cut some wire near the PUISIEUX Rd. and had damaged the CALVAIRE trench very badly. 11:30 P.M. to 12:50 A.M. 29/30 a considerable bombardment to the South, a raid being attempted by the 29th Division.	

Army Form C. 2118

WAR DIARY
or
INTELLIGENCE SUMMARY
(Erase heading not required.)

Instructions regarding War Diaries and Intelligence Summaries are contained in F. S. Regs., Part II. and the Staff Manual respectively. Title Pages will be prepared in manuscript.

Place	Date	Hour	Summary of Events and Information	Remarks and references to Appendices
In Billets BAYENCOURT	April 30th		Sunday. No work. Some of C & D Coys to Baths at SAILLY in the morning. A very well attended voluntary church service in Recreation Room. 2/Lt R. AFFLECK joined the Batt. for duty & was posted to B Coy. Still perfect weather except for a short thunderstorm in the afternoon.	
			Summary.— In trenches April 1-8th 16th-25th Remaining days at BAYENCOURT Casualties— Killed 1 Wounded 20 (1 since died of wounds).	

Rovey Lt.Col Comdg.
1/A Batt. Oxf & Bucks L.Infty

145th Brigade.

48th Division.

1/4th BATTALION

OXFORD & BUCKS LIGHT INFANTRY

M A Y   1 9 1 6

WAR DIARY or INTELLIGENCE SUMMARY

Army Form C. 2118

Place	Date	Hour	Summary of Events and Information	Remarks and references to Appendices
BAYENCOURT W/Billets	May 1st		Glorious weather. In the morning the Battalion again carried out the exercise practised on April 24th, moving along the N. side of valley from SAILLY to ROSSIGNOL FARM. The officers went over the ground first. The movement was carried out with fair success. It had been understood that the Battn. would be out of the trenches till May 11th. At 6.45 P.M. however orders were received to proceed to the trenches next day.	
HEBUTERNE In trenches G Sector	2nd		The Battalion relieves the 7th WORCESTERS in G Sector. First Coy left 2.15 P.M. Marched via SAILLY and LARREY track. As part of the garrison of the front line could not be relieved till after dark, relief not complete till 9 P.M. G Sector has been added to. Since the Battn. last occupied it, by the addition of the fire & support trenches to the RIGHT, as far as NAIRNE STREET. These trenches occupied by C Coy, A being in the main front line — formerly the whole Battalion front — was held by B Coy, D Coy on the Left. The Battalion on our right was the 12th YORK & LANCASTER REGT. — of the 31st Division, while the 1/5 GLOSTERS were on our Left.	
Do	3rd		A most unlucky day for the Battn. After a quiet night, about 9.30 A.M. the enemy started shelling our right Coy chiefly with 15 cm Hows & it is believed with 21 cm as well. They also put over trench mortars in twos & fired rifle grenades from the Grenade Battery. The french were ??? about. The shelling continued	Killed 2Lt KING J.S.C. "Lt HUGHES T.D. Slightly wounded 2/Lt AFFLECK R.

WAR DIARY or INTELLIGENCE SUMMARY

Army Form C. 2118

Place	Date	Hour	Summary of Events and Information	Remarks and references to Appendices
HEBUTERNE. In the trenches G. Sector.			most of the morning & afternoon and about 3 P.M. 2Lt KING and HUGHES were killed by the same shell. Lt KING was on duty and 2Lt HUGHES had gone down to the trench to arrange about working party in the trench. About the same time 2Lt APPLECK & a Sergt in B Coy were hit by shrapnel in B1 trench, & could not be got out till nightfall. Just after dark, 2 men in C Coy were hit by M.G. fire in the thigh. The left half of the Right Coy trench consists of a series of isolated posts, only held at night, & there men were hit while going out to their posts. A Corporal in B Coy was also hit, while relieving overland, by a stray bullet.	1901 Sergt BARNES Bay. Died at Field Ambulance. 2835 Gft SAUNDERS Bay. wounded. 3289 Pte CLEGG 4779 - REYNOLDS L.P. Both C. Coy. wounded.
Do.	May 4th		Night of the 3/4th Quiet. About 5.30 A.M. the enemy started shelling our right Coy trenches again and continued intermittently till 9.30 A.M. putting over about 140 shells in this period mostly 15 cm Howitzer shells, along CABER. One man in C Coy wounded. After this an fairly quiet day. Very fine. During the day the 167th Inf. Bde took over the Northern portion of Bde line down to the PUISIEUX Road. The only difference that this made to our disposition was that the 1/5 GLOSTERS took over the post at 2nd Barricade on the SERRE ROAD. One than front moved from BAYENCOURT to COUIN. About 10 P.M. enemy again active on our right. Few rifle Renches with shells & Trench mortar bombs and a few minenwerfer. Two men of A Coy who were working in trench JONES were hit.	2607 Pte WARREN G. Coy wounded. 2879 Pte COOK Atay. Wounded. W yrenades. 4929 PHUTSON Atay. Bullet in Shoulder.

Army Form C. 2118

WAR DIARY
or
INTELLIGENCE SUMMARY

(Erase heading not required.)

Instructions regarding War Diaries and Intelligence Summaries are contained in F.S. Regs., Part II. and the Staff Manual respectively. Title Pages will be prepared in manuscript.

Place	Date	Hour	Summary of Events and Information	Remarks and references to Appendices
HEBUTERNE in the trenches G Section	May 5th	2 AM	As one of the isolated posts of C Coy were retiring just before day light, they were fired at with rifle grenades, one man being killed and another slightly injured. On the whole fairly quiet day. The Right Coy got some 15 cm shells in the morning, and a few trench mortars bombs about noon, but no damage was done.	4486 Pte TOLLEY C Coy killed by grenade. 1916 Pte MITCHELL slightly wounded by grenade.
Do	6th	/	Company reliefs carried out in the evening. A Coy relieved C on the Right Bldg reliñed B on the left. It was noticed that when several of our posts which were relieving overland were fired at, a signal seems to be given on a whistle. Fairly quiet day. A little shelling round PIMLICO and elsewhere. But no damage or casualties. Draft 200R arrived LOUIN. To await Batt.	
Do	7th	/	Slight shelling all along front line causing 3 casualties in A Coy. The latter two were returned while trying to (Lt Pte BENNET up NAIRNS ST) L Col R L OVEY DSO to ENGLAND for investigation or leave (accompanied by Capt P. PICKFORD for investigation). Capt. E.W.R. HADDEN in Command.	2432 Pte OSTONE A. wounded by shell 2907 Pte BENNET R. wounded by shell Pte BENNETT up NAIRNS ST. Dgf Wounds 2256 C.S.M FINCHER E.F. wounded at Duty. All A Coy.
Do	8th	/	Battalion relieved by the 1/4th Royal BERKS in the afternoon. 1st Coy arrived about 4 PM. Relief completed in the trenches	

1875 Wt. W593/826 1,000,000 4/15 J.B.C. & A. A.D.S.S./Forms/C. 2118.

WAR DIARY or **INTELLIGENCE SUMMARY**

Army Form C. 2118

Place	Date	Hour	Summary of Events and Information	Remarks and references to Appendices
COUIN (Huts)	May 8th	10.30 PM	Lour Platoon (A) D Coy from 31.8.32 reached the Huts 1.30 AM 9TH. On relief the Coys marched via JENA track STAILLY, COIGNEUX, to Hut B in the Chateau Grounds at COUIN. Accommodation very fair. In fine weather shd be very pleasant.	
Do	May 9th		Usual day of rest after trenches "waked nil". Cheers a standing working party of 150 men to report to RE at QUIGNEUX church 7AM. In addition to this he had to supply 300 men to work on cable trench near SAILLY. Some of this party were unable to find their guide & returned. Rained all day.	
Do	16th		Working party of 250 to COLINCAMPS to dig CABLE trenches. In the evening 100 men to G Section to assist R BERKS in clearing derelict trenches.	
Do	10th		No parties by day except the usual 100 to COIGNEUX at 7AM. But a very very big party – 5 officers & 567 OR – was provided at night. This party in conjunction with a similar one from the 1/5 GLOSTERS was to dig a 6ft trench from a cable from DUBSCHEIN to the front to live near PRATTS RW along JENA, in G Sector. The cable was to be laid & the trench filled in by daylight.	

WAR DIARY
or
INTELLIGENCE SUMMARY

(Erase heading not required.)

Army Form C. 2118

Place	Date	Hour	Summary of Events and Information	Remarks and references to Appendices
COUIN Huts	May 11th		The digging was at very quickly & successfully carried out, but unfortunately the cable layers were not up to their task. As part of the job was left incomplete.	
Ditto	12th		Party arrived back about 4.30 A.M. 12th. Battalion had a lazy day after their nights digging, & in anticipation of another entertainment of the same sort on the night 12/13 - fortunately postponed. A football match between the Officers and Sergeants ended in a victory for the latter 3 goals to 1. The Officers not quite at full strength. Capt S. JACKSON, CF, attached to Battn, & Sgt Major (?) come some. A horrible pouring wet day. Besides the usual (?) at	
Ditto	13th		COIGNEUX. We had to provide a working party of 400 for cable digging in the neighbourhood of COUIN CAMPS. This party out 7.15 to 3 P.M. A draft of 37 O.R. who arrived the night before, were inspected & posted to their companies.	
Ditto	14th		Sunday. Weather too bad for a Church parade, but a service in the Recreation Room. 100 men at COIGNEUX and Baths were most of the day. In the evening the Battalion found a digging party of 10 officers & 520 O.R. for cable laying in the neighbourhood of COUIN CAMPS. Party moved off at 5.30 P.M. & returned between Mid-night and 2 A.M. 14/15.	

WAR DIARY
or
INTELLIGENCE SUMMARY

(Erase heading not required.)

Army Form C. 2118

Instructions regarding War Diaries and Intelligence Summaries are contained in F. S. Regs., Part II. and the Staff Manual respectively. Title Pages will be prepared in manuscript.

Place	Date	Hour	Summary of Events and Information	Remarks and references to Appendices
COUIN Huts.	May 15th	1	Battalion rested. After their night digging. Draft practice wire breaking. In the evening an excellent performance by the CURIOS in its Recreation Room, attended by many members of the Battalion. Pte Dawson D Coy, Fred Cuffern (at Hq of 1/5 GLOSTERS, on a charge of Conduct to the Prejudice of good order & military Discipline — a "green envelope" case. Accused found guilty & sentenced to 2 months F.P. No 1.	
Do	May 16th	1	12.20 AM to 2.25 AM Very heavy bombardment on Q Sector. From the noise it appeared about the heaviest bombardment yet experienced. This confirms when it was reported that the 4th Royal Berks has been raided and suffered heavy casualties. Beautiful day. German aeroplane over in the early morning. A piece of an anti aircraft shell has just dropped among the Huts. Companies engaged in company training. [Extract from London Gazette of May 13th — Lieut. B. B. B. Brooks to be temporary Captain. (Feb 20) 2 Lieut P. S. Bridges to be temporary Lieut. (Dec 29) 2 Lieut T. R. Patake ˮ do ˮ (Jan 11) 2 Lieut C. C. Harris ˮ do ˮ ˮ Lieut R. G. Lake ˮ do ˮ (Feb 20)	

WAR DIARY
or
INTELLIGENCE SUMMARY
(Erase heading not required.)

Army Form C. 2118

Place	Date	Hour	Summary of Events and Information	Remarks and references to Appendices
COUIN Huts	May 17th	—	Fine day. As it was known that the Brigade was to march to BEAUVAL next day, not much work was done, beyond various preparations for the move and inspection. In order to avoid the great heat, it was decided to start early, to be clear of COUIN by	
		5.15 AM		
		8.15 PM	Orders received that the times for the march were to be postponed 1½ hours.	
BEAUVAL Billets	May 18th	—	145 INF Bde marched to BEAUVAL via AUTHIE, MARIEUX, BEAUQUESNE. Order of march. Signals. Bde HQ, Berks, Bucks, Oxfords, Glosters, Glosters, B.M.G.Coy, T.M.Battery & Transport (Bde). [with exception of park ponies 5 A.T.a Limbers & Maltese cart which accompanied Battalion). Battalion left starting point — road junction just E. of ST LEGER Church — at 7.25 AM just before the Corps Commander, Lieut [General] HUNTER WESTON marched past. The Brigade marched in MARIEUX. The latter part of the march proved very trying, owing to the men being in bad condition, & because of the great heat. The men were also wearing shrapnel helmets for the first time on a long march. Consequently a considerable number of men fell out between BEAUQUESNE & BEAUVAL. BEAUVAL reached about 12.30 PM. Battalion billets in Rue de TANDAS and RUE DE L'EPINETTE. BEAUVAL two mules [RE] Ammunition very poor. [30 men under 2/Lt S. SMITH sent to BELLEVILLE two mule RE] Battalion handed in their long rifles, & re-equipped with new short rifles. A great improvement, as most of the old ones were quite unserviceable.	
Do.	May 19th	—	No cut-off on the new rifles.	

WAR DIARY
or
INTELLIGENCE SUMMARY

Army Form C. 2118

Place	Date	Hour	Summary of Events and Information	Remarks and references to Appendices
BEAUVAL Billets	May 20th		Divisional band performed in the Square in the afternoon and evening. A performance by the C of R.C.S. at 8 PM.	
	May 21st		Company training started. Owing to the fine hot weather the Brigade ordered that all training should be carried out between the hours of 7 AM & Noon. Routine as follows. Rouse 5 AM. Breakfast 6.15. Training 7 – Noon. The men allowed the afternoon free. 3 passes into DOULLENS granted up to 25%. Companies chiefly engaged in elementary musketry. The training areas allotted are universally small, & make anything like field work for anything larger than a section quite impossible.	
			A brigade church parade was held at 10 AM in a field outside BEAUQUESNE Road. Still magnificent weather.	
Do	May 22nd		Company training on same lines as before. Still extremely hot. 2 Lieut. A. N. HUNT joins the Battn. from the Base, and was posted to B. Coy. [Extract from London Gazette May 19th Capt. E. W. R. HADDEN to be temp. Major.]	

Place	Date	Hour	Summary of Events and Information	Remarks and references to Appendices
BEAUVAL Billets	May 23rd		Battalion route march 7AM to 10AM. Route. X roads N of Feu du ROSEL. BEAU QUESNE. Return to BEAUVAL. X Roads N of VERT GALANDE Fm. The Battalion marched very well. Weather rather cooler. The detachment at BRUE EGLISE returned to the Battn. An outdoor performance by the VARLETS in an orchard, in the evening.	
Do	May 24th		Company training as before. G.O.C. came round & inspected the Battn. at work. Coys started firing on the range. (miniature – 30-50 yards). C. Coy marched to HEM, & bathes in the Rue AUTULE. Cooker taken & some field work done out there. Rain in the afternoon.	
Do	May 25th		Wet. practically the whole Batt on fatigue. 200 men digging trenches for Bde Bomb Schl. 150 men out from 4.30AM to 11PM unloading trucks at AUTUBULE Station. 50 more men at same place unloading Field Gun ammunition. 50 men inoculated. Remainder of Battn mostly on Range.	
Do	May 26th		The whole Battalion marches to PEZAINCOURT to Platoons for Baths. Company training carried on as usual. When Coys is not at Baths. Weather fine again.	

WAR DIARY
or
INTELLIGENCE SUMMARY

(Erase heading not required.)

Army Form C. 2118

Place	Date	Hour	Summary of Events and Information	Remarks and references to Appendices
BEAUVAL in Billets	May 27th	7AM.	Brigade Route march. Order of March 9LOSTERS, OXFORDS, BUCKS, BERKS. Route CANDAS, MONTRELET, BONNEVILLE, & X roads N of VALHEUREUX. Near the latter point the G.O.C. met the Bde. In the afternoon the Corps Commander visited Batt. HQ & was introduced to the officers of the Battalion & made a short speech.	
Do	May 28th	10 AM	Bde church parade, attended by G.O.C. Orders received that Brigade would move on 30th to a training area NW of ABBEVILLE, about 20 miles distant.	
Do	May 29th		Company training as usual. In the afternoon the whole Brigade watched a Trench Mortar demonstration. (3" Stokes gun) given in a Quarry near Brigade Headquarters. Spectacle much enjoyed by the men. Draft of 47 O.R. arrived, mostly very young & small.	
Do	May 30th		Company training as usual in the morning. Battn completed grouping practice on the Range. No work in the afternoon in view of tomorrow's move. Every man in the Battn now has a steel helmet. 250 arrived today & re-equipped all the detail.	

WAR DIARY or INTELLIGENCE SUMMARY

Army Form C. 2118

Place	Date	Hour	Summary of Events and Information	Remarks and references to Appendices
BEAUVAL to ONEUX	May 31st	—	Whole Brigade moved into a new billeting area about 6 miles NE of ABBEVILLE. Order of March Bde HQ. OXFORDS, BUCKS, GLOSTERS, BERKS. Starting point about 3/4 mile outside BEAUVAL passed at 4.A.M. Route CANDAS, FIENVILLERS, BERNAVILLE, BEAUMETZ, COULONVILLERS, NEUVILLE, ONEUX. Halt for 1½ hours just outside BEAUMETZ for Breakfast. Battalion in billets by about 12 Noon. There is a large training area about 4 miles by 2, just north of the village.	

S Haldane Major Comdg. 2/Infy
1/4 Oxf. a Bucks

145th Brigade.
48th Division.

1/4th BATTALION

OXFORD & BUCKS. LIGHT INFANTRY

JUNE 1916

Army Form C. 2118

WAR DIARY
or
INTELLIGENCE SUMMARY
(Erase heading not required.)

Instructions regarding War Diaries and Intelligence Summaries are contained in F. S. Regs., Part II. and the Staff Manual respectively. Title Pages will be prepared in manuscript.

Place	Date	Hour	Summary of Events and Information	Remarks and references to Appendices
ONEUX Billets	June 1st	/	Battalion training carried out on the training area N of ST RIQUIER. 6 AM to Noon. Battalion practised advancing in attack formation across country.	
Do	June 2nd	/	Battalion carried out training as yesterday 12.30 – 5 PM. 8 Officers joined the Batt. from the Base. 2Lts SHEPHERD & LIDSEY posted to A Coy, 2Lts R.M.C. HUNT (returned from hospital) & LAY to B Coy, 2Lts JEFFERSON & TOWNSEND to C Coy, 2Lts SHERRINGTON & MILLARD to D Coy.	
Do	June 3rd	/	Brigade field day. Brigade assembled at YVRENCH at 7.30 AM & carried out an attack against a flagged position N of ST RIQUIER, about 600 yards away. Battalion B Buckx in front line.	
ARGENVILLERS Billets	June 4th	/	Battalion moved at 8.15 am to new billets at ARGENVILLERS about 4½ miles NW. New billets – vacated by 5/5th Bede, rather crowded. Church parade at 12 Noon. Major A.J.N. BARTLETT, Oxfordshire & Buckinghamshire L.I. from the Base & assumed Command. Draft of 5 O.R. arrived.	

Army Form C. 2118

WAR DIARY
or
INTELLIGENCE SUMMARY
(Erase heading not required.)

Instructions regarding War Diaries and Intelligence Summaries are contained in F.S. Regs., Part II. and the Staff Manual respectively. Title Pages will be prepared in manuscript.

Place	Date	Hour	Summary of Events and Information	Remarks and references to Appendices
ARGENVILLERS in Billets	June 5th	/	6 AM to 12 NOON, training in area E.S. of Village. 6-10 AM Companies practised extension. 10-12 NOON Batt. & Bn W's attacked a position on the ridge SW. of ARSENVILLERS, where the remainder of the Brigade had been digging in. 2Lt's H.F. PEARSON & G. PEARSON joined the Batt. & posted to B & C Coys respectively.	Major E.W.R. HADDEN to Hospital (appendicitis)
Do	June 6th	/	Wet morning. Batn paraded 5.30 PM & carried out a practise advance SW. in conjunction with remainder of Bde. 8-10 PM Brigade (Bucks excepted) & then carried out a night advance eastwards and coy up with an assault on an imaginary position from W of BOIS GRAMBOS, at dawn 7th. Bucks leaving followed by Booth. No work to remainder of day. Brigade horse show in afternoon.	
Do	June 7th	/	[Extract from Honours List in London Gazette of 3/6/16. Capt (T/Major) J.S. Amybene late Oxf. & Bucks ("Infty" awarded Military Cross 178. Sy Sergt L.R GRIFFIN awarded Military Medal 2645 Sergt J.H MATTINSON do.]	

WAR DIARY
or
INTELLIGENCE SUMMARY

Army Form C. 2118

Place	Date	Hour	Summary of Events and Information	Remarks and references to Appendices
AGENVILLERS in Billets	June 8th		Brigade assembled outside YVRENCHEUX 2.30 P.M. & carried out a practice attack in conjunction with the 144 Bde, in a S.W. direction. The 144 Bde advanced first & carried an imaginary line of trenches. 145 Bde then advanced through the 144 Bde, & captured a position on the ridge W of ONEUX. Very wet afternoon. Battalion not in billets till 8 P.M.	Report from L.G. of 6/6/16 & of 7/6/16 M.W. EDMUNDS Lte T/Capt 23/4/16.
Do	June 9th		Brigade assembled outside ONEUX 8 A.M. & advanced northwards towards AGENVILLERS carrying out a practise attack against the ridge S.t. AGENVILLERS. 144 Bde on our left. Battalion returned to Billets by about 1 P.M.	
March to MEZEROLLES (Billets)	June 16th		Brigade started march back to line. Battn marches off soon after 4 A.M. Order of march Bde. Bde Hrs. Bucks, Glosters, R. Berks, Bde HDQRS. Route: YVRENCHEUX – HEIRMONT – AUXI-LE-CHATEAU – WAVANS – PERNES (GRAND) Halt for breakfasts & dinners in a field near WAVANS, from 9.30 A.M. to 2.30 P.M. Much rain during the march. Capt. T.G. GRACE 2nd Scottish Rifles. attached to the Battn. joined for duty as Senior Major. Only the Battalion HQ and OUTREBOIS billeted in MEZEROLLES. The remainder of the Brigade billeted at FRESNES and OUTREBOIS.	

Army Form C. 2118

WAR DIARY
or
INTELLIGENCE SUMMARY
(Erase heading not required.)

Instructions regarding War Diaries and Intelligence Summaries are contained in F. S. Regs., Part II. and the Staff Manual respectively. Title Pages will be prepared in manuscript.

Place	Date	Hour	Summary of Events and Information	Remarks and references to Appendices
March to COUIN. (Bivouacs)	June 11th	/	Brigade continued march. Over French BIRKS, GLOSTERS, OXFORDS, BUCKS. Battalion marched at 5.20 AM Route GEZAINCOURT — HEM — BRETEL — DOULLENS — SARTON — THIEVRES — COUIN. The Grot. saw the Brigade march past outside HEM. The column considerably delayed, by a train intercepting the rear Battalion at a level crossing. Halt for about 2 hrs in a field between ORVILLE & SARTON. COUIN reached about 3 P.M. Battalion in Bivouacs on S. side of main road in valley.	
HEBUTERNE Trenches G. Sectn.	June 12th	/	Battalion Relieves 1/4th R. WARWICKS in Q. Sectn. 1st Coy stated from COUIN 8 AM. Relief complete about 1 PM. Coys disposed as under. C Coy Right Front cnl Coy B Coy Left Front cnl Coy A Coy Right B.H. Reserve Coy D Coy Left Battn Reserve Coy. Boundaries of sectn & disposition practically unaltered since last occupied by the Battalion. A new trench has been dug - KN 67 STREET, from IENA & JEAN BART between the front line and BRISCOU. Battn on our left 1/5 GLOSTERS. On our right 31st Division. Weather very wet & enemy extremely quiet. News received that Major EUR HADDEN died in hospital from effects of wounds.	11/6/16 9/197 Pte SMITH W.N. Killed by shell. 4737 Pte KEMP P. Army Sch Wound in face.
Do	June 13th	/	Weather still bad. Enemy on the whole quiet. 2 men in a carrying party hit during the afternoon. A great deal of work being done in the Sectn, especially on the front line and communicators. At night a party of 200 of the Bucks Battn	

Army Form C. 2118

WAR DIARY
or
INTELLIGENCE SUMMARY
(Erase heading not required.)

Instructions regarding War Diaries and Intelligence Summaries are contained in F.S. Regs., Part II. and the Staff Manual respectively. Title Pages will be prepared in manuscript.

Place	Date	Hour	Summary of Events and Information	Remarks and references to Appendices
HEBUTERNE Sect. in the trenches	June 14th		Came up to work. As Captain GRICE was setting the party to work at wiring in front of trench JONES, heavy Machine Gun fire was opened, & he was seriously wounded in both legs. An officer & a sergeant of the Bucks were also slightly wounded.	Capt. T.G. GRICE 2nd Suffolk Rifles attached 1/4 Oxf & Bucks L.I. Infy Wounded.
Do	June 15th		Coy relief. A relieved C in right fire trench. Dubens B is left fire trench. About 10 AM between 30 and 40 10.5cm & 15cm shells fired into VILLARS between VERCUNSTRIX & DUGGESCHLIN. No casualties but the trench badly blocked till nightfall. About 6PM PAPIN rdg. & the CARRIERE — now uninhabited — shells with 40 - 50 15cm shells & some shrapnel.	Capt T.G. GRIST died of wounds at Louvain
Do	June 16th		Weather still bad, & the work of cleaning up the trenches, so very urgently needed, consequently hampered despite a party of 200 from the Bucks each night. Enemy again shelled PAPIN & the CARRIERE. About 1AM night 15/16th a party of the 7th WORCESTERS attempted to carry out the enemy's trench just N. of the POINT. This raid has been previously planned & postponed. It was carried out, owing to a suspected enemy relief, although the 144 BDE was out of the line. One bridge of our artillery kept up a sweeping fire, whilst a party of RE attempted to blow a way through the	

r875 Wt. W593/826 1,000,000 4/15 I.R.C. & A. A.D.S.S./Forms/C. 2118.

Army Form C. 2118

WAR DIARY
or
INTELLIGENCE SUMMARY
(*Erase heading not required.*)

Place	Date	Hour	Summary of Events and Information	Remarks and references to Appendices
VISBOUTERNE (in the trenches G.Sector)	June 17th		Wire with Bangalore torpedoes. This was not successful. The party returned to our lines about 2AM, having failed to enter the enemy trenches, & having suffered several casualties. The Battalion relieved by the Bucks Battn. in the afternoon. The relief being completed by 4 P.M. Battalion moved via the Vicky Road into Bivouacs just South of the BEIL, on the CORCELLES-COIGNEUX ROAD. Weather fine but cold at night.	
Bivouac W. of SAILLY			While if B & C Coys out on fatigue on night of 16/17th. Weather fine. The whole Battn. out on working parties, chiefly at night, though there are a few small daily parties under the R.E. 200 here at broken G.S. etc. Lifting the Bucks at higher. Great preparations of all sorts being taken behind the lines, immense dumps of RE Material & Ammunition. As yesterday. Whole Battn. again at work. Besides the normal parties, a G. Seck, a party of 200 men are digging. Arrived on night of 18/19th.	
Do	June 18th		Great aerial activity. Several enemy aeroplanes over our lines.	

Army Form C. 2118

WAR DIARY
or
INTELLIGENCE SUMMARY
(Erase heading not required.)

Instructions regarding War Diaries and Intelligence Summaries are contained in F.S. Regs., Part II. and the Staff Manual respectively. Title Pages will be prepared in manuscript.

Place	Date	Hour	Summary of Events and Information	Remarks and references to Appendices
BIVOUACS W of SAILLY	June 19th		Battn still engaged on working parties. 2 companies on night of 19/20th. It was expected that the Battalion would be relieved and would go back to CORN ALLEY but this was postponed. Great aerial activity again. Perhaps the enemy are getting extra nervous owing to the continual registering by our heavies. Their aeroplanes in great numbers in the neighbourhood. Several of their planes on our lines again to-day.	4158 Pte CANTWELL MY [?] A Coy [?] Bullet wound in [?] 1689 Pte HURST G.B. C Coy Bullet wound in [?]
Do.	June 20th		The Balloon near ÉCRIN shelled he long gun to shells passing about directly over the Bivouacs. The usual working parties. 2 to work to BUTTES, A Section, 150 to D'Trench, 150 to BERLES in A Section. Baths allotted to the Battalion.	
Do.	June 21st		3 Officers — Lieut FORTESCUE, 2nd Lieut HALL & R.N.C. HUNT, & 220 Cpl Scott & BEAUCOURT to take over work of embarking trains from 1/6 GLOSTERS. Battalion still employed on various working parties. Open air performance by CURTIS in the evening. During the past week several officers have been to reconnoitre the trenches & approaches in the area to the South of the Divisional area.	

WAR DIARY or INTELLIGENCE SUMMARY

Army Form C. 2118

Place	Date	Hour	Summary of Events and Information	Remarks and references to Appendices
Bivouacs between COUIN and COIGNEUX	June 22nd		The Brigade relieved by 144th Bde. The Battalion moved into Bivouacs previously occupied by the 1/6 GLOSTERS between COUIN and COIGNEUX. Relief complete by 11.30 AM. As the accommodation left by the GLOSTERS was quite insufficient for the Battn. much time was spent in drawing fresh materials & erecting new bivouacs. Battalion also relieved of standing working parties by 144 Bde.	
Do	June 23rd		Battalion supplied following working parties. 2. 100 OR. Cable digging at COUIN CAMPS. by day. 40 OR. under R.E. at COIGNEUX. A digging party of 60 and another of 80 employed in carrying smoke bombs down to the trenches in Q Sector from HEBUTERNE. By night, one at C Coy having. A Bayards range dug on the hillside Rest of Battn Coy training. 1 Lieut. H.S. TAYLOR joins Battn for duty & posted to C Coy.	
Do	June 24th		Two Coys firing in Smoke helmet on range - Remainder Coy training as far bad weather & lack of ground permit. Bombardment started at 9 AM	
Do	June 25th		Sunday. Voluntary church Services. Firing on range continues. Otherwise no parades.	
Do	June 26th		Battalion struck the Bivouacs & carried & refitted them on a new site; about halfway between COUIN Church & ST LEGER, on the South side of the road.	

WAR DIARY
or
INTELLIGENCE SUMMARY

(Erase heading not required.)

Army Form C. 2118

Place	Date	Hour	Summary of Events and Information	Remarks and references to Appendices
Bivouac between CAGNICOURT & ST LEGER	June 27th		In the morning one company inspected in fighting over by G.O.C. Bde. Remainder of Battn engaged in company training on the terrain. In the afternoon some very successful Sports were held.	See Appendix
Do	June 28th		The detachment at GEZAIN COURT returned to the Battn at 7 PM. In the morning about half dozen shells fell within 300 yds of Bivouac vacated yesterday. Company training unavoidably interfered with by bad weather. It has been understood that the Battalion would probably move on the 29th therefore the day was free for the attack. Orders however received that the day for the attack was postponed two days.	
Do	June 29th		3 Coys to Baths in morning. 10 AM Orders received that Battn was to carry out a raid from G. Sector on night 29/30th. Lieut FORTESCUE selected to take command of party. Artist volunteers party 50 strong including 2 O's S. Smith & Lindsey, Covering party, 2 Lewis Guns & 25 men. While party trained equally by A & D Coys the orders to enter the German trenches just north of the POINT to capture prisoners. It was understood that the wire would be cut by late artillery, who were firing about the point of entry — K. 7. D. 13. all the afternoon. The party left the trenches near 1st Bavincourt 12.15 AM 29/30.	

WAR DIARY
or
INTELLIGENCE SUMMARY

(Erase heading not required.)

Army Form C. 2118

Place	Date	Hour	Summary of Events and Information	Remarks and references to Appendices
Between COPSE & STEGER	June 29/30		The first German wire was found badly damaged, and an existing gap was improved and the party passed through. The next two wires were against eight rows of concertina wire. Quite undamaged either about twenty five yards of the German parapet. In attempting to cut this wire the party was observed and countless flares were sent up. Bombs were thrown at the party & rifle fire opened. Attempts were made to get round and find other gaps on either side, but the enemy were very wide awake and the wire too strongly manned, and the party was successfully withdrawn, reaching our trenches at 2.10 A.M. The whole party returned in excellent order, and although the main object of the expedition was not attained, the while party was very creditably conducted. A Patrol also went out between 10.20 and 11.30 P.M. to examine the enemy wire along the front of Q Sector. There patrol was met by a Lewin. Another patrol also went out by the wiring party after they had returned to see if the enemy planes asp. Nothing was seen and the party returned just before daylight.	
B	30th		Company Training & inspections. Orders received that transport would be leaves by 7 A.M. following morning and Battalion standing by ready to move of 8 A.M. July 1st Probable destination MAILLY — MAILLET.	

Appendix to Vol XV
War Diary
1/4 Oxford & Bucks L.I.

SPORTS PROGRAMME.   27.8.16.

2 pm.   RELAY RACE.
        For teams of 8 men per Platoon.
        50 yards in Fighting Order. (Conditions below.)
            Winners:- Signalling Section.

2.45 pm. SIMULTANEOUS COMPETITIONS.
        (1) Lewis Gun Competition.
            2 teams per Company.
            Winners:- C Company. L.Cpl.Mattinson's Team.
        (2) Tug of War.
            10 men per Company.
            Winners:- Head Quarter Company Team.
        (3) Bombing Section Competition.
            10 men per Platoon.
            Winners:- 14 Platoon D Company.

3.15 pm. Obstacle Race for entire Platoons.
            Conditions below.
            Winners:- 13 Platoon D Company.

3.45 pm. Sergeants Race.
            Conditions below.
            Winner:- Sergeant.M.B.Wilkes. B Company.

3.55 pm. Officers Race.
            Conditions below.
            Winner:- Captain.E.C.Fortescue.

Teams for the Relay Race, Tug of War and Bombing Section are in no case to contain the same men.

CONDITIONS FOR COMPETITIONS.

1. RELAY RACE.   Heats. 8 men from each platoon of same Company.
                  Leading man of each platoon to carry his rifle and
                  hand to No.2. on completion of 50 yards and so on.
                  Final. Between the winning teams of each Company.
2. LEWIS GUN COMPETITION.
                  to be arranged by Lt.R.St.G.Lake.
3. BOMBING SECTION COMPETITION.
                  to be arranged by Lt.C.C.Craig.
4. TUG OF WAR.   Teams of 10 per Company.
                  Two Heats and Final.
5. OBSTACLE RACE. Complete Platoons in line with their Officers will
                  double 60 yards, pick up their equipment (Fighting
                  order) and Smoke Helmets, put same on and double
                  back to Starting Point. Platoon which has all its
                  men in in the shortest time will be the Winners.
                  Five Seconds will be added for every man arriving
                  at the Winning Post improperly dressed.
6 & 7 Officers and Sergeants Race.
                  100 yards in Clean Fatigue.
                  1 Yards start for every years service over 2.

145th Inf.Bde.
48th Div.

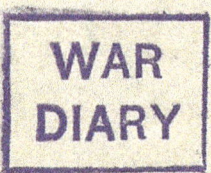

1/4th BATTN. THE OXFORDSHIRE & BUCKINGHAMSHIRE
LIGHT INFANTRY.

J U L Y

1 9 1 6

Attached:

Appendices 1 to 9.

WAR DIARY
or
INTELLIGENCE SUMMARY.

VOL XVI

WAR DIARY
of the
1/1 Battalion Oxfordshire & Buckinghamshire Light Infantry.
[145th Infantry Brigade
48th Division.]

for the month of
JULY 1916.

WAR DIARY or INTELLIGENCE SUMMARY

Army Form C. 2118

Place	Date	Hour	Summary of Events and Information	Remarks and references to Appendices
Bivouac betw. COUIN & SOUASTRE	July 1st	8 AM 9.20 AM	Battalion ready to move off according to instructions received over night. Battalion ordered to form ? between COUIN & SOUASTRE Roads. Men in marching order & also carrying 2 grenades, 2 sandbags apiece, while one platoon in every company puts on shovels & pt 5 & and ? N.C.O's has ? few aeroplanes flown overhead etc. Bde. marched to ? over GLOSTERS, OXFORDS, BUCKS, BERKS, 4th BDE near of 145 BDE. Route COUIN, COIGNEUX, BERTRAND COURT, BEAUSSART, MAILLY-MAILLET. Bde. bivouaced in fields S.W. of the village between in wood. Bivouac reached about 1 PM. Many clerks and delays owing to convoys of ammunition letters though the column. Heavy shelling audible all day & into the night. Many contradicting rumours circulated as to progress of the fighting, but no official news. Sleep somewhat disturbed by a 15 inch Howitzer about 40 yards away, which fired every half hour throughout the night. The following officers attended to Batt^n 's journey for duty. (? King 6th Marlboro Regt. W. MERRICK, PENWICK, PLOWMAN, HUTCHINS and THOMPSON all 5th Middlesex Regt. First 2 to Bde, next 2 to Coy, remaining 2 to C+D Coy respectively. The Bde & 144 Bde in Corps Reserve for the attack.	SKB

WAR DIARY or INTELLIGENCE SUMMARY

Army Form C. 2118.

Place	Date	Hour	Summary of Events and Information	Remarks and references to Appendices
MAILLY-MAILLET. Bivouac.	July 2nd	7 AM.	Bulletin received from which it appears that while French on the Somme, & Southern Corps of 4th Army have made good progress, the Northern Corps of 4th Army including VIII Corps have made no progress.	
		9.30 AM.	Commanding Officer & Adjutant sent for to Bde. H.Q. and preliminary orders issued to the effect that the Brigade would attack & capture the 1st & 3rd line of German trenches N. of ANCRE at dawn July 3rd. C.O. & Intelligence Officer — 2nd Lt. E. SMITH — went to 6 MESNIL to reconnoitre trenches from which Bn. would attack.	See Appendix 1
		2.30 P.M.	Capt. PICKARD returned from hospital. One new officer 2/Lt CARTER A.W. 5th Middlesex Regt. joined the Batt. & posted to D Coy.	
		5.30 P.M. 7 P.M.	Orders for attack issued. Batt. moved off, followed by BERKS & GLOSTERS, 5 Coy. of Men, each supplying officers [over 22] left behind at MAILLY when parks also attached. Batt. marched via ENGELBELMER, MARTINSART, to MESNIL which was reached at dusk. Battalion formed up river bank along Road leading N. from MESNIL. Bombing Party under 2/Lt WRONG went with R. BERKS up to HAMEL.	See Appendix 2
		11.30 P.M.	Operation orders cancelled. Battns. moved back to Bivouacs independently reaching there about dawn. One man hit by heavy shrapnel burst over the MESNIL Rd.	4726 Pte DAWSON J.E. wounded slightly artillery.
MESNIL & MAILLY.	July 3rd	Morning	Battalion resting.	
		4 P.M.	Orders received that Bde. would return to Bivouacs near COUIN in the evening.	
		6 P.M.	Brigade moved off in rear of 144 Bde. Order of march OXFDS, BUCKS, R BERKS, GLOSTERS, M.G. Coy, T.M. Battery. Bivouacs reached about 9 P.M.	B&B

WAR DIARY / INTELLIGENCE SUMMARY

Army Form C. 2118

Place	Date	Hour	Summary of Events and Information	Remarks and references to Appendices
Bivouac between COUIN & ST LEGER.	July 4th		Morning, one Coy to Baths. Much time spent in collecting the various articles issued to the Battalion for the attack. Afternoon extremely wet.	
		3 PM	Orders received that Battalion would relieve 1/7 WARWICKS in G Sector, starting at 4 PM. Owing to short notice and to fact that the disposition of the WARWICKS were different to our own [they had one Coy of BN, while part of TROSSACHS was allotted to us] relief was not complete till nearly midnight. Coys arranged as follows. R. Pulteney Coy, C. L Fretwell Coy, D. Right Reserve A. Left Reserve D Coy have post men hit while coming into the village. Cookers sent back as the village is distinctly unhealthy now-a-days, & looks very different to what it did formerly. 1/5 GLOSTERS [16 GHOSTERS?] (144 BDE) relieved 3/r Division on our right.	1656 Pte Mal EE Arly wounded Shrapnel
In the trenches HEBUTERNE G.Sector.	July 5th		A good deal of night shelling and M.G. fire, with the object of keeping open the gaps cut in the enemy's wire. Two men in A Coy hit while standing to in TROSSACHS. Orders received that the two Coys in the front line are to be relieved daily by the two Coys in Batt. Reserve, & that they are to take up shelter trenches overnight and act as if at an "outpost" State of trenches incredibly bad especially on the Right. Only one put by day, in the whole of the original front line. The trenches are in a bad a	2932 L/Cpl BATEMAN B.P.F. 3597 Pte MILLER RE Both wounded artillery

Army Form C. 2118

WAR DIARY
or
INTELLIGENCE SUMMARY
(Erase heading not required.)

Instructions regarding War Diaries and Intelligence Summaries are contained in F. S. Regs., Part II. and the Staff Manual respectively. Title Pages will be prepared in manuscript.

Place	Date	Hour	Summary of Events and Information	Remarks and references to Appendices
			Condition were in the depth of winter, except that they are chiefly full of water instead of mud.	3601 Pte McGee killed. 2723 Pte Hardwicke W. wounded
In the trenches HEBUTERNE G Sector	July 6th		3 men of A Coy killed while fetching rations from the village.	3531 Pte Holt C A Coy wounded by artillery
			Slight improvement in weather. The whole Battalion hard at work pumping out the trenches, several of which are now in a considerable improved condition.	SgtB
		9.30 PM	3 men in D Coy hit while pumping at the head of 1/ IENA.	
			The TROSSACHS handed over to the 144 Bde. Consequently the ammunition for the Battalion very considerably reduced, & A Coy sent to Bivouacs in the DELL, SW of SAILLY, where they arrived about 3A.	SgtB
Do	July 7th	7.30 AM	Weather perfectly atrocious, and the trenches filling up again rapidly. A smoke cloud discharge from the lines of the Battalion on our flanks with the object of "drawing" the enemy. Unfortunately the wind changed, and the cloud blew back over our own lines. Enemy however started shelling vigorously, especially on the Battalion on our right & on our right Coy. 2 casualties, in STAFFORD STREET, Coy Serg, Lewis Simmons.	16go Pte Marden E's Coy
			Night 7/8th part of B Coy, remain Gas cylinders from front trenches (K 23.10) near top of 1/IENA	4776 Pte Joeld F J A Coy Both wounded by artillery SgtB

1875 Wt. W593/826 1,000,000 4/15 J.B.C. & A. A.D.S.S./Forms/C. 2118.

Army Form C. 2118.

WAR DIARY
or
INTELLIGENCE SUMMARY
(Erase heading not required.)

Instructions regarding War Diaries and Intelligence Summaries are contained in F.S. Regs., Part II. and the Staff Manual respectively. Title Pages will be prepared in manuscript.

Place	Date	Hour	Summary of Events and Information	Remarks and references to Appendices
Trenches HEBUTERNE G Sub.	July 8th	/	Battalion relieved by Bucks Battn. relief being complete by 9 AM, in the Trenches. Some companies of 1/5th Bn going out with Bucks. Battalion moves to BENN track & valley Road, to Bivouacs between the HILL & COIGNEUX on the Hillside S. of the Road. Last party reached Bivouacs about 12.45 PM. One fort Bath at Bill. 6.30 PM 420 Men / A, B & D Coys sent up to G Sector to carry for working back to HEBUTERNE. Returned between 3 & 4 PM g/k.	B&D
Bivouacs between SAILLY & COIGNEUX	July 9th	/	Sunday. Voluntary church services. Aug 11 9/10th Clay from parties mending trench - hedge on the PENN, & taking "Gas bags" in VERCINGETORIX.	g/k
Do	July 10th	/	Good weather. On night of 10/11 inst. the Brigade Day & night French in Advance of H Sector. Guns front of G Sector. (see mem. attacks). Battalion Dug Southern half of Fire trench & Southern two Communications (BUGEAUD & ROBALT) A & B Coys dug fire trench. C & D by (a small detachment of 3) two Communicatns. Capt. PICKFORD in charge of whole party, 12 officers, 542 O.R. The work was successfully carried out, despite a good deal of enemy fire which caused several casualties. Actual work occupied under two hours. Party returned to	Appendix 3 2041 L/H TARRANT P.O. killed Shrapnel Bury 4447 Pte MAYO F Day killed M.G. 4930 Pte LOVERIDGE Bury 5193 Pte PAGER D/Y Bury 5185 Pte WHITE F. D/Bury Admitted to M.G. 2956 Sgt. (MAFF RT) Apr Bury 3447 Pte HERRING Bury 2877 Pte JARVIS Bury At Wounded Shrapnel

Army Form C. 2118

WAR DIARY
or
INTELLIGENCE SUMMARY
(Erase heading not required.)

Instructions regarding War Diaries and Intelligence Summaries are contained in F. S. Regs., Part II. and the Staff Manual respectively. Title Pages will be prepared in manuscript.

Place	Date	Hour	Summary of Events and Information	Remarks and references to Appendices
BUSNES between SAILLY & CARGNEUX	July 11th	1	Battalion silent 4 am 11th. Battalion resting after night digging party. Night of 11/12th practically whole of C & D Coy nr HEBUTERNE carrying & pick up parties up to trench for wiring new trench, & "dug-legs" in WHA. VERCIN PETORIX.	See PTE HAYNES B Coy wounded (Self inflicted) [?] E&B
To trenches HEBUTERNE Q Sector	July 12th	4 AM	Battalion starts for trenches to relieve Berks Battalion. A & B Coys Fire trench. B left Fire trench. D Batt Reserve. C supports. Enemy shell holes men too thick in the trenches. 2322 Pte ROUSE. C. tried by F. Gen. Ct Martial when reduced to on night of 6/7 July. Sentenced to 10 years P.S. Own artillery still firing action, but enemy reply methodical. Fealle. [?] Set 4 trench [?] our Battalion left at night. 1/5 GLOSTERS on our left 1/6 GLOSTERS on our right. Night of 12/13th practically all Coy up in HEBUTERNE carrying Smoke candles & R Bombs up to front trenches preparatory to our gas making - gas demonstration.	E&B
Do	July 13th	1	Morning: nothing particular to record. Weather fine. Not much enemy shelling	E&B

Capt. H.S.G. SCHONBERG 1st Batt. East Surrey Regt. attached to 1/4th Bn. @james for duty.

WAR DIARY
or
INTELLIGENCE SUMMARY

(Erase heading not required.)

Army Form C. 2118.

Instructions regarding War Diaries and Intelligence Summaries are contained in F.S. Regs., Part II. and the Staff Manual respectively. Title Pages will be prepared in manuscript.

Place	Date	Hour	Summary of Events and Information	Remarks and references to Appendices
In the Trenches N.E. BUTERNE G. Sector	July 13th (continued)		A programme of "considerable strafe" on the Capt. Front arranged for night 13/14th. About 10 PM 5th Div. Artillery on our right active. [Cdy. returns flag & DELL on right.] on right.	B/H Red attempted by G.H. POSTERS on G.S.5.
Do	July 14th	3.10 AM	Shrapnel discharges for half an hour also the Divisional front. 3.15 am Artillery opened on front line trenches. This provoked a very severe reply from the enemy who opened intense MG fire & put a tidy barrage with 15 cm shells 3 hand mortars, also JONES & CARTER Benches but line in front of J.W's & L6. Salient with shrapnel. Also some shelling mean left. Potentially only one casualty from P. Bomb. D Coy relieved B on left. Lewis guns attached from outer always. Men ordered to keep flat except over the top of parapet. Active patrolling evidence.	4775 Pte HAM BRIDGE H.J. (Blty. Wounds)
Do	July 15th	About 11.50 PM night 14/15th	"RAWLINSON took a patrol of 4 O.R. out from CARVER 12.10 PM Boats head. Shortly afterwards Capt EDMUNDS who was (missing) in post, has Whitton so came to help reported to him. He immediately went (out) to English & collected a last party including (Lieut.) HUTCHINS, which he took out to the place where the (Germans) seemed to come from. The party from 21 RAWLINSON tensely numbered in [illegible] 7 OR (Hour) practically as they became Hook practically, as the Germans & succeeded in bringing them in. Despite enemy fight falling all around & shrapnel being fired on party as they got back in a	BB

WAR DIARY or INTELLIGENCE SUMMARY

Army Form C. 2118.

Place	Date	Hour	Summary of Events and Information	Remarks and references to Appendices
In the trenches H. BUTTE NE G. Sect.	July 15th		The old front trench. Lieut RAWLINSON called & said the following. He noticed a yellow light in German trench & lay down & listened. (His party was in single file & he was leading.) On getting up again he remembers that he saw a bright light which knocked him over. Germans seemed to jump up in advance. As it believes that two men were killed outright (whether wounded or not he was uncertain) while the rest thought they were cut off & another out of his own devolver and started to search his private & The enemy were in a great hurry to get away. Lt Rawlinson pretended to be dead & thus he & little or some on the company had gone. Though extremely seriously wounded, Lieut Rawlinson was evacuated to 7th Ambulance Service July. Fine day. trenches now in fine condition except front line. CO & Adj of 16 Welsh Regt up in evening, as they were to take over next day. Lt 144 Bde on our right having relieved Bn relieved on our front, together with 141 Bde & Bucks & Berks. One of our aeroplanes came down just behind the PIPPIN Ridge after 7 P.M. & drew a good deal of shelling.	Lt G.M. RAWLINSON Clay Wounded Glanusk & Pork. 1897 Pte Cox W.P. Killed Rifle Clay 1303 (?Sergt ?) L Morris Clay 4159 Pte KINGHN M. Missing Clay 2591 Pte MAYWARD M. W. Clay Wounded R.B. remained at duty.

Army Form C. 2118.

WAR DIARY
or
INTELLIGENCE SUMMARY.
(Erase heading not required.)

Instructions regarding War Diaries and Intelligence Summaries are contained in F. S. Regs., Part II. and the Staff Manual respectively. Title pages will be prepared in manuscript.

Place	Date	Hour	Summary of Events and Information	Remarks and references to Appendices
In the trenches HEBUTERNE G Sector	July 16		Morning nothing to record. Awaiting relief orders.	
		4.30 P.M.	1st Coy of 1st WELCH Regt arrived. Relief complete about 7 PM except for LM gunners.	
			A Coy moved up from DELL and stores to WELCH for the night (one section stores to Earl platoon) WELCH	
			Batt. moved into Bivouacs between COIGNY and ST LEGER.	
Bivouac between COIGNY & ST LEGER	July 17th		Everything ready for a march to concentration pt of Q Sector.	R.B.
			A coy rejoined Batt. about 9 AM.	
		1 PM.	Batt. loaded into 36 lorries (transport moved independently) 2 PM Nosenter via AUTHIE — BUS — BERTRANCOURT — FORCEVILLE — HEDAUVILLE to BOUZINCOURT. Whilst the remainder	
		4.45 PM	Very bad traffic block on the road. Battalion in huts in orchards on West side of village. Transport at SENLIS.	
			It appears that 143 killed Boches are holding SILLIETRO and pushing to the line E & W. of POZIERES.	
Huts BOUZINCOURT	July 18th		Morning, inspections.	
		7.10 PM.	Received orders to attack between SILLIETRO and POZIERES 1.30 AM. 19th	See Appendix 4
		8.15 PM.	1st Company moved off through ALBERT & Dump on ALBERT – BAPAUME Rd. (on 30th mile) where R.E. Stores (also SAA etc) to be drawn to Batt.	
		10.45 PM.	Coys moved off up ALBERT-BAPAUME Road to get into position. B (in left) (in right) in front line, A Coy in support, D coy in Reserve.	

WAR DIARY or INTELLIGENCE SUMMARY

Place	Date	Hour	Summary of Events and Information	Remarks and references to Appendices
Between OVILLERS & POZIERES	July 19th	1.30 AM	Attack launched but held up. [See Appendix to pl. account]	Appendix 5
		About 3 AM	2nd attack ordered but abandoned owing to length of front covered being much too formidable	
		About 4.15 AM	Battalion returned to withdraw. This operation very difficult owing to state of French trenches. Coys reformed at Point (astride ALBERT) as marked but into	
		8 AM	Huts at BOUZINCOURT (when surplus officers & S.N.Cos who had been (49) left on going in about 12.35 PM). Remainder of day spent in rest. Total casualties 2 officers wounded [2/Lts JEFFERSON, & FENWICK (3rd Machine AR)] 5 O.R.'s killed, 47 missing believed wounded, 82 wounded & missing	B.B
BOUZINCOURT Huts	July 20th	—	[Night 19/20 Huts shelled by 4/5 Pooters from front 79 & 52] Bde reviewed that Battn wd be continued right of 20/21st Batt in reserve.	Appendix 6
		About 5 PM	Battalion moved off — bays at 5 mins intervals — through ALBERT as instructed in fall on 6 Ogn emplacement about 1/2 mile outside ALBERT just on SE side of ALBERT—BA-PAUME Road, reaches	
		1.15 AM 21st		
BOUZINCOURT near ALBERT	July 21st	6.30 AM	Information received [T248] that attack unsuccessful, & Bucks withdrawing to Bivouacs adjoining ours	B.B

WAR DIARY
or
INTELLIGENCE SUMMARY.
(Erase heading not required.)

Army Form C. 2118.

Place	Date	Hour	Summary of Events and Information	Remarks and references to Appendices
Bivouac outside ALBERT	July 22d	7.30 PM	Occupied by the Battalion. Battalion to relieve the Battalion in A line in afternoon. Battalion will be relieving more take over trenches. Instead 150 men parties to work under R.B.Eng. Right of (Btn) 250 for Sappers (on left) and 50 to cover R. Sussex who were laying new front & 3d (small) X.9.F (small).	
	July 22d	12.10 AM	B.M. 103 received intimation that stunt would be resumed, and carrying on different to resumed new trenches thing dug by Sussex.	See Appendices
		2.30 PM	All CO's with Bde HQ (CMR REDD.BT). Orders for attack issued.	
		9 PM	Battalion moved up to 81st trench position. The Australian Division on right were about to attack.	
		about 10 PM	Very heavy fighting afterwards in progress.	
In action but W.t PoZERES	July 23d	12.30 AM	Battalion attacks. A long right D on left B in support. Re. C in Reserve. For full account of their operations see appendices. Objectives as approximately shown on trace. Y.a.m.	See Appendices
			Left after a hard struggle to at least two counter attacks repulsed.	
		4 AM	Reinforced by two Coys of 4 R.BERKS Regt. Heavy shelling all day but no further attacks. In afternoon it became evident that Bn had suffered heavily & unfit to be relieved soonest was Bgd.	
			Would be relieved by the Bn of 143 Bde. Relieved by 1/5 R.WARWICKS. Relief not completed till after midnight 23/24th.	

WAR DIARY or INTELLIGENCE SUMMARY

Army Form C. 2118.

Place	Date	Hour	Summary of Events and Information	Remarks and references to Appendices
Bivouac outside ALBERT	July 24th		Coy moved as ordered to posn outside ALBERT, the Lab party getting in about 2.30 AM. Casualties Capt BROOKS missing believed killed. Capt BLAKE killed. Capt EDMUND'S 2Lts T.N. HALL, Q.M. PREDANE, E.E. SMITH, H.E. JONES, R. CLAY, S. SMITH & M. HUTCHINS [5th MD Shown Attd]. The following from wounds. Capt O.R. to killed 5. Missing Lthes killed 3 missing (wounded 16 & wounded) & missing O.R. 236. Battalion stayed in Bivouac till 4 pm Divison and then returned to huts at BOUZINCOURT via huts leaving to ANCRE between ALBERT & AVELUY.	
Huts BOUZINCOURT	July 25th		Battalion resting. A certain amount of German gun firing carried out, no Coy parties leaving Coy with any NCOs left.	N.B.
Do	July 26th	12.30 AM	News received that Brigade was being relieved and that Bn would probably go to VARENNES for Officers reunited for Batt to have in readiness to LEAVILLERS between 12.30 p.m. During harness their own cuttles. Eventually Brigade moved of 1.30 M. Over French OXFORDS, BUCKS, BEDS, FOSTERS, MARLBS & ARQUEVES via HEDAUVILLE — VARENNES — LEAVILLERS, arriving about 4 p.m. Parks carried on Motor Lorries.	B.B.
Billets ARQUEVES	July 27th		An easy day. Winter Sports. Many of the B.Coy visited the 2nd 6th Battalion at MUDLIERES. Draft of 15 O.R. arrived. Extra.	B.B

Army Form C. 2118.

WAR DIARY
or
INTELLIGENCE SUMMARY.
(Erase heading not required.)

Instructions regarding War Diaries and Intelligence Summaries are contained in F. S. Regs., Part II. and the Staff Manual respectively. Title pages will be prepared in manuscript.

Place	Date	Hour	Summary of Events and Information	Remarks and references to Appendices
Billets ARQUES	July 28th		Brigade marched to BETHUVAL starting at 8 A.M. & going on to the 11 A.M. Route via ORE Hill, BUIS BERGAIDEN, ROUES, RAINNEVAL & BLANQUESNE. Battalion to have billet in a barn & got a good reception. Snow with a Draft of 10 O.R. arrived.	
Billets BEAUVAL	July 29th		Brigade moved to new area comprising CRAMONT, DOMLEGER, AGENVILLE. Moved off about 8 A.M. Route CANDAS - FIENVILLERS - BERNAVILLE - BEAUMETZ - AGENVILLE where Battalion billeted. Great march 9 Offrs, R Berks (Oxfords Bucks). Battalion in billets by 1.25 P.M. Very hot indeed after about 9 A.M. Billets good on the whole, but the inhabitants rather suspicious of hostilities.	
Billets AGENVILLE	July 30th		Sunday. Church Parade in an orchard. Glorious weather. Draft of about 30 OR arrived.	
Do	July 31st		Coy training and wagonrying started, special attention being paid to bombing and musketry. Draft of 41 OR arrived.	

[signature] Col. Cmdg.
1st Bn. Oxf. & Bucks L.I. Infantry

APPENDICES to

VOL XVI [JULY 1916]

of

WAR DIARY

of

1/4 Batt. Oxf. & Bucks L^t In/try

Appendix 1. Advanced orders for attack July 3rd
2. Orders for attack July 3rd
3. Orders for trench digging night 10/11th
4. Orders for attack 18/19th
5. Report on attack 18/19th
6. Orders for attack 20/21st
7. Letter from G.O.^c Div. 22nd
8. Orders for attack 22/23rd
9. Account of attack 22/23rd. (with map).

Army Form C. 2118.

WAR DIARY
or
INTELLIGENCE SUMMARY.

(Erase heading not required.)

Instructions regarding War Diaries and Intelligence Summaries are contained in F. S. Regs., Part II. and the Staff Manual respectively. Title pages will be prepared in manuscript.

Place	Date	Hour	Summary of Events and Information	Remarks and references to Appendices

2353 Wt. W2544/1454 700,000 5/15 D. D. & L. A.D.S.S./Forms/C. 2118.

1. After yesterday's heavy fighting, our advanced detachments of VIII Corps were withdrawn to our old line.
X Corps still hold part of ground gained S of ANCRE but the situation is not clear.
Advance of Southern Corps of British Army and the French was maintained.
Germans in front of Northern Corps have suffered very heavy losses and no hostile reserves are reported.
The Northern defensive flank will not be pushed further than the high ground S of the ANCRE and the Spur to W of Station Road to Y Ravine inclusive.
29th Division will hold our front trenches from ANCRE to Hawthorne Ridge.
Fresh troops continue the attack S of the ANCRE.
48th Division (and 1 Brigade less 1 Battalion 29th Divn attached) will seize and form defensive flank N. of ANCRE.

2. <u>Objective.</u> 145th Brigade less 1 Battalion in Divisional Reserve - From ANCRE to Point 83 inclusive.
144th Brigade less 1 Battalion thence to Point 60 S. of Y Ravine inclusive.
<u>LIMITS.</u> First three lines of trenches and such forward points as are necessary to dominate Station Road and maintain Y Ravine.

3. <u>Formation.</u> The attacking Battalions of Brigades to be not less than four waves. Each wave three or four lines deep. Half Platoon of 5th Sussex(Pioneers) follow each wave for consolidating.
   1st Wave to take and hold 1st line of trenches.
   2nd " " " " " next line.
   3rd " " " " " " "

4. Brigade Reserve - One Battalion from each Brigade.
Divisional Reserve near ENGELBELMER.

5. <u>Covering fire.</u> Artillery Bombardment this afternoon and intense fire prior to and during attack.
Smoke clouds on each flank if favourable.
M.G.Fire from places in our Front Line, 29th Divn.assisting.

6. Roads and hours for moving into position will be allotted later.

7. The advance from our present Front Line will start at 3.30 am tomorrow morning.

8. <u>Supplies.</u> Rear Platoon to carry tools. Each Company to carry spare grenades.
Every man to carry rations for current day and Iron Rations.

Appendix 2

145th Infantry Brigade Order No. 28.

1. Situation is as given out this morning.

2. Brigade less BUCKS Battalion will march at 7 pm to MESNIL.
   Order of March.
   > OXFORDS.
   > R.BERKS.
   > GLOSTERS.
   > M.G.COMPANY.
   > T.M.BATTERY.
   > B SECTION 3rd F.AMB.
   > 1ST LINE TRANSPORT BRIGADED.

   Transport less L.G.Limbers and Bomb Limbers will be brigaded and all Transport will return to MARTINSART.

3. The objective as already made known will be gained by 4 R.BERKS. on right and 5th GLOSTERS on left.
   O.C.OXFORDS will detach a party of 25 Bombers under an Officer who will advance with Right of 1st Wave of R.BERKS and will bomb up Valley of ANCRE from Q.24.a. getting into touch with Bombers of 49th Division on our right almost opposite ST.PIERRE DIVION.
   4th OXFORDS in Brigade Reserve will be along road in Q.22.c. and Q.28.a.
   T.Mortars will remain in Brigade Reserve until further orders.

4. Advanced Dressing Station will be established in cellars in HAMEL.

5. 1st Line Transport will remain at MARTINSART.

6. <u>DUMPS</u>. For Grenades, S.A.A., Water and rations will be formed at Brigade Head Quarters in MESNIL at Q.28.c.7.8.(Last house S. side of Road.

7. Advanced Brigade H.Qrs. will be at R.A. O.P. in Jacobs Ladder Q.20.a.3.6½.
   Hourly Reports will be sent to Brigade Head Quarters at Q.29.c.7.8.

Dictated to Adjutants
    5.45 pm.
    2.7.16.

> <u>INTENSE BOMBARDMENT.</u>
> 2.15 to 3.15 am.
> 3.15 Infantry Start.
> 3.20 Lift off First Line.
> 3.25 Lift off 2nd Line.
> 3.40 Lift off 3rd Line.

Extracts from 145th Infantry Brigade 1093 date 10.7.16.

Appendix 3.

NEW TRENCH.

1. Advanced trench as per attached sketch (A) will be dug tonight 10/11th inst.

2. Digging will be done as before by groups.
   In the Fire Trench each party of 10 men will dig fire bay and two halves of adjoining traverses, vide attached sketch (B) and, in Zig Zag Communication Trench, each party of 16 men will dig two legs of the Zig Zag.

3. Each party of 10 (or 16) men will be under a N.C.O. and 4 parties of 10 or 16 men each will form one group under an Officer. Groups of each Unit will be numbered, leading Group being No.1., next group No.2., etc.

4. Trench will be dug 3' deep (length of pick helve) and it must be 3' broad at the bottom......................

9. Units will dig:-
   OXFORDS. Front Line from 1st BARRICADE to BUGEAUD and communications BOUALT and BUGEAUD.
   GLOSTERS. Remainder of front line and communication RICHARDS......

10. OXFORDS will provide:-
    518 Men.   41 N.C.Os   13 Officers..................

11. All earth in Fire Trench will be thrown forward.
    String marking trench is forward edge of Trench................

10.7.16.   (sd) T.J.Leahy. Captain.,
                                          Brigade Major.,
                                          145th Infy.Bde.

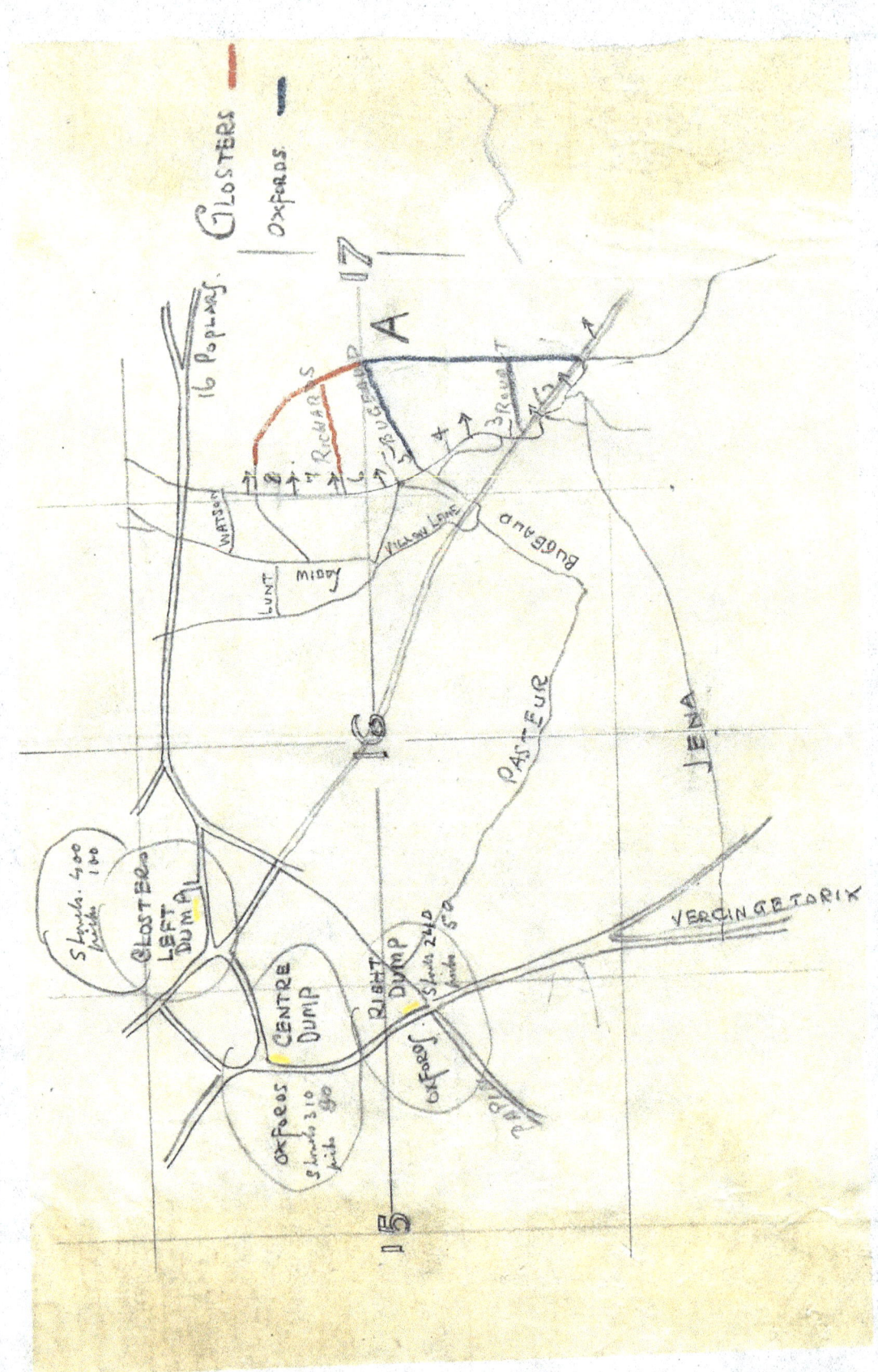

SECRET. Copy No.5.

145th INFANTRY BRIGADE ORDER No.98.   18.7.16.

1. (a) Present line will be advanced tonight to X.3.b.7.9. to X.3.b.1.1. and X.3.d.2.8.
   (b) and trench will be dug from X.3.b.1. to main ALBERT-POZIERES Road.

2. 4th OXFORD and BUCKS LT.INFTRY. will attack and capture above points (mentioned in 1 (a)).

3. The attack will start from front now held by 143rd Inf.Bde. at 1.30 am. An adequate artillery preparation has been arranged which lifts at 1.30 am. placing a barrage at 1.35 am.

4. Battalion in support will supply all carrying parties and will be prepared to relieve 4th OXFORDS on night 19/20th July.

5. All assaulting parties must carry everything necessary with them for 24 hours viz: Rations, Sandbags Ammunition, flares, artillery screens, etc.

6. All Officers above 20 per Unit will remain at BOUZINCOURT: Also the 5% to be drawn from each Company.

7. (a) Adv.Bde.H.Q. will be at Billet No.180 (W.29.c.89) ALBERT.
   (b) Report Centre on Road X.15.d.4.3.
   (c) Reports to ADVANCED Bde.H.Q. (or report centre).

8. (a) OXFORDS will reach Dump on ALBERT - POZIERES Road (J.24.c.8.3) at 9.pm. and there draw grenades, sandbags, etc.
   (b) 4th ROYAL BERKSHIRE REGT. will arrive at same dump at 10 pm. carry and bivouac in vicinity.

9. Battalions will march by Companies at 5 minutes interval.

Issued verbally 6.45 pm.
Copy (in writing) to follow.

T.J.LEAHY, Captain,
Brigade Major,
145th Infantry Brigade.

Appendix 5 to Vol XII   Appendix 5

Report on Operations night of 13/19th July 1916

1. The orders were for the Battalion to attack & capture and advance the line through the points X.3.c.7.9, X.3.B.1.1, X.3.D.2.8. The assault to be launched at 1.30 AM.

2. Disposition. Two Coys in front line formed up in trench from point X.3.D.20.15 to X.3.D.25.00. Right Coy to seize & hold R & C.52 points to enemy trench to left halfway to left point. Left Coy thence to left point & make good communication running thence to point X.3.c.12. Also if necessary seizing supposed tactical point X.3.a.30.15.

   One Coy in support immediately behind two leading Coys to occupy trench from which leading Coys exit etc., as soon as they were clear.

   One Coy in Reserve. Batt H.Q. at point X.9.c.4.5.
   Dressing Station trench junct. X.9.c.75.20

3. The leading Coys advanced at 1.30 AM and apparently lost direction somewhat to their left. At about 160 yards they struck a trench, not expected according to the map. The left Coy took this to be communication trench from the left point to X.3.c.12 & both Coys endeavoured to reform & get square with their objective. During this operation they were met by rifle fire from their left & enfilade Machine Gun fire from their right. They fell back to get their first alignment & there got mixed with the support Coy, which had moved up into the trench. The enemy then opened a heavy barrage with 15 cm: chiefly shrapnel all along the trench, causing considerable casualties, which owing to the shallowness of the trench, made reorganising very difficult.

4. During the first advance, the artillery which were due to lift at 1.30 AM of the 3 objective points, were observed to be still on them. This was reported back & subsequently rectified.

5. A second attack was ordered, but owing to the increasing casualties, & difficulties of reorganisation in the shallow trench it was about daylight, before it could be started and was finally abandoned.

6. Casualties 2/Lt FENWICK. C.J. 5th Middlesex Regt attached - wounded
               2/Lt JEFFERSON. H.   Wounded.

   Other Ranks - killed 12
                Missing, believed wounded 4
                Wounded   82
                Missing   1
                                        ___
                                         99

Army Form C. 2118.

WAR DIARY
or
INTELLIGENCE SUMMARY.

(Erase heading not required.)

Instructions regarding War Diaries and Intelligence Summaries are contained in F. S. Regs., Part II. and the Staff Manual respectively. Title pages will be prepared in manuscript.

Place	Date	Hour	Summary of Events and Information	Remarks and references to Appendices

2353 Wt. W2544/1454 700,000 5/15 D. D. & L. A.D.S.S./Forms/C. 2118.

SECRET.   Copy No 3.
          145th INFANTRY BRIGADE ORDER. NO.10 O.
                                                           20.7.16.   Appendix 6
Ref.Maps.   1
           ─────
           10000
57.D.SE. 20000

1. The Division will continue the attack tonight.

2. The 144th Brigade will be West of Point X.3.a.40 and the 145th
   Brigade will attack that point and also the following further East
   X.3.c.7.9. - X.3.d.2.8.

3. A Smoke Barrage will be established by Special R.E. if wind is
   favourable.

4. The attack will be carried out behind a short intense artillery
   barrage, the Infantry entering the hostile trenches almost in our
   own barrage which will lift at 0.0. (2.47 a.m.)

5. The 1/5th Gloster Regt will attack points X.3.b.4.0. and ~~X.3.b.1.1.~~
   X.3.c.7.9. and trenches adjoining. THE 1/BUCKS BN. will attack
   point X.3.b. 1.1. and X.3.d.2.8. and trenches adjoining these points.

6. The attack by each Battn. will be in four lines one behind the
   other.

7. The O.C. of each Battn. will be at Brigade Report Centre with
   Officers at forward observation points. The positions of these
   points are to be reported to Bde. H.Qrs as soon as possible.

8. O.C.Bde.M.G.Coy will arrange for close direct and also indirect
   fire on neighbouring to those being assaulted both in rear and on
   right flank, also on any Germans who show in a ~~certain~~ counter-
   attack.

9. Attacking Troops will go as light as possible but everyone must
   have bombs, water, food, ammunition also flares, artillery screens
   and pigeons will be worn on the back.

10. The 1/4th R. BERKSHIRE REGIMENT will evacuate the trench in X.9. h
    from POZIERES road to junction with 1/5th GLOSTER REGT. in order
    to leave it free for the 1/BUCKS BN. The will be done by 1.30 a.m
    tonight.

11. The 1/4th OXF & BUCKS L.I. will move from BOUZINCOURT so as to
    arrive at the bivouacs now occupied by 1/BUCKS BN. at 1.a.m. but
    not before, tomorrow morning (21st).

12. Dressing Stations   (1) X.14.b.3.1. (Mr BOISSELLES).
                         (2) OVILLERS.
                         (3) BAPAUME POST (near barrier on ALBERT-
                             BOISSELLES Road at W.24.d.5.7.)

13. Bde H.Q. will be at USNA REDOUBT.

14. Report Centre at X 14.a.5.6.

                                    (sd) T.J.LEAHY. Captain.
                                         Brigade Major.
                                         145th Infantry Brigade.

SECRET.

To:- OXFORDS.

T.239.   30.7.18.

Re.Bde. Order No.100 of todays date   aaa Please add:-

15. From 0.5. onwards O.C.Glosters and Bucks will each have one Battery at their disposal through F.O.O. who will be with them at Bde.Report Centre.   T.J.LEAHY. Captain",
                                                Brigade Major 145th Inf.Bde.

4.40 pm.

48th Division.
G.x.1583.

145th Inf. Bde.

Appendix 7

The Major General recognises how very gallant and determined the attacks were which the Bns made in the last few days and how very nearly they succeeded completely.

Those who took part in them may well be proud of their effort to break the German line here.

Those in the Brigades who were not engaged may well be equally proud of their comrades and the Brigade and Battalion commanders and staffs of having trained and directed such efforts.

Great successes have indeed already been gained by us. We must make one more effort and take advantage of all we have learnt about the position and show the Germans that in spite of all the difficulties and dangers we are going to beat them.

A victory gained after great efforts will be more really decisive as showing we are better fighting men than if we had gained it at our first attempt.

The decisive fights which lead to final victory are not those easily gained but those which like the first battle YPRES are gained by the determination to win no matter the odds in number and difficulties against us.

Here we are up against a strong position, the best German troops, machine guns and artillery fire.

Let our determination to win carry us through.

21.7.16.   (Sd) R.FANSHAWE. M.G.

O.C.
All Units.
Please communicate the above remarks to all ranks.

22.7.16.   T.J.LEAHY.
                            Captain.B.M.
                            145th Infy Bde.

SECRET.   145 Inf.Bde.Order No.101.   Appendix 8.

1. 145th Inf.Bde. will attack tonight in conjunction with the 144th Inf.Bde. - dividing line is the Railway in X.S.c.inclusive to 145 Bde.
2. 1/5th GLOSTERS will attack O.B. to 79 as their Right and the Railway as their Left. They will capture point 79 from West and Point 40 from East. 144th Bde. are attacking Point.40 from North.
   1/4th OXF.& BUCKS.LT.INFY. will advance - Left just East of Point 28 Right on Point.81. They will send flank parties to these and occupy points 97 and 81. They will cross Trench 28 - 81 and attack point 28 from East, sending a strong Bombing Stop up Trench towards point 54.
3. Such points in the Railway bank N. of Point 11 as are necessary will also be captured.
4. Every Trench and Post Captured must be consolidated and a sufficient garrison left to hold it.
5. Stokes Guns will fire on Points 39 & 40 under instructions given separately.
6. M.G.Coy. will carry out special duties which have been given them.
7.   Time has been notified to all concerned.
8. 1/BUCKS and 1/4th R.BERKS. will be prepared to continue or resume the operations under instructions already given and by order of this Office.
9. Flares are to be let off at 5 am., 8 am., 12 noon, 4 pm., 8 pm.,
10. Reports to this Office. O.C.ROYAL BERKS. will endeavour to get information about progress of operations on our right through his Right Company.
11. 7/R.WARWICKS with one Section of the 145 M.G.Coy.attached will move up and will be responsible for holding LA POISELLE and the 2nd and 3rd Lines of the defence should present garrison move forward, in accordance with instructions given personally to O.C. 7th Royal WARWICKS.
12. 1 Section R.E. is attached to each of the Assaulting Battalions and is at the disposal of Officers Commanding.

Issued verbally to C.Os 3.70 pm.
Copy (in writing) to follow.

                                          (sd) C.J.LYNN., Captain.,
                                                Brigade Major.,
23.7.16.   145th Inf. Brigade.

Account of Attack on 22/28th July 1916   Appendix 9

DISPOSITIONS.

A Coy: 1 Platoon to seize and hold point 97
        1 Platoon to seize and hold point 81
        2 Platoons in support of above.

D Coy. In two lines, 2 Platoons in each line.
        Objective: to reach trench running from 28 to 81; left wheel and
        take the trench running from 28 to 11 in rear.

B Coy. In two lines in support of D.

C Coy. 2 Platoons in new trench East of 31
        2 Platoons round point 46.

Battn HQ near BM 123.2 with POO at X.9.c.4.6.

PROGRESS of ATTACK [From 12.30 AM – 1.30 AM]

A Coy: 1 Platoon detailed for point 97, bombed out occupants, & worked up
        trench towards 81.
        1 Platoon detailed for point 81 bombed out garrison, who retired up
        trench towards POZIERES leaving tripod & belt of a Machine Gun behind
        1 Platoon remained at first in open in support.
        1 Platoon taken by Capt JONES into trench about X.3.b.65.90 &
        started bombing up towards 28. Finding himself rather isolated
        Capt JONES sent for the Platoon in support. Some men of the other two
        platoons also came up. Point 28 eventually gained after
        very considerable opposition, between 1.30 and 2 AM.

D Coy. On left situation is obscure.
        Right hand Platoon of front line [No 13] met by a barrage of bombs
        when about 30 yards from the trench from 28 to 81, & suffered
        heavily. A party of them led by Sgt CLARKE bombed into the trench but bombed out again.
        This party however was successfully rallied and joined in the
        successful attack on point 28 originated by A Coy.
        No 15 Platoon in support of No 13, met the same bomb barrage as
        No 13, & suffered heavily.
        No 14 Platoon in front line on left & No 16 in support, suffered
        heavy casualties from enfilade MG fire, & apparently got too
        far forward & to the left & got into our own artillery fire.
        These two platoons early became somewhat disorganised.

B Coy   Right hand Platoons After getting rather mixed up with D Coy, when
        the latter got held up, got into the trench about X.3.D.5.9.
        As at that time there was no sufficient room for all the men
        in the trench at this point, some of them were ordered to
        dig themselves in behind the main trench.
        Left hand Platoon Seem to have got in front of Point 28 before
        it was captured, & suffered very heavy casualties. The two
        platoons also became somewhat disorganised owing to loss of
        officers & NCOs.

Army Form C. 2118.

WAR DIARY
or
INTELLIGENCE SUMMARY.

(Erase heading not required.)

Instructions regarding War Diaries and Intelligence Summaries are contained in F. S. Regs., Part II. and the Staff Manual respectively. Title pages will be prepared in manuscript.

Place	Date	Hour	Summary of Events and Information	Remarks and references to Appendices

2353 Wt. W2544/1454 700,000 5/15 D. D. & L. A.D.S.S./Forms/C. 2118.

PROGRESS of ATTACK [2nd stage]

C Coy. About 1.30 AM received message asking for support. Two Platoons from 31 sent up & got into trench from 28 to 21 and helped in work of consolidating. Some of them were at first put to work digging & planting trench mines, & from main trench just E. of 29, but this was soon abandoned.

Meanwhile two platoons brought up from 26 to 31 & carried bombs up to the party which was bombing up towards 11 from 28. After getting two journeys, these two platoons remained in the captured trench, & the work of carrying continued by the R. Berks.

Meanwhile on the right C Coy had dispersed and driven back what appears to have been a carrying party bringing ammunition for the enemy on the top, while on the left a hard fight was going on for point 11. The bombers got to within 100 yards of point 11 but ran short of bombs and got driven back. The fight here lasted over an hour. Finally when the R. Berks brought up more bombs and one of our LGs was brought up, & fired a magazine down a thought length of trench full of Germans, the point was carried just before daylight.

COUNTER-ATTACKS Half an hour before dawn the enemy got onto their parapet Right & left of point 11 and advanced several times in close formation, but were driven back by our LG & rifle fire.

Another counter attack took place about the same time from point 23. This was only three strong & was easily driven back.

During the day there was a fairly heavy & continuous bombardment, which became intense, once during afternoon & once during the evening, but there were no further infantry attacks.

FLANKS. Communication established with the Bucks after their successful attack.

On the Right, R. Inniskillings seen bombing up the main trench in X.4.d, about 5 PM in the afternoon, with vanguard 50 yards. Bombing also heard in direction of point 54.

R.B.

Army Form C. 2118.

WAR DIARY
or
INTELLIGENCE SUMMARY.

(Erase heading not required.)

Instructions regarding War Diaries and Intelligence Summaries are contained in F. S. Regs., Part II and the Staff Manual respectively. Title pages will be prepared in manuscript.

Place	Date	Hour	Summary of Events and Information	Remarks and references to Appendices

2353 Wt. W2544/1454 700,000 5/15 D. D. & L. A.D.S.S./Forms/C. 2118.

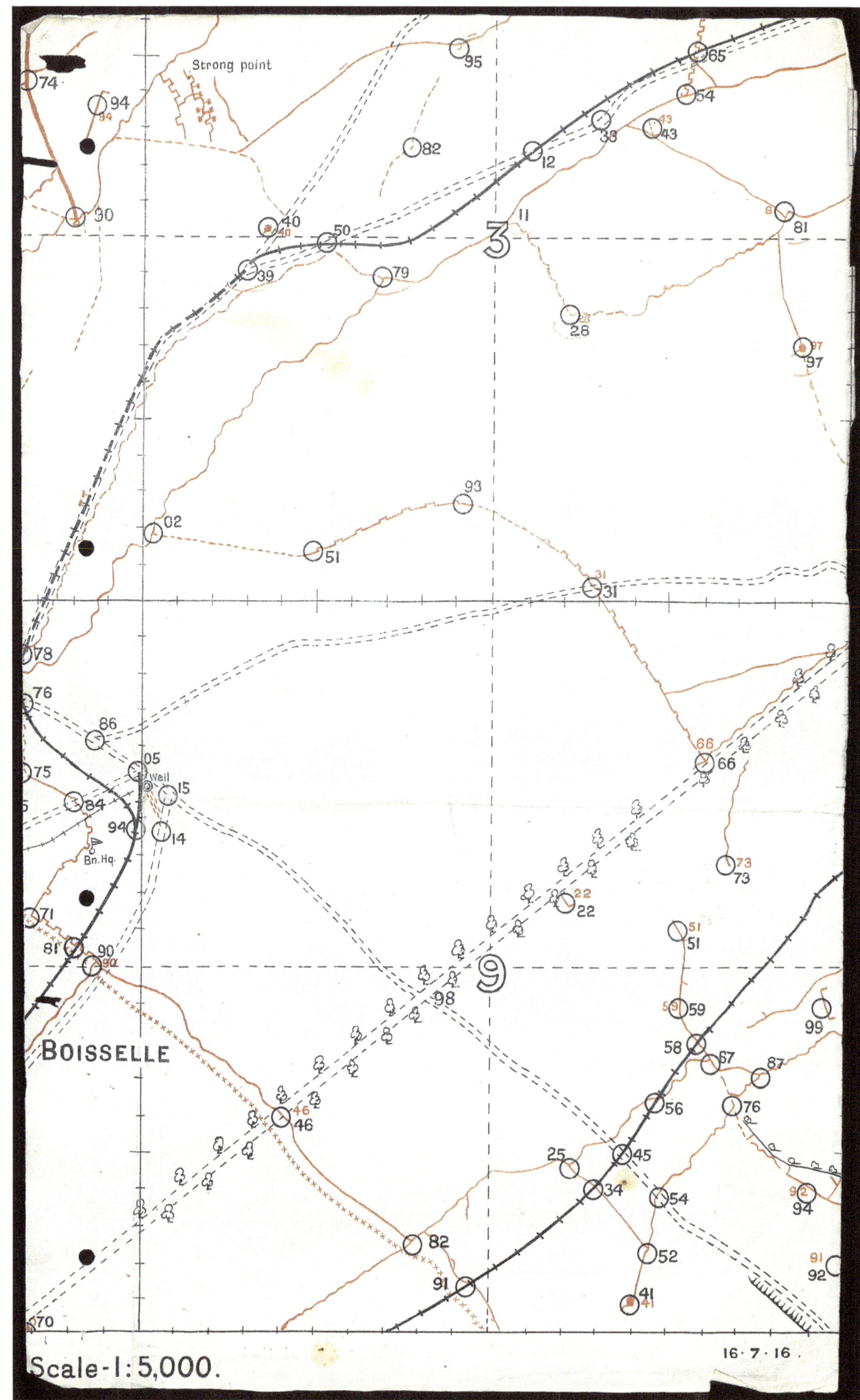

1. FORMATION IN ATTACKS 18/19th & 22/23rd JULY 1916.

In both cases Companies assaulted in two lines, two Platoons in each line.

Distance between lines in each Company 25 yards, and between Companies 50-80 yards.

2. TIME NECESSARY FOR ORGANISING THE ATTACKS.

On 18/19th the Battalion moved off from Billets 65 minutes after first warning was issued from Battalion Head Quarters, which allowed for issue of extra S.A.A. and explanations verbally to O.C.Coys.

1½ hours was allowed on the way to draw sandbags, bombs, flares, Artillery screens, and tools, which only just sufficed.

The Battalion was in position from which to attack with not more than ¼ hour to spare.

There was no time for previous reconnaisance, and very little for explanation.

IN THE ATTACK 22/23rd.

There was sufficient time for reconnaisance, and explanation and the same periods for drawing stores allowed as before, which proved ample on the recent occasion.

On the second occasion orders were issued from the Battalion Head Quarters at 3.30, and the Battalion moved from Bivouacs at 9 p.m., stores being collected before 7 p.m.

145th Brigade.
48th Division.

1/4th BATTALION

OXFORD & BUCKINGHAMSHIRE LIGHT INFANTRY

AUGUST 1 9 1 6

Attached - Report on Operations 11th-28th
Trench Maps.

Headquarters
145 Infantry Brigade

Herewith War diary for August
1916. Kindly acknowledge receipt.

E.L.Bulger Lt.A/I/ for OC

1/4 Oxf & Bucks Lt Infty

1/9/16

WAR DIARY
or
INTELLIGENCE SUMMARY.
(Erase heading not required.)

Army Form C. 2118.

Instructions regarding War Diaries and Intelligence Summaries are contained in F. S. Regs., Part II. and the Staff Manual respectively. Title pages will be prepared in manuscript.

Place	Date	Hour	Summary of Events and Information	Remarks and references to Appendices
AGENVILLE H.BVILLE	August 1st	/	Company training starting at 6 A.M. Not too very fine the day. A Coy firing on 75 yards miniature range. C Col'd to fire in A.V.R. AUTHIE has BEAUVOIR RIVIERE. A lot of MG's posted on 2nd Btn: Holding from the BUCKS Batt: That man Bowman has for the 4 Bn & New Bn to R Bucks about a week ago.	
Do	August 2nd 3rd	/	As yesterday J.B Coy on range. C Coy firing two miles alone, A. & B. near AUTHIE	3B
Do	August 3rd 4th	/	Company training - weather. C Coy on range. B Coy firing. D Coy on range & weather afternoon. B.H.Q. in AUTHIE	3B
Do	Aug 4th	/	As yesterday. D Coy on range. A Coy firing. B Coy lecturing in AUTHIE	3B
Do	Aug 5th	/	Coy training. D Coy firing. H.Q. returned to battle near AUTHIE	3B
Do	Aug 6th	/	Sunday. Voluntary church service. 2 officers visited 3rd Bn at BIRVEILLE (gunner members)	3B
Do	Aug 7th	/	Coy training. One Coy firing in Brisk relief on range. Lt J.C.B. GWILLIAM L.W. HUNTER joined the Battalion. A Bomb of 5 Br awards Brass	3B
Do	Aug 8th	/	Coy training. Two Coys firing in Brisk trench in the afternoon a rubber bullet match against the BUCKS Batt	3B

Army Form C. 2118

WAR DIARY
or
INTELLIGENCE SUMMARY.
(Erase heading not required.)

Place	Date	Hour	Summary of Events and Information	Remarks and references to Appendices
AGENVILLE Billets	August 9th		Brigade moved to BEAUVAL. Order of march L.R.BERKS, OXFORDS, GLOSTERS, BUCKS. Battalion moved off at 8AM. Route BEAUMETZ - BERNAVILLE (Canadas Battalion) got into usual billets at BEAUVAL by 12.45 PM. A very hot march & a great many men of the Brigade fell out. Incidents been brought from AGENVILLE in lorries.	
BEAUVAL Billets	August 10th		Brigade moved to VARENNES. Route VAULEN & VERT-GALAND FARM - BERNAQUESNE - ARQUEVES - LEALVILLERS. Battalion move off at 5.10AM Over 1 M&L BUCKS, OXFORDS, GLOSTERS, BERKS. A very hot morning and a little rain. Mens packs came on ambulances. Battalion got into very crowded billets about 10.30 AM. A draft of 58 O.R. from 5th Battalion at VARENNES. The New Divn General (Major Genl Fanshawe) Deft went for DIVN Lates on of July an (Major) 7th Interprete on his Battery took North for North to BOZINCOURT on his Orders received that Battn WINDMILLGARAN at VARENNES on 11th Order received That Battn would march to BOZINCOURT at 7AM on 11th	
VARENNES Billets	August 11th	6.30 PM 8.15 PM 10.30 PM 6.55 AM	Brigade marched to BOUZINCOURT via SENLIS. Order of march OXFORDS, GLOSTERS, R.BERKS, BUCKS. Battalion got into huts & bivouacs at N.E. end of village by	

Army Form C. 2118.

WAR DIARY
or
INTELLIGENCE SUMMARY.
(Erase heading not required.)

Instructions regarding War Diaries and Intelligence Summaries are contained in F. S. Regs., Part II. and the Staff Manual respectively. Title pages will be prepared in manuscript.

Place	Date	Hour	Summary of Events and Information	Remarks and references to Appendices
Bivouac While West of BOUZINCOURT	Aug 13th	2.30 PM	9 AM. Considerable shelling of the village at intervals during the day and at 3.30 PM Orders issued to move Battalion to open position in Cornfield about ½ mile West of BOUZINCOURT.	
In the line NE of OVILLERS	Aug 13th	3 AM	Orders received that Battalion would relieve two Battalions of the 12th Division early on 13th in the line East of OVILLERS. Reconnaissance of line by C.O. & Adjt Bn. Battalion moved off from Bivouac by Companies and marched via BOUZINCOURT and infantry track crossing ANCRE by bridge ½ mile North of ALBERT, to neighbourhood of USNA REDOUBT, where Bn halted.	
		7 AM	Battalion moved off & took over trenches from 7th NORFOLKS on right and 9th ESSEX on left. Front line — SKYLINE TRENCH — had been taken by these two Battalions the previous night [12/13th] with very little opposition. Disposition as follows. C Coy. Right front Coy. 2 Platoons in SKYLINE TRENCH with their Right at point 81. Where line joined up with ANZACS. 2 Platoons in RATION TRENCH with their left hyle on POZIERES-MOUQUET ROAD. D Coy Left front Coy. 1½ Platoons in SKYLINE TRENCH with its Left at Point 99. (having touch maintaining on the left.) 2 Platoons in RATION TRENCH ½ platoon from 23. B Coy in Support. 1 Platoon from 89. 3 Platoons 79 – 54. A Coy in Reserve. 2 Platoons in THIRD	see Map Appendix I.

WAR DIARY or INTELLIGENCE SUMMARY.

(Erase heading not required.)

Army Form C. 2118.

Place	Date	Hour	Summary of Events and Information	Remarks and references to Appendices
In the Line NE of OVILLERS (continued)	August 13th (continued)		AVENUE 79-62. 2 Platoons in OVILLERS. Heavy enemy shelling started at 8am on the 13th which was complete, & continues throughout the whole day, over the whole area, but especially on RATION & SKYLINE TRENCH. It later especially being attenuated by the shelling. Heavy enemy fire in C & D Coys. [It is practically certain that our own heavies were also dropping on the trench.] During the evening (about 7.30 PM) LIEUT WAYMAN was reported missing, having been last seen going to the left of his line, presumably to make a reconnaissance. About 9 PM, enemy shelling became intense round Bath. HQ & all the lines were cut. At the same time 2/Lt SHERRINGTON in charge of D Coy front trench detailed signs & enemy movement, and sent back 5 messages, none of which got through. Shortly after 10 PM, enemy attacked our front & left flank, with apparently his Battalion. Our Centre, which was weakly held, was pierced. On the left, 2/Lt SHERRINGTON	
	Night 13th/14th		was in great danger of being cut off & captured, but he succeeded in extricating himself by great bravery & leading by a task up the position in RATION TRENCH thinly securing on left flank. On the right of 2 Platoons in Clay under Sergt CROWE were cut off by an attack in force in the latter, but succeeded in hacking out a SKYLINE TRENCH near point 81 with the rest of the Battalion.	

WAR DIARY or INTELLIGENCE SUMMARY

Army Form C. 2118.

Place	Date	Hour	Summary of Events and Information	Remarks and references to Appendices
In the Line N.E. of OUVILLERS	Night of Aug 13/14th (continued)		From the front forming attacks were organised down the trench, with the assistance of the ANZACS, and the bottom of the trench was held till this party was relieved by 2 platoons of 1/5 GLOSTERS on evening of 14th. A bombing stock was also organised from RATION TRENCH up the communication trench, led by 2/Lt HUNTER. This officer was killed and the attack broken off when close to SKYLINE TRENCH.	Casualties 13/8/16 Lieut MA YARMAN Missing 2/Lt W HUNTER Killed Wounded Lieut CLARKIN 2/Lt A W CARTER 2/Lt J V KING 6th Middx 2/Lt G PEARSON 147 Str. —
Do	Aug 14th		Owing to the length of time occupied & the casualties already sustained, no further counter attack by the Battalion was practicable. 2 Coys of 4 R BERKS were sent up to counter attack about 5am without success. The line of RATION TRENCH was then held, as front line.	248
		2PM	Battalion relieved by (Bucks Battalion) & up to the rear USNA REDOUBT & line Ward Battalion (Bivouac) and to trenches in ALBERT—BOUZINCOURT line Where Battalion rested.	300
Bivouac ALBERT—BOUZINCOURT Line	Aug 15th		Battalion resting. Beds written, & very little shelter from the rain.	
Do	Aug 16th	1AM	Orders received to relieve 1/Bucks Batt in the same sector of line. Way Coy to reach OUVILLERS at 10AM. Relief completed 1PM.	

WAR DIARY
or
INTELLIGENCE SUMMARY.
(Erase heading not required.)

Army Form C. 2118.

Place	Date	Hour	Summary of Events and Information	Remarks and references to Appendices
In the line N.E. of OVILLERS	Aug 16th (cont.)	—	Dispositions. B on right & A on left, holding SKYLINE & RATION trenches with two platoons each only by day: (the two remaining platoons being in reserve behind OVILLERS). By night, the two rear platoons moved up & took up a position in shell holes on the site of SKYLINE trench. D Coy in support. 3rd AVENUE down as far as Batt. HQ. C Coy in reserve behind OVILLERS. Shelling not nearly so severe as last time the Battalion was in, but fairly heavy all day.	
	Night 16/17th	—	During the night, patrols sent out to reconnoitre trench X28 74—78 (which was found strongly held) & trench leading up to MOUQUET FARM (R32 D23 — R33 A54) which was found held. Patrols also sent out 2 find trench (with ANZACS on our right). With these examinations, the situation on the POZIÈRES–MOUQUET FM Rd being very obscure.	Ends
D.	17th	—	Shelling which has been fairly heavy since the Batt. came in abated considerably early in the morning. Two artillery trams fired up in SKYLINE TRENCH. Coys relieved about 5 P.M. C relieving B on Right, D relieving A on Left, B moving into Support & A into Reserve	

WAR DIARY
or
INTELLIGENCE SUMMARY.

(Erase heading not required.)

Army Form C. 2118.

Instructions regarding War Diaries and Intelligence Summaries are contained in F.S. Regs., Part II. and the Staff Manual respectively. Title pages will be prepared in manuscript.

Place	Date	Hour	Summary of Events and Information	Remarks and references to Appendices
In the line	Night	9 PM	Hostile shelling considerably increased, on SKYLINE & PATTON Trench & THIRD AVENUE	
N.E. of OVILLERS	17/18th August	9.45 PM	Enemy movement suspected on our left front.	
		10.15 PM.	Suspicion of actual attack increased and a barrage was put on. Their two guns arrived and kept up for some time, with all reserves stood to again. From information received from prisoners it appears that an attack by the enemy was actually intended by a Division owing to the casualties caused by our barrage. Patrol under 2/Lt THOMPSON reconnoitred Trench X.28.b 74-78, and found it unoccupied, and fairly knocked about.	See Appendix II
In the line N.E. of OVILLERS	Aug 18th	7 AM.	Relief of Battn. by 1/4th R. BERKS Regt. commences. Very complete by 12 NOON. Gun pits in rear, & USNA REDOUBT. On relief Battalion moved to USNA REDOUBT and leave R. ANCRE.	Casualties 16-18th Lieut G.H. GREENALL wounded at duty 45 O.R.
USNA REDOUBT	Aug 18th	12.10 A.M.	Orders received to move to ALBERT – BOUZINCOURT line before 8 A.M. unless further orders received by 7 A.M.	
ALBERT–BOUZINCOURT line		7.30 A.M.	Moved to ALBERT – BOUZINCOURT line.	
		6.30 P.M.	Orders received to move into billets at BOUZINCOURT, sending billeting party to report at 5.30 P.M. Battalion moved off and got into billets by about 9 P.M.	
BOUZINCOURT				

WAR DIARY
or
INTELLIGENCE SUMMARY.
(Erase heading not required.)

Army Form C. 2118.

Place	Date	Hour	Summary of Events and Information	Remarks and references to Appendices
Billets BOUZINCOURT	Aug 20th	—	Battalion resting, and occupied in reorganizing. 2 Coys billets on the MARTINSART Road and 2 in billets at the same end of the village.	
Do	Aug 21st	—	Battalion doing Company training in the morning	BB
		3.30 PM.	Orders received to be ready to move off at short notice in case the Battalion was required to support an attack by the 144 BDE.	
		7.15 PM	Orders received to move immediately to OVILLERS POST. Battn moved off by Coys via usual infantry track & reported to HQ 144 BDE. Battn was not required and spent the night — 2 coys in OVILLERS REDOUBT 2 coys in gunpits in rear.	BB
Neighbourhood OVILLERS REDOUBT	Aug 22nd	—	Two Coys in BSNA REDOUBT, orders to move out & occupy gunpits closer to R. ANCRE before 10 AM.	
		6.15 PM	Orders received to relieve 17th WORCESTERS in the line N of OVILLERS	See Appendix III
In the line N of OVILLERS	Aug 23rd	9 AM	Battalion moved off to relieve 17 WORCESTERS. Relief being complete by 12 NOON. Sector of line from X 2 B 48, on right (where in touch with 143 BDE) to about X 2 A 66 on left (where in touch with BUCKS Battn.) Front line held by two Coys, kit very hard in depth, junction between coys being X 2 B 06. The greater part of front two coys in depth along 3rd & 4th Streets. A Coy in left B on right. Clemen support	

WAR DIARY
or
INTELLIGENCE SUMMARY.
(Erase heading not required.)

Army Form C. 2118.

Place	Date	Hour	Summary of Events and Information	Remarks and references to Appendices
In the line N. of OVILLERS (continued)	Aug 23		about points 88, 18, 47, 92. D Coy in Reserve between points 88 and 79. A bombing stop between 76 and 79. At this point bombing almost continuous except when orders to withdraw to enable our heavy artillery to bombard point 79. About 35 yards of ground gained and our bombstop pushed up to within twenty yards of point 79, but the attack [on?] point junction could not be forced by direct frontal attack alone.	
		3 PM	BUCKS attacked on our left, 1st Oxfords being trench 33-79 2nd objective 91. Battalion responsible for making close communication between X28AB & X2A 79. Buths Divisor through R32c 91 or straight across open. Bucks only partially successful, the greater part of the trench X2a 28-79 being won, though the Eastern portion of this trench remained in enemy's hands	
		8 PM	Enemy artillery active on front area till 10.30 PM. Between only intermittent and not very accurate shelling through the day. During the night working parties engaged on digging out trench 76-48 which was badly blown in, & in digging new trench from 49 towards point 79. Patrols reports trench 31-79-91 very strongly held. An MG position doubtful or	
			91. On the left trench A8-20-12 was found to have been completely obliterated.	see

WAR DIARY or INTELLIGENCE SUMMARY

(Erase heading not required.)

Army Form C. 2118.

Place	Date	Hour	Summary of Events and Information	Remarks and references to Appendices
In the line N of OVILLERS	Aug 24th	—	Constant touch with enemy near point 79, but general situation unaltered. Coys relieved during the morning. D relieves A on left, C relieves B on right.	
		4 PM	Artillery bombardment for attack by 25th Div: on LEIPZIG SALIENT on our left commenced, the actual assault being delivered at 4.10 pm. Plans had been made to take advantage of this to make an attack on point 79 assisted by two Stokes Mortars. This had to be abandoned as orders received from Corps to withdraw our bombing posts to smaller heavier to pus on 79.	
		5.10 PM	A good deal of hostile artillery activity on our trenches. A good deal of shrapnel fired on our front trenches during the night impeding work of consolidation. Plans made for a combined attack with Bucks on 79, about midnight, abandoned owing enemy activity. Enemy front line trench again reported as held in great strength. Prisoner of 5th GRENADIER GUARDS taken opposite our right Coy. Prussian Battalion had relieved during night.	20.
Do	Aug 25th	5 AM.	Some hostile shelling. Otherwise very quiet throughout day.	
		6-8 AM	B Coy relieves D on left. D moving into Reserve, and A moving up into Support.	
		—	1/5 GLOSTERS relieves 1/1 BUCKS on our left	

WAR DIARY or INTELLIGENCE SUMMARY

Army Form C. 2118.

(Erase heading not required.)

Instructions regarding War Diaries and Intelligence Summaries are contained in F. S. Regs., Part II and the Staff Manual respectively. Title pages will be prepared in manuscript.

Place	Date	Hour	Summary of Events and Information	Remarks and references to Appendices
In the Line N. of OVILLERS	Aug 25th (continued)	10-11 PM	Orders received that Consolidation only required. So no further attack made on point 79. Hostile artillery very active on our right front Coy. Doing much damage to trenches around +3. Patrols during the night got well up to trench 79-91 and reported enemy digging energetically and apparently the garrison of the trench in many cases rest in the actual trench, but in Shell holes just behind. 80.	
Do	Aug 26th	8 AM	Relief of Battalion by 1/A. R. BERKS Regt commenced, being completed by about 10 AM. On relief Battalion moved into dugouts in RIBBLE STREET near OVILLERS Post. Remainder of day nothing to report.	Casualties 23-26th 1/Lt A.C. THOMPSON wounded. 57 O.R. 30
RIBBLE STREET	Aug 27th	—	Two Companies employed on various carrying parties etc during the day	
		4.30 PM	A Coy sent up to OVILLERS KEEP in support of 1A R. BERKS who were attacking	
		8.15 PM	Urgent message received to send up one Coy stronger in support of 5 PLATOONS. B Coy left in and most of at 8.30 PM. These two Coys up in the trenches all night, engaged in carrying etc, & returned to the Battalion about 7 AM next day. Orders received to move off to BOUZINCOURT at 7 AM 28th.	45

Army Form C. 2118.

WAR DIARY
or
INTELLIGENCE SUMMARY.
(Erase heading not required.)

Instructions regarding War Diaries and Intelligence Summaries are contained in F.S. Regs., Part II. and the Staff Manual respectively. Title pages will be prepared in manuscript.

Place	Date	Hour	Summary of Events and Information	Remarks and references to Appendices
RIBBLE STREET	Aug 28th	2 AM	Orders received that Battalion not to move off till the 9th L.N.LANCS - 74th BDE, had passed SVILLERS POST.	
Busnes W of Bouzincourt		9 AM.	Battalion moved off by companies & marched to Busnes W. of BOUZINCOURT (via central) via AVELUY & Infantry track N of AVELUY - BOUZINCOURT Road. On arrival an advance party of a Batt. of 7th Brigade [25th Div] found in possession: This party joined some afterwards by representative of another Batt. of same Brigade. Eventually about 12.30 PM, compromise effected and Battalion left in possession.	
Do	Aug 29th		Brigade moves to BUS via HEDAUVILLE - FORCEVILLE - BERTRANCOURT. Over it Mud Busses, OXFORDS, GLOSTERS, BERKS. Ten minutes clear allowed between units. Battalion moved off at 6.55 AM and reached BUS about 9.35 AM. Men quite carried in lorries.	
Huts in BUS WOOD			Battalion in huts at SW corner of BUS WOOD. Wet weather and very muddy in the wood. All the furniture carried off by the last occupants.	
Do	Aug 30th		Wet day. Usual inspections etc carried out. 1 Company of the 2nd Batt. now in CURCELLES.	

2353 Wt. W2544/1454 700,000 5/15 D. D. & L.   A.D.S.S./Forms/C. 2118.

Army Form C. 2118.

WAR DIARY
or
INTELLIGENCE SUMMARY.
(Erase heading not required.)

Place	Date	Hour	Summary of Events and Information	Remarks and references to Appendices
Huts in Bus Wood	Aug 31st		Fine day. Company training carried out during the morning. 2 Coys to bathe during the afternoon. Detachment of 50 OR under Lieut WRONG sent to BEAUVAL. [signature] 1/5th Bn. West Yorks. I/C Bn. 31st a Brits. I hutm	

Instructions regarding War Diaries and Intelligence Summaries are contained in F. S. Regs., Part II. and the Staff Manual respectively. Title pages will be prepared in manuscript.

REPORT OF OPERATIONS AUGUST 11th to 18th 1916.

Aug.11th. Battalion arrived in BOUZINCOURT from VARENNES at 9 am.
Two Companies in Huts and two in Bivouacs - edge of Village.
3 pm. Ordered to leave vicinity of Village on account of
shelling. Moved forthwith to Bivouacs N.W. of Village.

Aug.12th. Orders received at 2.30 pm to relieve two Battalions 12th
Division in line East of OVILLERS.
3.30 pm to 8.30 pm. personal reconnaisance.

Aug.13th. Battalion marched at 3 am. and took over line in early
morning from 7th Norfolks and 9th Essex. Front Line -
SKY LINE Trench taken the previous evening with little
opposition.
7.30 am. Shelling commenced. All our area very heavily
shelled all day. Nothing less than 15 cm. (Front line
almost obliterated by evening) somewhat assisted by our
own Heavies during the afternoon).

Night of
13/14th. Enemy showed signs of movement soon after 9 pm. opposite
left of line. Five messages sent back failed to get through.
Region of Batt.H.Q. very heavily shelled and all Infantry
and Artillery Lines cut.
Enemy attacked front and left flank at 10 pm. with
apparently 2 Battalions. Centre of Line pierced - Right
Flank held out with remains of two Platoons till isolated
when they joined with the Anzacs on our right, and remained
in possession till following evening when relieved by
5th GLOSTERS. This party made repeated Bombing attacks
and remained in possession of right half of original front
line. Garrison of left flank which was exposed was nearly
cut off and remains of 2 Platoons under 2nd Lt. SHERRINGTON
withdrew and kept secure the left flank.
Local counter attacks did not relieve the situation and
1/4th R.BERKS. counter attacked with 3 Coys. at 5 am.
without success.
Line as then held consolidated and enemy shelling decreased.

Aug.14th. Battalion relieved by BUCKS at 3 pm. Moved to Bivouacs
in ALBERT - BOUZINCOURT Line.
Casualties:- 6 Officers and 147 Other Ranks.

Aug.15th. Resting.

Aug.16th. 1 am. orders received to relieve BUCKS in same line at
10 am. Relief complete at 1 pm.
Sector held by two Coys in front line with small posts
only by day - Whole of both Coys by night occupying shell-
-holes on site of original SKY LINE Trench and in RATION
Trench.
Heavy shelling up till early morning 17th. Patrols during
night to gain touch with ANZACS with whom communication was
unsatisfactory. Patrols towards enemy front and left
reported no movement.

Aug.17th. Enemy shelling moderated during the day. Front Coys.
relieved by those in rear between 2 and 4 pm.
Enemy shelling slightly increased with darkness. About
9.45 pm. suspicious movements of enemy opposite left front.
10 pm. Suspicions increased of probable attack. Barrage
by our own guns asked for and immediately given.
(From prisoner's statements subsequently obtained an
attack apparently was intended and prevented by this barrage).

Aug.18th. Our patrols after midnight reported no enemy movements.
Remainder of night quiet. Battalion relieved by R.BERKS
8 am. Moved to USNA REDOUBT and gunpits in rear.
Casualties. 1 Officer (at duty) 45 other ranks.

Aug.19th

Aug.19th.   12.15 am. Orders received to move at 7 am to ALBERT -
            BOUZINCOURT Line. Batt. in that line 9 am.
            6.30 pm. Orders received for Battalion to move to Billets
            at BOUZINCOURT, Billeting party to report to that place
            at 5.30 pm. Billeting party sent forthwith.
            Battalion in Billets at BOUZINCOURT 9 pm.

Aug.20th.   Rest.

Aug.21st.   3.30 pm. Orders received to be ready to move at short
            notice.
            7.15 pm. Orders received to move immediately to OVILLERS
            Post, in support of 144 Brigade.
            7.40 pm. Battalion moved off.
            Not required by 144 Brigade and spent the night in USNA
            REDOUBT and gun pits in rear.

Aug.22nd.   Battalion moved during the morning to gunpits closer to
            RIVER ANCRE.
            6.15 pm. Orders received to relieve 7th WORCESTERS in 1st
            line N. of OVILLERS early next morning.

Aug.23rd.   Personal Reconnaissance 5.30 am to 8 am.
            9 am Battalion started to move off. Relief completed by
            12 noon.
            Sector of line held from X.2.a.66 on left, where in touch
            with BUCKS to X.2.b.48 inclusive joining up with 5th R.
            WARWICKS on our right.
            Two Coys. in Front Line - One in Support - One in Reserve -
            all very much in depth. Bomb Post in contact with the
            enemy at 79. Bombing at this Point continuous throughout
            the next 48 hours, except for intervals when ordered to
            withdraw to allow Heavies to fire on Point 79.
            BUCKS Bn. attacked on our left at 4 pm. Our leading Coy.
            prepared to co-operate at Point 79 and join hands.
            BUCKS attack not wholly successful - Situation as before. Attempt to
            join up during the night by forward trench with BUCKS
            prevented by enemy activity. All our front area fairly
            heavily shelled throughout the night.

Aug.24th.   Constant touch at Point 79 with enemy but only about 30
            yards gained. Actual Trench Junction too strongly held
            by the enemy.
            Front two Companies relieved.
            25th Division attack on LEIPZIG SALIENT at 4.10 pm.
            Previous arrangement to take advantage of this prevented
            by orders received during afternoon to withdraw our Bomb-
            ing Post to allow Heavies to fire.

Night of
24th/25th   Plans made for a combined effort with BUCKS. Ourselves
            at 79 - BUCKS at R.32.c.51. abandoned owing to enemy
            activity.
            Patrols sent out after midnight reported enemy in front
            in great strength.
            Our lateral Communication Trenches now obliterated by shell
            fire redug during the night.

Aug.25th.   Prisoner taken at about 5 am. of 5th Grenadier Guards just
            arrived in line opposite us.
            Hostile shelling moderate during the day but warmed up
            towards the evening.
            3 pm. Left front Company relieved and plans made for
            attack on 79. This attack cancelled as orders received
            for further consolidation only.

Night of 25/26th.
            Night quiet. Patrols sent out after midnight got well up
            to line 79 - 91 and reported enemy digging energetically
            and line strongly held.

Aug.26th.   Battalion relieved by R.BERKS. 9 am. and moved to Trenches
            in RIBBLE STREET.
            Casualties:- 1 Officer, 57 Other Ranks.

Aug.27th.   Two Companies employed on various carrying parties etc.
            during the day.
            One Company moved at 4.30 pm to OVILLERS KEEP in support
            of 4th R.BERKS.
            8.15 pm.Urgent message received for One Coy. to move up
            immediately in support of 5th.GLOSTERS. This Coy. moved
            off at 8.30 pm.
            Orders received during afternoon for Battalion to move
            at 7 am next day 28th to BOUZINCOURT.

Aug.28th.   5 am. Orders for time of move changed to 9.30 am. when
            relieved by Battalions of 74th Brigade
            Battalion arrived Bivouacs area N.W. of BOUZINCOURT at
            11 am and found advance party of Batt. of 7th Brigade
            already there.   11.30 am. the representatives of another
            Battalion of the 7th Brigade arrived to claim the area.
            Compromise effected and Battalion settled in 12.30 pm.

Aug.29th.   Battalion left Bivouacs 6.55 am.

29/8/16

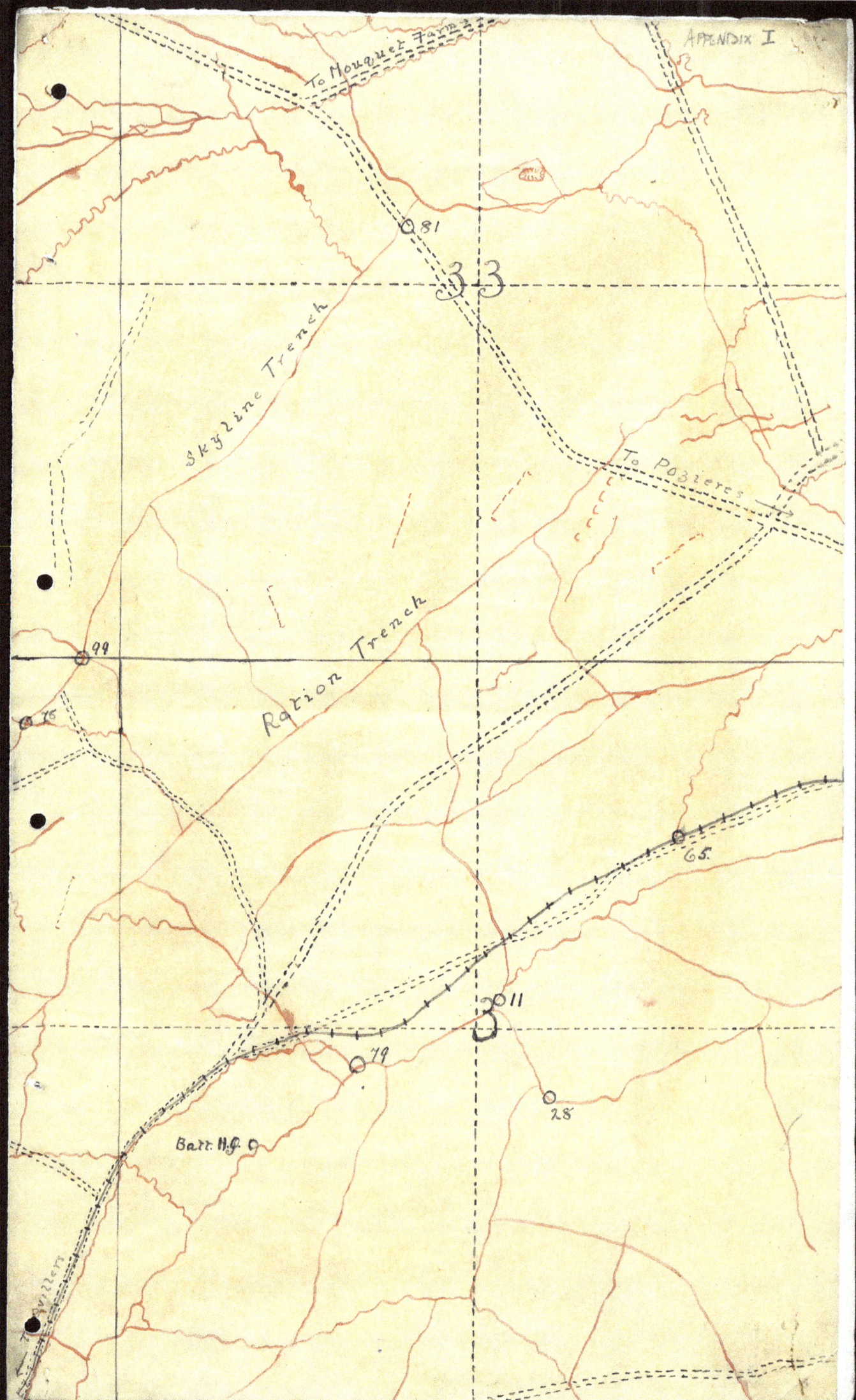

Appendix II to Vol XVII War Diary.

1/4th OXFORD and BUCKS LT. INFANTRY.

REPORT OF EXAMINATION OF A WOUNDED LANCE CORPORAL OF THE 5th COY., 86 th REGIMENT, CAPTURED ON THE 18th IN THE TRENCH X.9.b.70.74.80.

1. The prisoner is an educated man, 24 years of age, who was a student of BONN University at the outbreak of the war and 'eingezogen' in December 1914.

2. RECENT MOVEMENTS OF THE REGIMENT.

The Regiment arrived with the rest of the Division in this area on the 26th July. It spent some time in the back area in the neighbourhood of BAPAUME and on the 13th the two battalions went into the front line to retake the portion of SKYLINE TRENCH which had been lost by the 62nd Regiment.

The battalion captured the trench but was again driven out with the exception of their right which established itself round X9.b.7.8. The battalion then took up its position South of the barricade and was there when we attacked last night.

On the 17th/18th the 1st and 3rd Battalions were to make another attack on the SKYLINE TRENCH but such heavy losses were suffered during the organization of the attack through our artillery fire that they/ operation had to be abandoned.

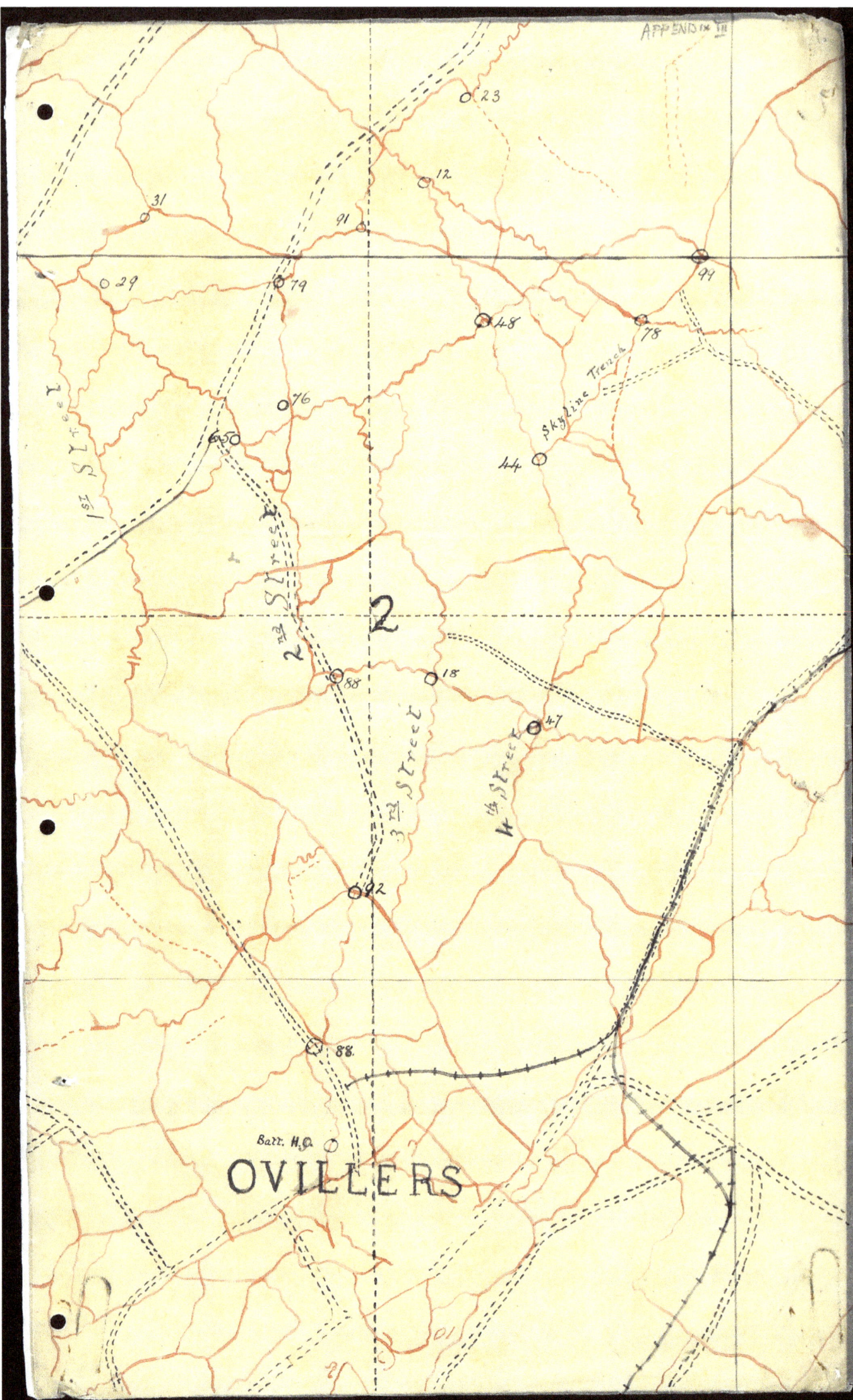

The following Decorations have been awarded to Officers
N.C.O's and men of the Battalion, for acts of gallantry
and especial good work during recent operations.

MILITARY CROSS.

2/Lt. F.E.JONES On the night 23/23 July though wounded in the leg,
led his Platoon in a charge into the enemy's trenches
which they successfully captured, before he would
return to have his wound dressed.

2/Lt. C.E.R.SHERRINGTON On the night 15/16 August was in command of
left half of SKYLINE TRENCH, N.W. of POZIERES when
the enemy made a strong counter-attack both from his
front and his left flank. He sent five messages,
none of which reached their destination. He held on
till almost surrounded and then withdrew his force
in a most able manner, maintaining his guard of the
left flank the whole time. His masterly withdrawal
in the face of enormous odds kept the line intact
and enabled a counter-attack afterwards to regain
more easily the position evacuated.

Rev. R.C.JACKSON On the night 19/20 July, S.W. of POZIERES, as Regi-
C.T.F. attached   mental Chaplain accompanied the Bn. Medical Officer
1/4 Bn. Oxford's and a relief party for evacuating wounded from a
Bucks Lt. Infy.   trench in front line, whence it had not been possible to move them before the Battn. was relieved.
He was not intended to go beyond the Field Ambulance
but when Stretcher Bearers were found to be scarce
he voluntarily accompanied the party and himself
carried a wounded man from the front line trench
upwards of half a mile to a position of safety,
notwithstanding a barrage of gas shells through
which he had to pass.

DISTINGUISHED CONDUCT MEDAL.

1440 Sgt. H.A.CLARK In the attack on the night 22/23 July commanded
D. Coy.   the leading Platoon of the assault, and when all the
Officers and the Coy. Sgt. Major were casualties took
charge of the remainder of the Coy., organized and
led further attacks in the enemy's trenches till he
himself was wounded. His prompt action held back the
enemy's counter-attacks till reinforcements arrived.

2249 A/Cpl H.BAILEY On the 23rd July in the attack S.E. of POZIERES
C. Coy.   when his own section was depleted, of his own init-
iative organized a bomb section from another Coy.
and was successful in forcing back the enemy's bombers
thereby securing the left flank which was exposed.
Again on the night 13/14 August N.E. of POZIERES
when the enemy had obtained a footing in our trench
and a local counter-attack was in progress, he
himself rushed alone along the parapet throwing bombs down
amongst the enemy, till he himself was wounded,
losing an eye.

1389 Sgt. L.CROWE On the night 13/14 August was in charge of his
C. Coy.   Platoon in SKYLINE TRENCH, N.W. of POZIERES, when
the enemy made heavy counter-attacks and gained a
footing in that trench. He collected the remainder
of his own and another platoon that were not casualties
and made repeated bomb attacks down the trench till
relieved the following night, thereby preventing
the enemy consolidating the position they at first
gained.

MILITARY MEDALS.

4364 Pte. A. MARGETTS
B. Coy.
After the attack S.W. of POZIERES on 19th July, acting as Stretcher Bearer in an exposed piece of trench whence the wounded could not be moved, remained voluntarily with them after the Batt. were relieved, till they were safely evacuated the following night.

3530 Sgt. A. HUSTONE
A. Coy.
During the attack on the night 22/23 July, S.W. of POZIERES, did continuous good work with his Section, and though twice wounded would not leave his post to be attended to till the position was consolidated.

3037 Pte. L. MARTIN
A. Coy.
During the attack S.W. of POZIERES on the night 22/23 July and during the morning of the 23rd, constantly carried messages and things from the front line across the open and under heavy shrapnel fire.

3637 Pte (now L/Cpl) ####
A. Coy.
During the attack on the night 22/23 July single handed held back for ten minutes a German party bombing up a trench, whilst a front attack was being organized and more bombs fetched.

3616 Pte F.G. MILLER
C. Coy.
During the attack S.W. of POZIERES on the night 22/23 July and after daylight 23rd, when acting as runner from Batt. Headquarters carried several messages across the open to the front line under very heavy fire.

1582 L/Cpl B.F. HARROD
C. Coy.
3341 Pte. E.E. STEVAN
C. Coy.
After the attack S.W. of POZIERES during the morning 3rd July, working as Stretcher Bearers between the lines, carried many wounded across the open to safety, regardless of personal safety.

4615 L/Cpl T.W. HUDSON
D. Coy.
Since died of Wounds.
On the night 15/16 August was in charge of a Lewis Gun on the left flank of SKYLINE TRENCH, N.E. of POZIERES. When heavily attacked from front and flank handled his gun in a most able manner; when the party were almost surrounded completely he withdrew the gun, himself firing it all the while from the shoulder, till they got back to a position suitable to cover the exposed flank, when he himself was wounded. His action kept the exposed flank secure, and inflicted great loss on the enemy.

1700 A/Cpl R.W. HEWSON
B. Coy.
On the 16th August, N.W. of POZIERES, when in charge of an advanced post, the remainder of the trench on either side was obliterated and garrison withdrawn, he maintained his position and consolidated the post in a most able manner.

145th Brigade.

48th Division.

1/4th BATTALION

OXFORD & BUCKS. LIGHT INFANTRY

SEPTEMBER 1 9 1 6

WAR DIARY or INTELLIGENCE SUMMARY

Army Form C. 2118.

Place	Date	Hour	Summary of Events and Information	Remarks and references to Appendices
Huts BUS WOOD	Sept 1st	—	Battalion engaged in company training. Classes for Lewis Gunners and bombing. Several officers and men visited the 52nd at COURCELLES.	
Do	Sept 2nd	9 AM	Battalion inspected by Major-General R. FANSHAWE Gen. Div., who congratulated the officers, NCOs & men of the Battalion on their work when engaged in the offensive during July and August, and urged them to prepare for further effort.	
Do	Sept 3rd	—	Sunday. Voluntary Church Service.	
Do	Sept 4th	—	Draft of 22 O.R. arrived early in the morning. About half of them SA Horse reinforced.	
		2.30 PM	Orders received that Battn. would probably take over trenches from 7th Worcs. on Thursday 7th. 2nd in C. & Adjt. to reconnoitre trenches E. of AUCHONVILLERS.	
Do	Sept 5th	8.15 AM	1st Coy moves off to relieve 7th WORCS. Battn. marches via BERTRANDCOURT – BEAUSSART between Coys. Rehit completed by 12.15 PM. Boundaries of Battalion area BRITTANY on South, and NEW BEAUMONT Road on North. Disposition. Two Coys holding front and support lines – MARLBOROUGH & HUNTER & SEAFORTH trenches. Each with one platoon of support Coy attached. Remaining two platoons of support Coy in Tunnel 88 (with Battn H.Q.). Reserve Coy in AUCHONVILLERS.	see Appendix I

WAR DIARY
or
INTELLIGENCE SUMMARY.

(Erase heading not required.)

Army Form C. 2118.

Place	Date	Hour	Summary of Events and Information	Remarks and references to Appendices
In the trenches E. of AUCHONVILLERS	Sept 5th (continued)		in cellars. A Coy on right. D on left. B on support. C in Reserve. 1/6 GLOSTERS on our left. B on our left. 1/Bucks relieved 1/8 WORCESTERS during the afternoon. Battalion under 144 Bde. 2/Lieuts. C.H. POWELL & R. AFFLECK rejoined the Battalion & posted to D & C Coys respectively. Village shelled about 3.20 PM.	Pte L/ BARTLETT to Hospital Major BARNSLEY to Hospital
Do.	Sept 6th		A certain amount of sniping (especially during the night), & some shelling with field guns. Otherwise a fairly quiet day. Battalion engaged on laying & improving communication etc. Trenches deep & narrow but muddy & practically unrevetted. Battalion on our right relieved by 17th K.R.R.C./ 15 Inf Bde took over Command of line at 3 PM.	Sgt TP. WELDON J. Coy wounded shell.
Do	Sept 7th	2.30 – 3 A.M. 3 – 6 PM	Enemy artillery active. Batteries a light shrapnel barrage on our left. communications to support trenches. Medium minnenwerfer also active, especially on B Coy on our left. Nothing developed. Nothing doing. Fairly quiet day. bursting of A.R. BERKS Regt. carrying empty	Cpl. PT BATES M.C. (Coy) wounded Arm Sgt PT BIGNELL A Coy wounded at Dim wounded at gut.

WAR DIARY
INTELLIGENCE SUMMARY

Army Form C. 2118.

Place	Date	Hour	Summary of Events and Information	Remarks and references to Appendices
In the trenches E of AUTHUILLE AVILLERS			Gas cylinders out of trenches.	
Do	Sept 8th	5-8 PM	Enemy artillery fairly active, especially on our Emplacements. Battalion relieved by 1/4 R. BERKS Regt. relief being complete by about 10.15 AM.	
Billet - BUS	Sept 9th		Gr. relief Baker march by Coys to billets in BUS, last Coy being in billets by 1PM. Coy training. Physical drill. Bayonet fighting etc. 2 Coys to Baths.	
Do	Sept 10th		Very fine day. Sunday. Church Parade. Anglican Service. Other services then Bath. March down to BEAUVAL on following day.	
Do	Sept 11th		Morning physical drill only. Afternoon Bde. marched to BEAUVAL via AUTHIE - MARIEUX - Northern edge of BEAUQUESNE - TERRAMESNIL. Divis. 17th march BERKS, BUCKS, GLOSTERS, OXFORDS. 300 yards between each. Battalion head of Bde. Battalion arrived in billets — same as before — by 7PM. This the 4th time Battn has been billeted in the area.	
Billet BEAUVAL	Sept 12th		Preparations made for company training. Bombing, trench dig. Range enlarged etc. Coys training started. Coys to Baths.	
Do	Sept 13th		Coy training. 1 Coy on average firing 5 rounds, grouping. 1 Coy throwing live bombs.	

WAR DIARY
or
INTELLIGENCE SUMMARY.

Place	Date	Hour	Summary of Events and Information	Remarks and references to Appendices
BEAUVAL BUIRE	Sept 14th		Remainder throwing dummy bombs, bayonet fighting, physical drill, open order drill etc. Saved for firing NCOs starts.	
Do	Sept 14th		Coy training as yesterday. Following officers joined the Batn. 2/Lieut A.M. KIRKWOOD, J.A.S. MACLEAN, & R.G. RAMSAY of 7th Bn Scottish Rifles, and Lieut A. ALLEN A.S. WOTHERSPOON & D.W. DINWOODIE of 8th Bn Scottish Rifles. First two attached to C Coy, other two to Bn. HQ, L/A & Scott to D Coys.	
Do	Sept 15th		Coy training as yesterday. The Battalion practices artillery formation in the open ground towards CANDAS. Leave starts again — with a very small allotment for special cases — having been closed since June 23rd. Battalion ordered to be ready to move at 2 hours notice.	
Do	Sept 16th		8 – 9.30 p.m. Brigade practices having alarm enemy, the formation adopted being Coys both in column of route, with wide interval & distance between coys, and two cemetery files. The remainder of day, Coy training carried out, Batn. still ready to move at two hours notice.	

WAR DIARY or INTELLIGENCE SUMMARY

Army Form C. 2118

(Erase heading not required.)

Instructions regarding War Diaries and Intelligence Summaries are contained in F. S. Regs., Part II. and the Staff Manual respectively. Title Pages will be prepared in manuscript.

Place	Date	Hour	Summary of Events and Information	Remarks and references to Appendices
Billet BEAUVAL	Sept 17th	/	Sunday. Voluntary Church Service. Brigadier inspects billet. Information received that Brigade no longer liable to be called upon, and would move into an area further back, on 18th.	
Do	Sept 18th	/	Brigade moves into area round FIENVILLERS. Battalion moves 10.15 A.M. Groupment. Bucks Oxfords & Berks. Battalion marches to FIENVILLERS which was reached about 12 Noon. Raining throughout the march and during the afternoon.	
Billet FIENVILLERS	Sept 19th	/	Another wet day. Training being very considerably interfered with. Major BARTLETT rejoined Bn from hospital. 2/Lt N.R. PAXTON. 8th Scottish Rifles, joined Battalion and attached to B Coy. Inoculation started. Bourne being done.	
Do	Sept 20th	/	Company training continued. A draft of 26 n.s. arrived. (5 of them being O.S. hands returned to the remainder draft.) Inoculation continued.	
Do	Sept 21st	/	Coy training as yesterday.	

1875 Wt. W593/826 1,000,000 4/15 J.B.C. & A. A.D.S.S./Forms/C. 2118.

WAR DIARY or INTELLIGENCE SUMMARY

Place	Date	Hour	Summary of Events and Information	Remarks and references to Appendices
In Billets FIENVILLERS	Sept 22nd		Coy training as before. 16 officers and 160 O.R. inoculated. In the afternoon Bn made a reconnaissance into Bryas(?) scheme on next day. Draft of 8 O.R. mostly (A) kinds.	
Do	Sept 23rd		Bryas scheme. Battalion practices attack on a position taken up by RFC kites.	
Do	Sept 24th		of ETOCAMPS – opposition provided by 1/6 M.G. Coy. Performance by CoRs in afternoon.	
Do	Sept 25th		Sunday. Voluntary Church Services. Draft of 59 O.R. arrived, less apparently originally intended.	1st 5th - 13 Sep.
			Coy training as before. 10 rounds rapid on 30 yards range. Draft of 54 O.R. arrived.	
Do	Sept 26th		Coy training as yesterday.	
Do	Sept 27th		Ditto	
Do	Sept 28th		Battalion tray scheme in morning. Battalion marched through BERNAVILLE to a point about half way between BERNAVILLE & LE MEILLARD and returned to FIENVILLERS arms country in artillery formation. About 10 P.M. orders received that Battalion would not leave its billets were on the 29th, as a move was probable. Draft of 6 O.R. arrived.	

Army Form C. 2118.

WAR DIARY
or
INTELLIGENCE SUMMARY.
(Erase heading not required.)

Place	Date	Hour	Summary of Events and Information	Remarks and references to Appendices
In Billet FIENVILLERS	Sept 29th	3.15 PM	Orders for move received.	
		9.10 AM	Battalion moved off & marched through CANDAS (Brigade starting point) DOMNEUX, Eaten en-route of DOULLENS - 9 Roches - LUCHEUX - HUMBERCOURT to NARUZEL the Battalion billets. Advance march OXFORDS, BERKS, BUCKS, GLOSTERS. Very rainy wet march. Battalion halted for dinners between LUCHEUX and HUMBERCOURT between 1.50 and 3.30 PM. Battalion reached WARLUZEL about 4.30 PM. for billets.	
Billet WARLUZEL	Sept 30th	—	Coy training etc.	
		11 PM	Intimation received that Brigade would probably have next day.	

A.M. Knutton Lt Col Comdr
1/4 Oxf + Bucks L. Infty.

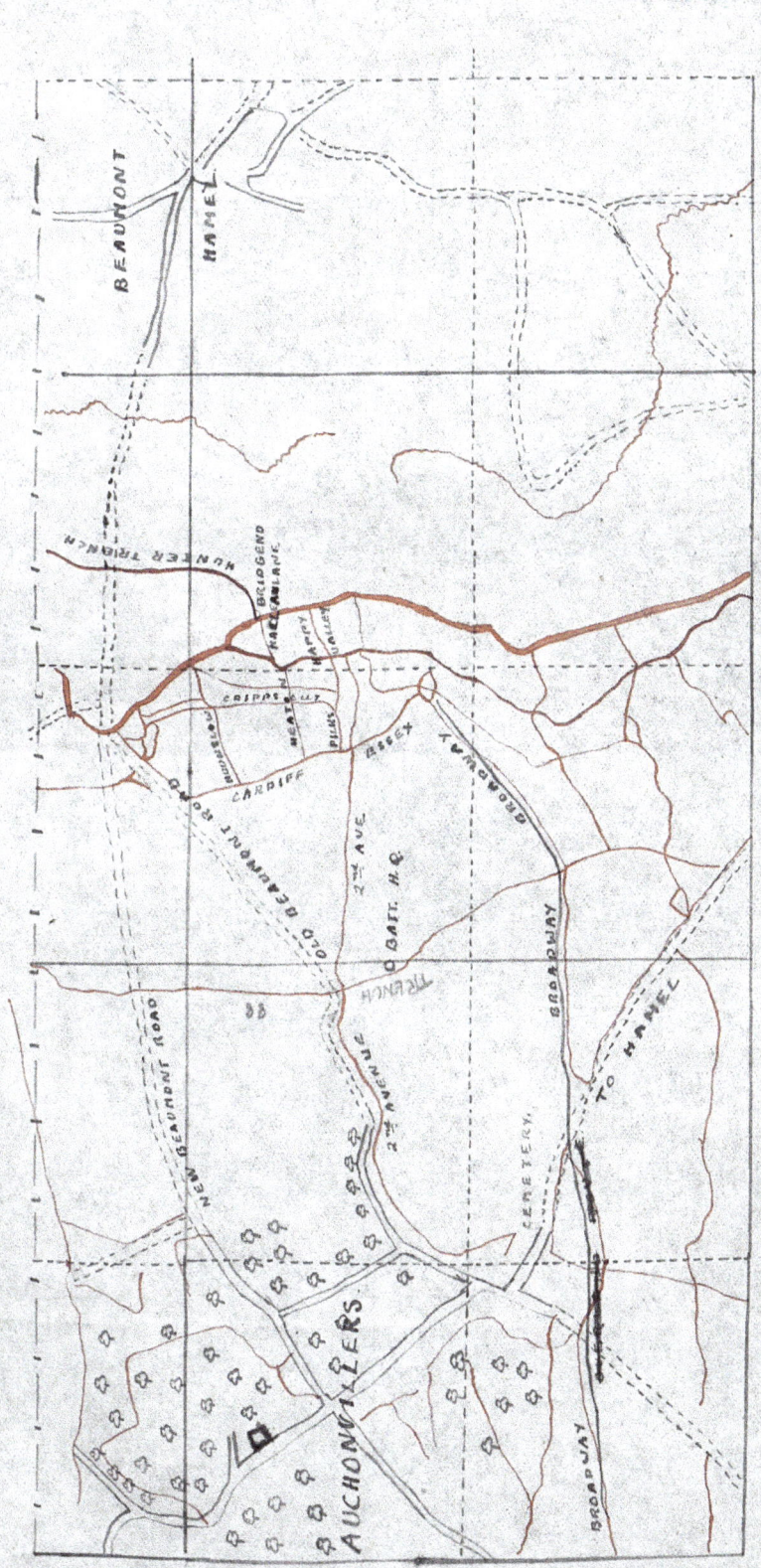

145th Brigade.

48th Division.

1/4th BATTALION

OXFORD & BUCKS. LIGHT INFANTRY

OCTOBER 1 9 1 6

WAR DIARY
or
INTELLIGENCE SUMMARY.

(Erase heading not required.)

Army Form C. 2118.

Place	Date	Hour	Summary of Events and Information	Remarks and references to Appendices
In Billets WARLOZEL	Oct 1st	9 AM	Orders received to move to WARLINCOURT area	
		10.45 AM	Battalion moved off and marched via COTURELLE and WARLINCOURT Halte. Billeting area — huts on hillside just N. of WARLINCOURT — reached 1 P.M. Huts still occupied. Battalion had dinners in field and moved into huts about 4 P.M. Accommodation very cramped, and huts not weather proof (Draft of 5 OR only) handed [?].	
Huts at WARLINCOURT	Oct 2nd		Wet day. Company training very curtailed. In the evening the question of ammunition became even more difficult owing to the arrival of the Divisional Artillery into the area.	Do
Do	Oct 3rd		Very wet in the morning. Cleared up in the afternoon and a certain amount of company training possible. All available tailors at work making canvas covers for steel-helmets.	R.B. [illegible]
Do	Oct 4th		Another wet-co-day. Company training carried out as far as possible.	W.B. [illegible]
Do	Oct 5th		Company training as yesterday. Brigade Headquarters moved to SOUASTRE from WARLINCOURT and their billets taken over by Bn. H.Q.	RNC Hunt [illegible] 4th Army 4.8.16

WAR DIARY
or
INTELLIGENCE SUMMARY.
(Erase heading not required.)

Army Form C. 2118.

Place	Date	Hour	Summary of Events and Information	Remarks and references to Appendices
WARLINCORT	Aug 6th		Company training continued as before. Physical drill, rifle exercises etc.	See
Do	Aug 7th		Company training. Final stage of attack practised. Co. & N. C. O.'s & Westerns to recommend rewards etc.	B/15
Do	Aug 8th		Sunday. Voluntary Church Service. Weather fine (x) Practically all B Coy. & paths to village. The rest of the Brigade. Practically having to be seen brilliant.	B/5
			MENU & GOWRIES but Hot Baths made enough & hours on Some pines.	
Do	Aug 9th		Company training continued. Lecture to CSMs & NCO's of HOBSTERNE & recruits. Resume practice in afternoon.	B/5
Do	Aug 10th		Company training. Lectures on bayonet fighting given by Major CAMPBELL. Assistant instructor in bayonet fighting.	B/3, see B/15, B/15
Do	Aug 11th		Company training. Practice in hen hunting started.	
Do	Aug 12th		Training carried on as before.	
Do	Aug 13th		Co. training. Football match Officers v Sergts. Won by letter 2-1.	B/5
Do	Aug 14th		Co. training. Football match between Officers and Officers of the Battalion. 16 Bucks. Bucks won 3-1.	B/6

WAR DIARY or INTELLIGENCE SUMMARY.

Army Form C. 2118.

(Erase heading not required.)

Place	Date	Hour	Summary of Events and Information	Remarks and references to Appendices
Bellue & Huit	Oct 15th	/	Sunday. Voluntary church service. 2 Coys on fatigue all day in MARLINCOURT. Covering up water pipes. Rest of Battalion to baths.	
Do	Oct 16th	/	Enjoying a Leper Information received that B Battalion would relieve 1/8 WORCESTERS in trenches on 18th inst.	Res.
Do	Oct 17th	/	Three Coy working party near GAUDIEMPRE. Rest of Battalion any training.	R.B.
Do	Oct 18th	/	Battn due to start for trenches 10 AM	
		8.30 AM	Relief cancelled. Battalion to remain in WARLINCOURT. Coy training resumed.	
		11.30 PM	Advance parties received that Battalion would move to WARLUZEL on 19th starting	Res.
Do	Oct 19th	10 AM	Battalion moved off	
		10.35 AM	Orders received that B Head to return to WARLINCOURT and not start before 2 PM. These orders cancelled on telephone from BELLEVUE and Battalion arrived at WARLUZEL via BELLEVUE & COUTURELLE, in drenching rain. MARLUZEL reached 12 Noon. Are instructed by 4th Div. that 1.30 PM. Billets crowded.	Res.
			Lieut W.D SCOTT joins Battalion	

Army Form C. 2118.

WAR DIARY
or
INTELLIGENCE SUMMARY.
(Erase heading not required.)

Instructions regarding War Diaries and Intelligence Summaries are contained in F. S. Regs., Part II. and the Staff Manual respectively. Title pages will be prepared in manuscript.

Place	Date	Hour	Summary of Events and Information	Remarks and references to Appendices
Billet WARLUZEL	Oct 20th	/	Continuous Weather cold but fine. Blowing strong from the East. 2/13 J.L. ETTY, T.A. HILL and H.H. DYE reported to B.D. & Coys respectively.	/15
Do	Oct 21st	/	Continuing. Good Weather. Orders received to move to BEAUVAL on Oct 22nd.	/15
Do	Oct 22nd	/	Battalion moved off 9.45 a.m. Order of march: Bde, GLOSTERS, BERKS, BUCKS, OXFORDS. Marched via HUMBERCOURT – LUCHEUX – GROUCHES – Eastern Edge of DOULLENS to BEAUVAL, which was reached at about 3 P.M. Halt for about 20 minutes but N of DOULLENS otherwise no long halts. Dinners on arrival. Battalion billets a same area for the 4/5th time. Cinema show in evening.	/15
Billet BEAUVAL	Oct 23rd	/	Brigade moved to TALMAS. Order of march: BERKS, BUCKS, BUCKS, GLOSTERS, OXFORDS. Battalion moved off 1.45 p.m. &c billets TALMAS before 4 o'clock. Fine sunny afternoon: cold but good for marching.	/15
Billet TALMAS	Oct 24th	/	Battalion moved off 7.40 a.m. Order of march: Byne. BUCKS, OXFORDS, GLOSTERS, BERKS. Marched via RUBEMPRÉ – PIERREGOT – MOLLIENS-AU-BOIS, MONTIGNY – BOUZENCOURT to LAHOUSSOYE, where Battalion & Bde HQ were	

WAR DIARY
or
INTELLIGENCE SUMMARY.

(Erase heading not required.)

Army Form C. 2118.

Place	Date	Hour	Summary of Events and Information	Remarks and references to Appendices
In Billets LAHOUSSOYE	Oct 25th		Brigade billeted in BUSSENCOURT. Billets cleaned about 12.30 P.M. Very bad day for marching. Raining hard and roads hilly and in very bad condition.	BWD.
Do	Oct 26th		Next day. Men occupied in cleaning up etc. Detachment of 45 O.R. under 2/Lt PLOWMAN sent to MERICOURT to work under No 6 R.E. Park.	BWD.
Do	Oct 27th		Coy training. Weather still bad. Following officers joined Battalion 2/Lts C.F. DADLEY, V GARLICK, and E.H. FAWCITT, posted to D, B & C Coys respectively.	BWD.
Do	Oct 28th		Coy training. Coy training. Orders received for Battalion to march to MILLENCOURT on next day. Later in day, orders received that move postponed till 30th.	BWD. BWD. BWD.
Do	Oct 29th		Sunday. Voluntary Services. A detachment of 50 O.R. under 2/Lieut AFFLECK sent to MILLENCOURT, to keep billets "warm". Weather still unsettled and rainy.	BWD.

Army Form C. 2118.

WAR DIARY
or
INTELLIGENCE SUMMARY.
(Erase heading not required.)

Place	Date	Hour	Summary of Events and Information	Remarks and references to Appendices
In Billets LAHOUSSOYE	Oct 30th	—	Coy training. Orders received to march to MILLENCOURT on 31st inst	S.3.
Do	Oct 31st	8.40	Battalion marched to MILLENCOURT via the AMIENS-ALBERT Road and LAVIEVILLE. 100 yards interval kept between Platoons on account of heavy traffic along the main road. Battalion in billets by 11.15 am.	S.3.

[signature] Lt Col
Officer Comdg 2 A.I.F.

145th Infantry Brigade.

48th Division.

1/4th BATTALION

OXFORD & BUCKS. LIGHT INFANTRY

NOVEMBER 1 9 1 6

WAR DIARY
or
INTELLIGENCE SUMMARY.

(Erase heading not required.)

Army Form C. 2118.

Place	Date	Hour	Summary of Events and Information	Remarks and references to Appendices
MILLENCOURT	Oct 31st	11.30 PM	Orders received that Battalion would probably move to CONTALMAISON on 1st prox.	B3.
Do	Nov 1st	9 AM	Co. Adjt & O.C. B & C Coys to reconnoitre Support trench between MARTIN PUICH and LE SARS.	
		11.45 AM	Battalion ordered to move at 12.30 PM. Manched via ALBERT and FRICOURT to BAZENTIN. Battalion started with 10 yards between platoons but much cut into and delayed by transport and other units. Very muddy and wet and surroundings of BAZENTIN almost impassable for transport. BAZENTIN reached about 4.30 PM.	* Ref 57c SW 20,000
BAZENTIN between FRICOURT & CONTALMAISON	Nov 2nd	10 AM	Verbal orders received to relieve 6/7 Royal Scots Fus. [45th Infantry Brigade 15th Divsion] in trenches reconnoitred the previous day.	B3
		5 PM	Battalion moved off by Platoons carrying hot days rations and leaves to CONTALMAISON (where Tpts were picked up) - thence via Tramway in Company tracks. Fine moonlight night made conditions comparatively easy and relief completed by 10.45 PM. Front line held by 5/ Glosters. Buch in reserve round MARTINPUICH. [Front line held by 5/ Glosters. Buch in reserve round MARTINPUICH.]	

WAR DIARY
or
INTELLIGENCE SUMMARY.

(Erase heading not required.)

Army Form C. 2118.

Place	Date	Hour	Summary of Events and Information	Remarks and references to Appendices
Support trench between LE SARS & MARTINPUICH			Dispositions – Front Coy. (B) 1 Platoon DESTREMONT FARM (2 yards diagonal) (Rear is Left Support B") 3 Platoons down Junction of DESTREMONT TRENCH & 26TH AVENUE. Battalion HQ. 26TH AVENUE M 27 A 1A. 2nd Coy. (A) 26TH AVENUE [between Battn HQ and 76TH STREET. 3rd " (D) 3 Platoons 76 STREET. 1 Platoon Junction of 76TH STREET & 26TH AVENUE. 4th " (C) 26TH AVENUE West of 76TH STREET [Surplus Officers and S.L. & ALBERT. Transport and QM/Stores at CAPPES SPUR]	See Appendix I
Do.	Nov 3rd		Fine day. Comparatively little shelling of Battn HQ area. Enemy in engaged in (heavy up trench (enemy) fire is unavoidable) and improving the very limited accommodation. No troops. A few Verey lights shots but not at Kite. While area is on forward slope and consequently has to be in full view to be walking over the top, which is the only way of getting about. Fortunately enemy take no notice of this. Rations brought up in Pack ponies to junction of 26TH AVENUE & MILL ROAD. A.A. cart parts engaged in Carrying rations for 5/9 platoons.	NP.

WAR DIARY
or
INTELLIGENCE SUMMARY.

Place	Date	Hour	Summary of Events and Information	Remarks and references to Appendices
Support Trenches between MARTIN PUICH & LE SARS	Nov 4th	—	Work as yesterday. Not very much shelling of Battalion area except	
		10.15 PM	DESTREMONT FARM which received considerable attention. Intense bombardment of enemy front on our left for about 10 minutes. During the evening command of the line taken over by 144 Inf Bde, to whom Bn started for the tactical purposes.	
	Night 4/5th	—	Relieved 4/5 POSTERS in front line. Owing to inexperience of guides, relief which started at 9PM not complete till nearly 2AM.	
Front line in front of LE SARS	Nov 5th	—	Disposition: (Battn in Left Front Sector). Right Flank French Coy. (B) 2 Platoons in SCOTLAND TRENCH (just beyond M.6.b.3&). 2 Platoons in CHALK TRENCH (in rear of above platoons) Left Flank French Coy. (C) 1 Platoon in SCOTLAND TRENCH 3 Platoons in CHALK TRENCH (with p.t. in RAVINE TRENCH) Right Support Coy. (D) GGI & II Jnct SE of ALBERT-BAPAUME Rd. Left Support Coy. (A) GGI & II between Rd & RAVINE Trench. 26th AVENUE. M.27.B.29. Battalion HQ. In our right, 144 Bde. on our left 44th Canadian. (4th Canadian Division)	See Appendix II

Army Form C. 2118.

WAR DIARY
or
INTELLIGENCE SUMMARY.
(Erase heading not required.)

Place	Date	Hour	Summary of Events and Information	Remarks and references to Appendices
Front line in front of LE SARS	Nov 5th (contd)	9.16 PM	56th Division (on our right of 144 Bde) started BUTTE DE WARLENCOURT. Attack appears successful. Enemy retaliates with 77 mm and 15 cm on front and support and LE SARS. Considerable intermittent hostile artillery activity throughout the day. Enemy snipers busy all day on our left flank enfilading AQUEDUCT ROAD. This troublesome enemy to trouble state of trenches.	Casualties 6 OR Killed 9 OR Wounded
	Night 5/6		Intercompany relief. Detached Bombs. A relied On left. Patrols out during the night reported enemy wire weak opposite our left. Patrol on left also got into touch with 47th CANADIANS (who had relieved 44th) in ROUGE TRENCH N.3.	1 OR Wounded
Do	Nov 6th		Enemy artillery showed more than usual activity. LE SARS, DESTREMONT FARM, AQUEDUCT ROAD and intervening ground with branches, especially during afternoon. Coy Hd Qr front line received special attention.	
			Three prisoners of 64th A.I.R. 1st GUARDS Division. Guards Reserve Corps captured opposite our left Coy, & despatches to Brigade.	
	Night 6/7		Battalion relieved by Bucks Batt. Relief not complete till after midnight. On relief Coys moved back into trenches in support area previously occupied.	[illegible signature]

P.B.

Place	Date	Hour	Summary of Events and Information	Remarks and references to Appendices
Support trenches Between LESARS & MARTINPUICH	Nov 7th		Quiet day. Weather conditions very bad. 1 Platoon of each Coy engaged in carrying up rations to Brooks after dark. In the evening Battalion relieved by 4th R. Berks Regt, relief being complete by 8 PM. On relief Bn. moved into Reserve Area around MARTINPUICH. Disposition. Battalion HQ. M 32 A 41. 2 Coys (A & B) SW end of Village. 2 Coys (C & D) in Pulpit in S.I.B* (Very bad accomodation both huts & dugouts)	Casualties 1 O.R. Killed 5 O.R. wounded *A. dug out with types that [illeg] Ref. 57 SW 1 20,000
MARTINPUICH	Nov 8th		Battalion found fatigue & working parties. E.D. from 1/3 AM, 3.0 AM & 3.5 PM - 50 & 5 PM. R.E.D. various for men carrying and water parties. B Coy Casualties 6 O.R. wounded	
Do	Nov 9th		Battalion engaged on working parties to Yesterday. Originally orders for B to march to attack or major 9/10th. However received other relief [illeg] much later Recognition in dumps as well. Major 10/11th. D Coy who has the most disagreable dumps as well B Coy in the morning. Are to take B from B who were on relief remained. Recognition - except for Bn. HQ - ML.	

WAR DIARY or INTELLIGENCE SUMMARY

Army Form C. 2118.

Place	Date	Hour	Summary of Events and Information	Remarks and references to Appendices
MARTINPUICH	Nov 18th		Working party of 150 OR required by day. All available details & 50% brought up to BAZENTIN-le-PETIT WOOD and a detachment under an officer sent over from each Coy from MARTIN PUICH. The party worked hard all day & eventually Bivouac in three Coys but up in BAZENTIN-le PETIT WOOD [S.7.B.a.D] and shallow Bivies for fourth Coy (A) "Keep Thursm" NW [from] NW corner of WOOD. Thirty by the Bn as output lay and had a post on ridge to watch Divisional front. Battalion relieved by 1/8 R.WARWICKS (exclit firing complete by 7.45 pm) and on relief to quarters in above. [1/5 FORESTERS] and [1/5 KK] in reserve— from 1/3 FORESTERS] 2nd Bn	Casualties 1 OR wounded Sgt J H ABRAHAMS 1/5 2 Lieut
BAZENTIN-le- PETIT WD.	Nov 11th		Battalion resting. Each Coy from 1.30pm to 5.30pm for work in MARTIN PUICH one by night. (Sunday) Voluntary Church Service. B Coy & 13 OR as - BECOURT	
Do.	Nov 12th		Working Parties changed to 150 by night and 50 by day. B Coy & Bath at BECOURT. Orders received for 2 Coys to be kept intact & ready to move at short notice. Something afoot here from last 2 days. [Extremely heavy bombardment on North morning News of unanks]	

2353 Wt. W3544/f454 700,000 5/15 D. D. & L. A.D.S.S./Forms/C. 2118.

WAR DIARY or INTELLIGENCE SUMMARY

Army Form C. 2118.

Place	Date	Hour	Summary of Events and Information	Remarks and references to Appendices
BEAUCOURT-SUR-PETIT WOOD	Nov 14th		News that BEAUMONT-HAMEL has been captured.	
		5.30pm	Originally meant to be (Br Gds) right line hijk 14/15th. The new Bn pushes 24 hours. Division on our right sent up S.O.S. Considerable commotion but nothing developed.	
Do	Nov 15th		No working parties.	
		6.30pm	Battalion started to relieve 1/4 WARWICKS – Left Support Battalion. Dispositions have been changed and the line is held by one Brigade with two Battalions in the line and two in Support – instead of two Brigades with each having one Battalion in the line, one in Support and one in Reserve. Relief uneventful and completed by 10 P.M.	
			Dispositions Batt HQ. M32 A 41.	
			2 Coys (A & B) in SW end of village.	
			1 Coy (D) – 1 Platoon DESTREMONT FARM.	
			3 Platoons. Junction of DESTREMONT TRENCH & 26th AVENUE.	
			Coy HQ Sunken Road	
			1 Coy (C) 26th AVENUE from in Support Bn HQ. [M 27 a 11]	

WAR DIARY
INTELLIGENCE SUMMARY

Place	Date	Hour	Summary of Events and Information	Remarks and references to Appendices
In Support MARTIN PUICH	Nov 18th		Battalion engaged on working parties, which together with return to water carrying parties occupy our two men. Clear frosty weather. Enemy artillery fairly active near MARTIN PUICH.	
Do	Nov 17th		Further clear day. Enemy aeroplanes up early in the morning, fairly in evening now of the SW end of village shelled heavies continuously from about 1-5pm. 1 Section to a 19 of B Coy Funkers sent by a direct hit in a relay. Moon 3pm - Shell fell about 15 yards N of Bn HQ & wounded 2 officers & 16 airmen. Battalion HQ Killins Beer LAKE and a 15" MG Group who were just outside. Battalion relieves Bucks Battn in front line.	Casualties Lieut Lipsett 2nd Lieut Ritchie 2 OR Killed 9 OR Wounded
"	Night 17/18th		Relief received (about 6.30pm) and relief complete by 11.15pm. Coys disposed as under. B Coy Right. Fire Trench C Coy. Clay Left Fire Trench. D Coy Right Support. A Coy Left Support. Dispositions slightly altered from last time in. Coy left support by	
Front line			moved closer up to the front line & two Coys 4 pts forward. Left / Right in RAVINE TRENCH. 1/i R. BERKS more night.	
In front of LE SARS			A good deal of work done to front line on our left / Right during the night.	

WAR DIARY or INTELLIGENCE SUMMARY

Place	Date	Hour	Summary of Events and Information	Remarks and references to Appendices
Front line in front of LE SARS	Nov 18th	6.10 - 6.40 AM	Attack on our left. Our guns put up a barrage on enemy's lines opposite us, which drew a heavy retaliation practically obliterating the road on the left which has been worked at during the night. Frost broke during the morning and wet weather set in. Fairly heavy intermittent shelling throughout the day.	Casualties 1 O.R. wounded
Do.	Night 18/19th		H Company relieved Duties B on night. A relieves C on left. Enter on pm Support Battalion. 1/2 platoon Right Support Coy. W.R. BERKS on right. Relieves by 1/5 YORKS. Orders received Lt. Butts would be sent forward. Being inches of 2.	O.B.
Do.	Nov 19th		Heavy shelling during the night causing considerable slushing casualties.	Casualties 5 O.R. killed 15 O.R. wounded
		Fm 5 AM	Patrols out between trenches and BHQ encountered no enemy patrols. Enemy was putting up a great number of lights. Found very difficult owing to thick mud and number of shell holes & continuous downpour of rain. Condition very bad. Practically no shelter from the weather or shells (in fact except any but front). Men getting tired and wet but gradually improving - digging up and getting small.	

WAR DIARY
or
INTELLIGENCE SUMMARY

(Erase heading not required.)

Army Form C. 2118.

Instructions regarding War Diaries and Intelligence Summaries are contained in F. S. Regs., Part II. and the Staff Manual respectively. Title Pages will be prepared in manuscript.

Place	Date	Hour	Summary of Events and Information	Remarks and references to Appendices
Frontline in front of LESARS.	Night 19/20 Nov 20	—	Exhausted. The overland routes are also very bad "going". The trenches are not bogged and the ground is extremely heavy & sticky. Artillery more than usually active throughout the day. Intercompany relief. [B & C relieving A & D.]	2nd
Do	Nov 20	—	Patrol out in early morning but nothing to report. Enemy artillery showed much activity. AQUEDUCT Road, 25TARES, 09J32 being shelled. Aircraft which has been hindered by the bad weather in the main active today. Several aerial duels being witnessed. (The last 2 w/t Boar who went red this March 1915 & had not so before most firing) Battalion relieved by 1/BUCKS Battalion. Relief complete. On relief Coy B moved via MARTINPUICH — the tanks by 10.45 P.M.	R/57. SW
	Night 20/21 Nov	—	Thence to VILLA STATION (where Sp (posts) to PEAKE WOOD CENTRE CAMP [X 22 B] Progress from trenches exceedingly slow, owing to darkness & state of ground, & exhaustion of men. Bt Hd of first 3 Coys in by 2 A.M., but the whole Battalion not in — till after 7 A.M. C Coy suffered some casualties on the way out. Lieut SCOTT being	Casualties 20.11.16 Lieut Scott wounded 1 OR Killed 8 OR Wounded

WAR DIARY or INTELLIGENCE SUMMARY

Army Form C. 2118.

Place	Date	Hour	Summary of Events and Information	Remarks and references to Appendices
PEAKE WOOD CENTRAL (approx)	Nov 21st		Wounded 3 men killed a & and 1 wounded. Battalion resting. Following officers who had to Battalion has arrived at transport lines have joined the Battalion: 2/Lt W.H. ENOCH (rejoined) J.E. ELLIS, A.O.W. KINDELL, W.H. LEEMING, W.B. BOWLER, 2/Lt FOSKETT detail Arm Adjt. Remaining officers attached to B.A.&C Coy Infantry.	1B
Do	Nov 22nd		Battalion finding 250 men (a) day for work on BAZENTIN – MARTINPUICH Road & 50 men by night for same work.	1B
Do	Nov 23rd		Battalion finding working parties as yesterday. 2/Lt J.E. ELLIS & 2/Lt W. WINDER proceeded to join 2nd & 5th Army having been ordered to do so. 1 day & 2 days leave respectively. Several officers visited 4th 2/4th Bn Loyal North Lancs and have been to dinner.	1B
Do	Nov 24th		No working parties. Battalion to relieve 4th R. BERKS Regt on line on night 24/25th. This postponed till night 25/26th. Battalion ordered to have its PEAKE WOOD LEFT CAMP in order that the CENTRAL CAMP might be struck. This order also cancelled. Major R.R.S. ROWELL resumed B. a took over command of B Coy.	1B

WAR DIARY or INTELLIGENCE SUMMARY

Army Form C. 2118.

Place	Date	Hour	Summary of Events and Information	Remarks and references to Appendices
PEAKE WOOD CENTRAL CAMP	Nov 25th	4 PM	1st Bn moved off to relieve 1/4th R. BERKS in left Section. 458 horse ration sent up by light railway & picked up en route just beyond MARTINPUICH. Relief works well, being completed in Coy's way by 10 P.M. A good deal of hostile shelling round MARTINPUICH & 69.1+2 but fortunately no casualties. Very wet afternoon & evening.	
Front line in front of LESARS [Left Sect]	Nov 26th		Coys disposed as under. D Right front. A Left front. B Right Support. C Left Support. Disposition slightly altered since last in the line. The front line now lightly held. Enemy not disturbing us in 1/5 R. WARWICKS on our right, as CANADIANS on our left, though their right was somewhat exposed. Hostile artillery active about 4 AM. Otherwise quite. Two men round 16 R. Warwicks Battalion when remnants of 143 Inf Bde, who are holding reinforcements of Division arty front.	Casualties
Do	Night 26/27		Support Coys largely engaged in carrying up RE material, especially inverting frames to improving part of front line. 2 platoons of each of A & D Coys in front relieved by 2 platoons in support tranch. Patrols out during the night but nothing exceptional to report. Enemy wire not set up again.	1/13

WAR DIARY
or
INTELLIGENCE SUMMARY

(Erase heading not required.)

Army Form C. 2118.

Instructions regarding War Diaries and Intelligence Summaries are contained in F. S. Regs., Part II. and the Staff Manual respectively. Title Pages will be prepared in manuscript.

Place	Date	Hour	Summary of Events and Information	Remarks and references to Appendices
Trenches in front of LE SARS. 2nd (Left Sect)	Nov 27th		Cold day. Morning quiet. Afternoon fine enemy artillery active from 3 – 5.30 PM on in usual points. Many enemy planes up in afternoon. Evening driven off by our A.A. fire.	Casualties see App. No.
Do	Night 27/28th		An Exploration Patrol returns having brought up by limbers via PoZiÈRES - ALBERT - BAPAUME Rd. to Junction of GILBERT ALLEY and Rd (Afternoon was) successfully returns heavy up by J.5.40 PM. M.G. Company relief C & B railway A & B respectively. 51st Division took over on our left (Black watch 1/6th B. watch) H.Q.	
Do	Nov 28th		Very foggy morning. Hostile artillery a bit remarkable, especially in & at support B.SR.MEAD. Coy H.Q.	
Do	Nyt 28/29th	9.15 PM	Inter platoon relief as on night 26/27th. Rather peaceful along SCOTLAND TRENCH team same as first. No enemy was seen to exhibit. Prisoner a young German N.C.O. of 1st BRIGE (? Reg) west forces to find a German who threw down his arms & came in. It belongs to 1st Coy, 1st Bn. 1st Marine Infantry Regt. 2nd Mar. I. Division, 4th W. Group). Reserve Divn. This Div. the extension very late in line as much uncertainty as to who occupies the sects opposite on left.	

2449 Wt. W14957/M90 750,000 1/16 J.B.C. & A. Forms/C.2118/12.

WAR DIARY or INTELLIGENCE SUMMARY

Army Form C. 2118.

Place	Date	Hour	Summary of Events and Information	Remarks and references to Appendices
Trenches in front of LESARS [Left Scots]	Night 28/29	10.30pm	Patrol under 2/Lt BOWLER saw a party of enemy. Bn. Post were warned and then tried to cut off the enemy & drive them on to our posts. Owing to the great darkness patrol soon lost sight of & escaped. Our patrol only numbers 4.	Casualties
	Nov 29	—	Bn came in sight relieved by 1/6 R. WARWICKS.	1 O.R. Killed
Do			Foggy morning. Enemy Artillery fairly quiet till the afternoon when our right Coy. very heavily shelled. The trench bay of shelters or places	1 O.R. Wounded 2 O.R. shell shock
Do	Night 29/30	5PM	Considerably hostile artillery activity on our Lt. Northern developed. Battalion relieved by 1/5 GLOSTERS. Relief went well being completed 9PM. Coys moved by road into Scots REDOUBT CAMP (SOUTH). The camp comprised of the new Nissen huts and the men are very content. The Battn had during the month Battalion all in camp by 11.15PM except for a few stragglers who had lost feet.	SAA
SCOTS REDOUBT CAMP SOUTH BTH	Nov 30	—	Battalion resting. Clothing inspection etc.	

W. White Lt Col
Comm'g
1/4 Oxf & Bucks L.I.

TRENCH MAP, 4th ARMY FRONT.

Attached as Appendix II
WAR DIARY VOL XX
1/4 C of S Bn & Letter

145th Brigade.

48th Division.

~~944449444~~

1/4th BATTALION

OXFORD & BUCKS. LIGHT INFANTRY

DECEMBER 1 9 1 6

Army Form C. 2118.

WAR DIARY
or
INTELLIGENCE SUMMARY
(Erase heading not required.)

Instructions regarding War Diaries and Intelligence Summaries are contained in F.S. Regs., Part II and the Staff Manual respectively. Title Pages will be prepared in manuscript.

P. 21

Place	Date	Hour	Summary of Events and Information	Remarks and references to Appendices
SCOTTS REDOUBT	Dec 1st		Inspection of kits by Commanding Officer. Company training continued & Lewis Gun Classes continued under Company Lewis Gun Officers.	
Do	Dec 2nd		Work of improving camp continued.	Mus West
Do	Dec 3rd		Fine cold day. The greater part of the Batt. on working parties, so their little training could be carried out. Rumour that great deal of work on huts, being nearly a mobilisation & parking in stores. 2nd Lieuts RYE & GARLICK joined the Divisional Bomb School. Orders received to move to MIDDLE WOOD CAMP.	
Do	Dec 4th		Reveille 5:30. Pre Warkots collected & dumped before working party of 350 moved off at 7:30. P.M. Heat cleaned on return at 3 P.M. 4 P.M. Companies moved independently to MIDDLE WOOD CAMP & relieved 1/4 Royal BERKS. 'D' Coy relieved the outpost Coy (A) of the Berks. Relief complete by 6 P.M.	
MIDDLE WOOD CAMP	Dec 5		During day work was carried out on the improvement of the camp. Chalk path was made through the mud & the men's shelters were made weather proof. Order received to relieve the outpost Company of the 1/7 ROYAL WARWICKS in the vicinity of BAZENTIN WOOD. This carried out by 'C' Company & relief reported complete at 6 P.M. The Battalion supplied a working party of 350 men at night.	
Do	Dec 6		Work continued in camp & improvement of open shelters. Working Company formed & assembled in bivouacs vacated by C Coy the day before. Composition of Company:- 2nd Lieuts AFFLECK & ALLAN, one effective N.C.O., 12 L/Cpls & 18 min from each Company, & 2 cooks. This Company supplied working party at night, working from 5:30 P.M. to 11:30 P.M.	

2449 Wt W14957/M90 750,000 1/16 J.B.C. & A. Forms/C.2118/12.

Army Form C. 2118.

WAR DIARY
or
INTELLIGENCE SUMMARY
(Erase heading not required.)

Instructions regarding War Diaries and Intelligence Summaries are contained in F. S. Regs., Part II. and the Staff Manual respectively. Title Pages will be prepared in manuscript.

Place	Date	Hour	Summary of Events and Information	Remarks and references to Appendices
MIDDLE WOOD CAMP	Dec 7		The Working Company' suppllied working parties. A great deal of work done on the Camp; paths made to the entrance & to the Medical Tent. Headquarters' latrine visible. The training of Lewis Gunners continued, with the object of having at least three teams per Company. 2nd Lieut MILFORD returned to duty from the Divisional School.	
MIDDLE WOOD CAMP	Dec 8		A very wet day. Morning spent in preparation for moving. Manifests, rations etc. preparatory to move. Antishing huts at the end of the extension to the Camp.	
		2 P.M.	'A' Coy moved off by half Coys at 6 minutes interval to relieve Coy of WORCESTERS at SHELTER WOOD NORTH CAMP. 'B' Coy moved in similar formation at 3.15 P.M. 'C' & 'D' Companies moved in same formation when relieved. Relief was held up by 6 P.M.	
		8.30 P.M.	Received warning by telephone that Battalion might picket the 143 Bde in the lines on the following night. The Commanding Officer & Company Commanders left at 9.30 P.M. for 143 Bde Headquarters to take over dispositions.	
SHELTER WOOD CAMP NORTH	Dec 9		Continued to recce the whole day. The camp, which consisted of huts, known very recently.	
		9.30/M	Received order by telephone that the Battalion would relieve the 6/R.W.Kents on picquetting in the Centre Area 10-night. Orders about rations, rangers, & working Coys issued.	
		Noon	Received message cancelling order of morning.	
		2 P.M.	The training of Companies by Company Commanders continued.	
Do	Dec 10		The Reverend Bothe attached to the Battalion between the hours of 8A.M & 2P.M. Company training continued. Voluntary Church Service in the morning & evening held in Curios' Tent at SHELTER WOOD. 2nd Lieut M.P. POWELL joined the Battalion.	

Army Form C. 2118.

WAR DIARY
or
INTELLIGENCE SUMMARY

(Erase heading not required.)

Instructions regarding War Diaries and Intelligence Summaries are contained in F.S. Regs., Part II. and the Staff Manual respectively. Title Pages will be prepared in manuscript.

Place	Date	Hour	Summary of Events and Information	Remarks and references to Appendices
SHELTER WOOD CAMP NORTH	Dec. 11	3.45 P.M.	1st Coy moved off to relieve 1/6 ROYAL BERKS in the line. Carriers at corner of GILBERT ALLEY & ALBERT–BAPAUME road. Rations for 24 hours dumped well from huts at same place. Relief went well, all Coys being in position by 9.30 P.M. The BAPAUME Rd was shelled during relief & 2nd LIEUT KIRKWOOD & his servant were badly wounded. Coys disposed as under:– C Coy Left Front; B Coy Right Front; A Coy Left Support; D Coy Right Support. At 8.40 P.M. an enemy patrol of six to eight men approached CHALK PIT from N.N.W. & orders to watchers 10 yds of our post before being seen. Known to melt bombs & rifles, but unfortunately remainder of party in shelter at bottom on hearing noise rushed out & received bombs in their midst, killing one & wounding 5. Two men of front moving. A patrol of four men kept M.15.B.65, went straight out to watch 50 yds of exit. Our enemy patrol of about 20 men, which watchers almost immediately. They followed up to mg post but could see no sign of more. Later. 2nd BOMBER & 1 N.C.O. left our trench just west of same place & general area. Saw no enemy or enemy work.	
Front line in front of LE SARS [Left Sector]	Dec. 12		Raining of preceding night kept to snow & sleet & made trenches & dug outs in a hopeless condition. Coys worked all day on keeping trenches & shelters clear. Enemy shelling not more active than usual. 2nd LIEUT PATTON sighted an enemy patrol about 150 yds from SCOTLAND TRENCH opposite the junction of that trench & GILBERT ALLEY. Unfortunately whilst doing so he was sniped in the neck & wounded on side of head, but carried in until the arrival of MAJOR POWELL in the evening. Received instructions that Bn. would be relieved on following night by 1/5 GLOSTERS – guides unexpected.	
		6 P.M.		
		9.30 P.M.	Patrol of 1 Sgt & Lewis Gun team from Reserve Coy went out from M.15.B.6500. Located enemy	

WAR DIARY or INTELLIGENCE SUMMARY

Army Form C. 2118.

(Erase heading not required.)

Instructions regarding War Diaries and Intelligence Summaries are contained in F. S. Regs., Part II. and the Staff Manual respectively. Title Pages will be prepared in manuscript.

Place	Date	Hour	Summary of Events and Information	Remarks and references to Appendices
		10.30 P.M.	Posts at M9 D72 + M9 D83 about 500 yds apart. Approached to within 30 yds of W. post & observed Machine Gun, which opened fire on front of Right Front Coy. Report enemy is NOT digging trench between our line & GALLWITZ. The DYKE is manned. No sign of sigs observed. Track observed running from about M9 D56 to front between the two posts discovered. Patrol returned 10.45 P.M. Patrol of Lewis Gun & three men, supported by 5 others leyes right front line at 10.30 P.M. & located small trench at M9.C.01, held by from 10 to 15 men. Patrol were spotted & fired on by machine gun. Two men hit & had to withdraw.	
Front Line in front of LE SARS	Dec 13th		Continued to rain the whole of the day. Enemy shelling not particularly active. A few gas shells fell near BESTRENCONT FARM during the morning. Bn relieved by 1/5 GLOSTERS. Relief went well being complete by 9 P.M. Coys billeted moved to SCOTTS REDOUBT SOUTH. Last Coy arrived at 12 Midnight.	
SCOTTS REDOUBT SOUTH	Dec 14th		Bn moved to D Camp at BECOURT. 1st Coy moved at 11.15 A.M. & took over from the 7/8 K.S.O.L.I. Move complete by 12 Noon. Camp composed of NISSEN HUTS & very comfortable, except for the mud.	
D Camp BECOURT	Dec 15th		Companies at the disposal of Coy. Commanders for training & cleaning up. Quartermaster unspected Baths allotted to the Bn from 2 P.M. to 5 P.M. Nothing during the morning.	
Do	Dec 16th		Bn found working party of 262 men. Few men left for work in camp or for training.	
Do	Dec 17th		Working parties found by Bn. All available men employed on improving camp, making huts & drains.	

Army Form C. 2118.

WAR DIARY
or
INTELLIGENCE SUMMARY

(Erase heading not required.)

Instructions regarding War Diaries and Intelligence Summaries are contained in F. S. Regs., Part II. and the Staff Manual respectively. Title Pages will be prepared in manuscript.

Place	Date	Hour	Summary of Events and Information	Remarks and references to Appendices
D Camp REDOUBT	Dec 17		For all ranks not on morning parade this was an hours training from 8.30 AM to 9.30 AM in minor drill & Musketry. A class was started for the instruction of NCO's with the Reg.t Sgt Major & C.S.M. Hawker, hours 10 AM to 12 Noon & 2 PM-3 PM. All available men continued work on camp from 10 – 12.30 PM & from 2 PM to 4 PM.	
D Camp REDOUBT	Dec 18		Only a small working party paraded by Reg. so that a larger number of men were available for work on the Camp. Many dugouts dug, not sandbagged & further made. The class for NCO's continued & all available NCO's & men attended. An hours training from 8.30 AM to 9.30 AM in Physical Training, saluting & arms drill. Weather very cold. A little snow fell during the afternoon.	
"	Dec 19		Weather still cold. 13° registered midday. An hour training from 8.30 – 9.30 AM. Work on Camp & NCO's class continued.	
"	Dec 20		Training & work as yesterday. Draft of 15 O.Rs arrived. Appear with transit.	
"	Dec 21		Work on Camp & NCO's class continued	
"	Dec 22		Rained hard all the morning. Work & training had to be suspended until 11 AM. In the afternoon weather cleared up & we were able to do a great deal of work on the camp. Training of NCOs continued.	

WAR DIARY
or
INTELLIGENCE SUMMARY

(Erase heading not required.)

Army Form C. 2118.

Place	Date	Hour	Summary of Events and Information	Remarks and references to Appendices
D Camp BECOURT	Dec 23		Working parties supplied by Bn. Bn. available men in Camp continued the sandbagging of huts. The N.C.O's class under R/Sgt Major & C.S.M Martin continued. Drafts of 30 ORs arrived at 3 P.M. Quite a gratifying lots met on Two N.C.O's from the 5th Bn. At 4 P.M another draft of 154 ORs arrived. These came from the Queens Own Oxfordshire Hussars, & knew very little of Infantry training. Many had only fired a two days emergency musketry course. Nevertheless they took on if they went out well with a little training.	
Do	Dec 24.		Work in camp finished. The N.C.O's class was continued.	
"	Dec 25		Christmas Day went off very well in spite of the sudden increase in the strength of the Bn. By order of the Brigadier General no parade or training was carried out. Tables had been made in the Nissen Huts, so that all the men were able to sit down to their Christmas dinner.	
"	Dec 26	4.30 P.M. 6 P.M.	The training of Lewis Gunners, & Bombers was continued under By arrangements. Training was carried out from 8-30 A.M. to 12.30 P.M. & from 2 P.M to 4 P.M. The training of Scouts was started under 2/Lt WHITE, & that of Snipers under 2/Lt MOULDEN. The signalling class under Cpl HILL was continued. Training had to be cut short during the afternoon owing to the rain. Lectures for all Officers by the Brigadier General A tactical scheme was set to all Officers by the Commanding Officer.	
"	Dec 27	9.30 A.M. 6 P.M.	Training continued as yesterday. Lectures for all Officers by the Brigadier General. The Commanding Officer received the Report of the Medical Officer set the stay before to all Officers.	

Army Form C. 2118.

WAR DIARY
or
INTELLIGENCE SUMMARY
(Erase heading not required.)

Instructions regarding War Diaries and Intelligence Summaries are contained in F. S. Regs., Part II. and the Staff Manual respectively. Title Pages will be prepared in manuscript.

Place	Date	Hour	Summary of Events and Information	Remarks and references to Appendices
Camp at BRESLE	Dec 28		The Bn. arrived into camp at BRESLE & took over from the 6th Northumberland Fusiliers. Line of march: A Coy, B Coy, C Coy, D Coy. Headquarters Details, with distance of 100 yds between platoons. The first platoon left at 7.55 A.M. Route BECOURT—MEAULTE—ALBERT—AMIENS road through D.15.c. Fine frosty morning, & the Bn. marched well, there being no stragglers. Relief completed by 11.30 A.M. New camp consists wholly of Bell Tents.	
Do	Dec 29		The training of Coys continued. Hours of work: 8.30–12.30 & 2–4 P.M. The training of signallers continued under 2nd Lt ALLAN, snipers under 2nd Lt MACLEAN, scouts under 2nd Lt WHITE, Lewis Gunners & Bombers under Coy. arrangements.	
Do	Dec 30		Training continued as yesterday. Draft of 44 ORs from Bucks Hussars arrived, mainly men of good physique.	
Do	Dec 31	7.35 A.M.	Bn. formed up in line & marched to the CONCERT HALL in PRINCES STREET, BRESLE to attend Divine Service. Service held by CAPT JACKSON. C.F.	
		11.30 A.M.	Coys route marched for half-an hour under Coy. arrangements.	

A.B.L. Johnston Major
Commdg 1/4 Oxford & Bucks L.I.

Army Form C. 2118.

WAR DIARY
or
INTELLIGENCE SUMMARY

(Erase heading not required.)

CONFIDENTIAL

ORIGINAL

VOL. XXII
of the
WAR DIARY
of the
1/4th Batt. OXFORDSHIRE & BUCKINGHAMSHIRE LIGHT INFANTRY
[145TH INF BDE. 48TH DIVN]
for
JANUARY 1917.

Army Form C. 2118.

WAR DIARY
or
INTELLIGENCE SUMMARY

(Erase heading not required.)

Instructions regarding War Diaries and Intelligence Summaries are contained in F. S. Regs., Part II. and the Staff Manual respectively. Title Pages will be prepared in manuscript.

Place	Date	Hour	Summary of Events and Information	Remarks and references to Appendices
Camp at BRESLE	Jan 1st		Section & Platoon training carried out from 8.30 A.M. – 12.30 P.M. & from 2 P.M. – 4 P.M. Specialist classes continued – Signallers under 2nd Lt ALLAN & Cpl. HILL, Scouts under 2nd Lieut PLOWMAN, Lewis Gunners under Sgt COGGINS, Bombers under Sgt DUKE.	
Do	Jan 2nd		Training continued as yesterday	
Do	Jan 3rd		Ditto	
Do	Jan 4th		Training continued as before	
Do	Jan 5th		Ditto	
Do	Jan 6th	9.30 A.M.	The Batt. was inspected by the Corps Commander, Sir H.P. Pulteney. Batt. drawn up on three sides of hollow square at 9.30 A.M. on high ground S.W. of range at D 8 G.33 – 5th GLOSTERS right flank, 1/4 Oxfords right centre base, 1/4 ROYAL BERKS left centre base, M.G. Coy, T.M. Battery & 1st BUCKS left flank. The Gen. was complimented on the good work it had done whilst in the fighting & the last few months. It had been raining hard in the early morning, but the weather cleared up for the inspection.	
		10.45 A.M.	Training continued as yesterday	

2449 Wt. W14957/Mgo 750,000 1/16 J.B.C. & A. Forms/C.2118/12.

Army Form C. 2118.

WAR DIARY
or
INTELLIGENCE SUMMARY
(Erase heading not required.)

Instructions regarding War Diaries and Intelligence Summaries are contained in F. S. Regs., Part II. and the Staff Manual respectively. Title Pages will be prepared in manuscript.

Place	Date	Hour	Summary of Events and Information	Remarks and references to Appendices
Camp at BRESLE	Jan 7		"B" Coy had Baths from 1.30 P.M to 4 P.M.; "A" Coy from 4 P.M to 6.30 P.M. A Bde Concert was held in the evening in the CONCERT HALL, BRESLE	
Do			A Church Parade had been ordered in the morning but owing to CORPS TROOPS being sick, this was cancelled. "C" Coy bathed from 12 Noon to 2.30 P.M.; "D" Coy from 2.30 P.M to 5 P.M.	
Do	Jan 8.		Training continued as before.	
		8 A.M.	Transport started for CERISY-BULEUX [stopping night at ST SAVEUR, about 4 miles from AMIENS]	
		3.20 P.M	The Brigadier lectured all Officers in the CONCERT HALL, BRESLE.	
Do	Jan 9	4.50 A.M.	The Rev. Père in Law the usual outlook the Coups to moved off by Coys into 200 yards intervals to HEILLY STATION. After ½ mile 2-I-O, 2 Coys, Police, Quarter details. HEILLY was reached at 7.5 A.M. & here the men unpacked to the men before entraining. The entraining was carried out punctually & the train started at 8.20 A.M. route AMIENS - LONGPRE - ONGEMONT. The Bn detained at OISEMENT at 1 P.M. & moved off in the same order as before to CERISY-ROLLEUX, which was reached at 3.45 P.M. Billets rather scattered. Billets on the whole very comfortable.	

2449 Wt. W14957/Mg0 750,000 1/16 J.B.C. & A. Forms/C.2118/12.

Army Form C. 2118.

WAR DIARY
or
INTELLIGENCE SUMMARY
(Erase heading not required.)

Instructions regarding War Diaries and Intelligence Summaries are contained in F. S. Regs., Part II. and the Staff Manual respectively. Title Pages will be prepared in manuscript.

Place	Date	Hour	Summary of Events and Information	Remarks and references to Appendices
CERISY-BULEUX Billet	Jan 10th	—	Training started on area just N of OISEMONT Station. Some snow & Weather very cold. Training only carried out in the morning, owing to the long trip the Batt had yesterday.	P.3.
Do	Jan 11th	—	Training carried out as yesterday. Four and a half hours work to be done in the morning and the afternoon free for Games, lectures, etc.	P.3.
Do	Jan 12th	—	Training as yesterday. A letter known mine has been found on NW side of the village. Employés near passing with their toys for training.	P.3.
Do	Jan 13th	—	Do.	P.3.
Do	Jan 14th	—	Sunday. Corps route-march in morning. Draft of 29 O.R. arrived about 7.30 pm.	P.3.
Do	Jan 15th	—	Training continued as before.	

Army Form C. 2118.

WAR DIARY
or
INTELLIGENCE SUMMARY

(Erase heading not required.)

Instructions regarding War Diaries and Intelligence Summaries are contained in F. S. Regs., Part II. and the Staff Manual respectively. Title Pages will be prepared in manuscript.

Place	Date	Hour	Summary of Events and Information	Remarks and references to Appendices
CERISY-GAILLY Billets	Jan 16		Training continued during morning. In the afternoon all officers visited the Lewis Gun.	
Do	Jan 17		Training as yesterday. 'A' Coy fired on range in N corner of Vaux. In the afternoon all Officers & NCO's attended a lecture by the Divisional Bombing Officer LIEUT. WALKER, M.C.	
Do	Jan 18		Training as yesterday. 'B' Coy fired on range. In the afternoon CAPT CHAMBERS M.C. of the 1st M.G. Bn French Mortar Battery gave a demonstration with the STOKES Gun to all Officers & NCO's.	
Do	Jan 19	2 P.M.	Training continued as yesterday. The range was at the disposal of 'C' Coy. All Officers & NCO's attended a demonstration by LIEUT. WALKER M.C. & how to fight in the attack.	
Do	Jan 20		Training continued. The football match between the Bn & Bde H.Q was cancelled owing to the bad state of the ground.	
Do	Jan 21		Sunday. Coys route marched in morning. Coy Commanders met at MYLEN COAT to lay out ground for cloth attack to-morrow. Voluntary Church of England service in Non-Conformist service at 7 P.M.	

2449 Wt. W14957/M90 750,000 1/16 J.B.C. & A. Forms/C.2118/12.

Army Form C. 2118.

WAR DIARY
or
INTELLIGENCE SUMMARY
(Erase heading not required.)

Instructions regarding War Diaries and Intelligence Summaries are contained in F. S. Regs., Part II. and the Staff Manual respectively. Title Pages will be prepared in manuscript.

Place	Date	Hour	Summary of Events and Information	Remarks and references to Appendices
HAPPY AUBIGNY Billets	Jan 22		Bde. carried out their trench attack at HALLENCOURT. Bn moved off at 8 P.M. except C Coy & H.Q. details. Buglers. D.9.B. sig'n. Contact patrols at 9.35 P.M. Attack finished at 1 P.M. Bn halted outside HALLENCOURT for dinners. Billets reached at 4.45 P.M.	
Do	Jan 23rd		Company training in the neighbourhood of CERISY. A Coy on Range. 2 Coys done Bombing. Several Officers attended a tactical scheme held by Lieut. WANEL 3. SFREL.	M.B.
Do	Jan 24th		Bn carried out Drill attack near HALLENCOURT on same ground as on Jan 22nd. Bn moved off at 9.30 A.M. Dinners eaten outside HALLENCOURT about 12.30 P.M. A demonstration in Aeroplane contact patrol was given in conjunction with the attack, which finished about 3 P.M. Billets reached at 6 P.M.	M.B.
Do	Jan 25th		Company training in neighbourhood of CERISY. Weather 8th Extremely cold. Very hard frost & ground covered with Snow. B.O.R. held conference of C.O.s at HALLENCOURT.	M.B.
Do	Jan 26th		Continuing as yesterday.	
Do	Jan 27th		Company training as yesterday. Transport left CERISY spending night 27/28th at ARGOEUVES and night 28/29th at AUBIGNY, rejoining Battalion on 29th. Billeting party started under Major ROWELL.	M.B.

2449 Wt. W14957/M90 750,000 1/16 J.B.C. & A. Forms/C.2118/12.

Army Form C. 2118.

WAR DIARY
or
INTELLIGENCE SUMMARY

(Erase heading not required.)

Instructions regarding War Diaries and Intelligence Summaries are contained in F. S. Regs., Part II. and the Staff Manual respectively. Title Pages will be prepared in manuscript.

Place	Date	Hour	Summary of Events and Information	Remarks and references to Appendices
CERISY-BULEUX	Jan 28th	—	Sunday. Coys did half an hour rapid marching. Voluntary Non-conformist service.	113.
Do	Jan 29th	—	Battalion fell in at 8.10 AM and marched to OISEMONT Station. 2 trains conveyed Battalion to station. Battalion, Bucks, Berks & 2nd F.A. entrained at about 10.15 am. Trains started and H.Q.H., Route LONGPRÉ – AMIENS – VILLERS-BRETONNEUX – WARFUSÉE – CERISY-GAILLY, where Battalion detrained at about 5.30 P.M. Thence marched to HAMEL which was reached at about 7.30pm. Battalion accommodated in 10 large ADRIAN huts in SW edge of Village.	Draft of 22 OR joined Battn. Twenty OR (Rank reported) SWB
HAMEL	Jan 30th	/	Battalion route marched. Route VAIRE – SOUS – CORBIE – HAMELET – thence South in to FOUILLOY – WARFUSÉE Road – West edge of BOIS DE VAIRE. More snow fell during the day. 2/Lieut. G.G. SMITH joined the Battalion & posted to C Coy.	113.
Do	Jan 31st	/	Company training carried on in huts & their immediate vicinity.	do

W. Richardson Lt.Col Comdg
1/4 Bn Oxf & Bucks L. Infy.

Army Form C. 2118.

Vol 2 B

P.23

WAR DIARY
or
INTELLIGENCE SUMMARY.
(Erase heading not required.)

CONFIDENTIAL

VOL XXIII
of the
WAR DIARY
of the
1/1st Bn OXFORDSHIRE & BUCKINGHAMSHIRE LIGHT INFANTRY
[145 INF BDE 48th DIV]
for
FEBRUARY 1917

ORIGINAL

Army Form C. 2118.

WAR DIARY
or
INTELLIGENCE SUMMARY
(Erase heading not required.)

Instructions regarding War Diaries and Intelligence Summaries are contained in F. S. Regs., Part II. and the Staff Manual respectively. Title Pages will be prepared in manuscript.

Place	Date	Hour	Summary of Events and Information	Remarks and references to Appendices
HAMEL. Huts.	Feb 1st	/	Weather still very cold. Company training carried out in the vicinity of huts occupied by the Battalion.	S.B.
Do	Feb 2nd	/	The rest of the Brigade — except 1/5 GLOSTERS & ourselves moved to CAPPY — ECLUSIER area. Coy training and medical inspection in morning. Battalion practised attack in afternoon.	S.B.
Do	Feb 3rd	9.15 AM	Battalion moved off, order of march D. A. B. C. 200 yards distance between coys, to allow for Halts in traffic. Route (URISY-GAILY — MORCOURT- MERICOURT-SUR-SOMME — CHUIGNOLLES to MARLY CAMP. (3 mile S of FRAISSY) Camp still occupied by French troops who moved out at 2.45 P.M. to handed over BARLEUX. Battalion had dinners in timber yard opposite camp — moving in at 8PM. Eight ADRIAN huts allotted to Bat. with three small shanties for officers.	S.B.
MARLY CAMP Feb 4th Huts		/	Sunday. Voluntary services. Quiet day. Padre sent from each div to Memorite RIBEMONT AREA. Orders received to stand by ready to move at H.E. Div front invaded. 9.5 P.M. One & thirs down received.	S.B.
		9.5 pm		S.B.
Do	Feb 5th	/	Small Bx Respirators issued to Batt. Company training carried out as far as possible. Weather still very cold. Draft of 35 O.R. arrived.	S.B.

Army Form C. 2118.

WAR DIARY
or
INTELLIGENCE SUMMARY
(Erase heading not required.)

Place	Date	Hour	Summary of Events and Information	Remarks and references to Appendices
MARLY CAMP Feb 6th HdQ	Feb 6th	—	Company training carried out as far as conditions permit. In the evening the Battalion again warned to be ready to turn out at short notice, as heavy shelling has been directed on to back of the Divisional front & future raids anticipated on 1/4.	30
Do	Feb 7th	—	In the morning, all companies carried out the new French parade tour relinquishment for trench feet.	
		2.30 pm	Battalion moved off by companies at 200 yds interval to relieve 1/8 Works in Brigade Reserve SOPHIE TRENCH 1¼ miles N of HERBECOURT Marked via FROISSY & CAPPY. All in by 5.15 PM Alternative Employ. A Coy in trench leaving N from HERBECOURT. Battalion to 1/5 Gloster at present attached to 144 Bde. [the Divisional front being held on the following principle:— that each of the four Battalion sectors shall be "Worked" by the same three Battns in rotation; the accompanying 2 Bn attending 145 to 143 and 2 Bn 145 to 144.]	26
SOPHIE TRENCH HERBECOURT	Feb 8th	—	Very cold weather still. Coys employed in cleaning up trenches & improving entrances to dugouts etc. In the afternoon information received that Battalion would probably relieve 1/8 Works in front line on afternoon of 9th inst.	9B

Army Form C. 2118.

WAR DIARY
or
INTELLIGENCE SUMMARY
(Erase heading not required.)

Instructions regarding War Diaries and Intelligence Summaries are contained in F. S. Regs., Part II. and the Staff Manual respectively. Title Pages will be prepared in manuscript.

Place	Date	Hour	Summary of Events and Information	Remarks and references to Appendices
SOPHIE TRENCH MARBECOURT	Feb 9th	3 PM	Orders received to relieve 1/8 WORCESTERS in front line in evening.	
		1.5 PM	Reconnaissance of front trenches by CO, Adjt & O.C. Coys. It appears that Battalion relieving 1/8 WORCS. will take over Right Coy frontage of left Brigade [1/5 WARWICKS]	
		4.30 PM	Coys. moved off to trenches — 200 yards distance between platoons. Relief noted very smoothly, being completed by 1/15 Avl. Batt. gives men under 145 Bde [The system of hitherto Divisional front has now altered. One Right & larger Sector being hot alternately by 1st and 145 Brigades with 2 Battns in line, 1 in Support & 1 in Reserve; the Left & smaller Sector being hot by 143 Bde providing its own reliefs.] 1/5 Glosters on Right, 1/5 R. Warwicks on Left.	
			Disposition:	
			Right Coy. [B]. 3 platoons front line @ I a 10.15 — @ I 6.25.55.	
			1 Platoon in Support.	
			Centre Coy [C] 3 platoons front line @ I 6.25.05 — @ I 6.05.73.	
			1 Platoon in support.	
			Left Coy [A] 2 platoons front line @ I 6.05.73 — I 31.0.30.73.	
			1 Platoon in Support.	
			1 Platoon in Reserve.	
			Support Coy [D] Trench STETTIN & QUIBERT.	
			Battn HQ. @ I A 60.25.	
Em Plane apperule LA MAISONETTE	Night 9/10	1.35 AM	Some trench mortar trails on front trenches & Shrapnel — Quiet night.	Bks.

WAR DIARY
or
INTELLIGENCE SUMMARY

(Erase heading not required.)

Army Form C. 2118.

Place	Date	Hour	Summary of Events and Information	Remarks and references to Appendices
Front line opposite LA MAISONETTE	Feb 18th	—	Some artillery activity on our centre & left coys between 8.9 and 13 AM. Otherwise quiet day. 2 other ranks wounded. Ground in trenches frozen. Very hard making work extremely laborious. Enemy aeroplanes over our lines. Several seen during the day. Parties of 7th R. BERKS up in evening to assist in improving trenches.	7923 Private ROBINSON 20364 Pte WILLIAMS (Both wounded)
Do	Feb 19th	—	Between 8 and 9 AM hostile enemy artillery activity, chiefly on about 60 shells falling in the area in the hour. 1.40 pm a few more shells on our trenches. 3 O.R. wounded by artillery during the day. Enemy also active with rifle grenades — which are favoured by short distance between trenches — to which we replied.	B.B. 1803 Pte BARBER P. Bdy 3562 Pte WATER H.W. Coy 5550 Pte SMITH J. Also All wounded
		10 PM	Several enemy aeroplanes again over our lines. Orders received to extend our line to the left, to take over two more pts from the 1/5 WARWICKS. This completed by about midnight. [NB Return sent up brought to point that RUTLAND DEFENCES came FLAG CORP. — TRENCHES R & J]	No
Do	Feb 20th	—	Frost still holding. Enemy again fairly active with grenades & artillery. Between 8 & 10 AM and again about 3 pm. Our snipers claim a hit on a German who was exposing himself in a sap. Very little aerial activity. One casualty, caused by sniping, a pte of French troops.	7253 Pte EVANS. E Bdy wounded (Snipers wound)

WAR DIARY
or
INTELLIGENCE SUMMARY

(Erase heading not required.)

Army Form C. 2118.

Place	Date	Hour	Summary of Events and Information	Remarks and references to Appendices
Authuile SOMME LA MAISONETTE	21st Sept	4 am	which were being returned for the trenches. P.R.I. in B/Coy informed the general... There was an A/coy near Clanwith B/C in from brickfield on the north side of the artillery encampment artillery in support. Enemy shelling fairly active again on way forward to try to B/C. They relieved 1st R.B. at B Bns in the early morning. Relief was not completed by 8:45 pm (5 copies of common zone 2 (3.65.f)) or relief Bns were at Brigade support - pushed forward pairs (Bng) at dugouts in M5 a.7.11. Coys disposed as follows A x B in DESIRE VALLEY R36 A x B, D coy dugouts N6A (1300) C coy — Bn H.Q. — Bomb dugout M5 a 7.11	Sos B.3
Bryan Fer Snapnt 4th 15th E. of FLAUCOURT		After 10 am regimental H (Bn R? Snap pm Wound d.O. 3 light wound d.O. Battalion worked on support trench making further in line for Burying Parties for SAN. Bns R.E. PLEANS 8th along with the lighter in... Working parties as before gearing in the killed Buried	26th Wembly 5.24 Bd 11th... Mc(iv?) ... ...28.

Army Form C. 2118.

WAR DIARY
or
INTELLIGENCE SUMMARY
(Erase heading not required.)

Place	Date	Hour	Summary of Events and Information	Remarks and references to Appendices
Brigade Support Trenches E of FLAUCOURT	Feb 15	9.30 AM	Several hostile aeroplanes over which were "strafed" by our Lewis Guns.	1/LB VOKES slightly wounded 11552 Pte BURTON slightly killed
		9.45 AM 10.15 AM	Shelling of neighbourhood of Battalion HQ commenced. This continued, without cessation, till 1 PM, being most unduly fierce for about the first 3/4s of an hour. Several hundred shells were fired, principally 15cm. Thus several direct hits were scored on Dugout occupied by "B" Coy HQ & Coy. also — a dump of trench tools on the road close by. Casualties 2/Lt B. VOKES — from shell which had just missed entrance to Coys HQ, B 1 OR wounded 5 OR.	7380 Pte VOKES slightly killed 7917 L-Cpl NEWMAN 5373 Pte KENNEDY Coy Atton wounded 11415 Pte VINCENT (since died of wounds)
Do	Feb 16th	—	Battalion on wiring party at night as usual. Am relieved by King taken over by 2/A BURKS. Remaining this platoon & SOPHIE trench for the night. Accommodation for B platoons of A Coy found in FLAUCOURT, where 2 platoons from SOPHIE trench went in afternoon. Very heavy working and carrying parties found on night 16/17. Large parties being required to carry tools left to last front Battns. Patrols sent out under 2/Lt POWELL and 2/Lt ALLAN from R BURKS trenches. Both these patrols did excellent work & got much valuable information as to the enemy wire & the mouths of hidden their trenches.	J/B B.B.

Army Form C. 2118.

WAR DIARY
or
INTELLIGENCE SUMMARY

(Erase heading not required.)

Instructions regarding War Diaries and Intelligence Summaries are contained in F. S. Regs., Part II. and the Staff Manual respectively. Title Pages will be prepared in manuscript.

Place	Date	Hour	Summary of Events and Information	Remarks and references to Appendices
Bryan Bridge E. of FONQUENT	Feb 17th		Battalion relieved by 1/1 Worcesters Relief complete 2.15 p.m. On relief Bn's moved via Valley of PLAME DETRUIT [illegible] & HEBUTERNE and thence through ECLUSIER & Camp 56 between ECLUSIER & CAPPY. Troops was at disposal of Battalion. Burgd. Battalion & 2 Coys of 1/4th Bn Beds in same camp. Cap arr 6 & 6.30 pm. Thaw started & heavy rain during the night.	
CAMP 56 CAPPY	Feb 18th		Sunny. Violent thunder shower between 3 & 4 pm. Much rain & heavy wind during the night. 6 hrs of drill.	
Do	Feb 19th		Only finding working party of 35 in camp. Remainder of Coys training. Baynes Attacks &c.	
Do	Feb 20th		Coys to bath at ECLUSIER. Afternoon Coys training. Parties furnished from Co to wash. 6.15 am. Coys marched 20-ex to ECLUSIER QUARRIES 3pm, and Do 1 Bn'd [illegible]. Training of [illegible] furnished by Battalion on line of possible	

Army Form C. 2118.

WAR DIARY
or
INTELLIGENCE SUMMARY
(Erase heading not required.)

Place	Date	Hour	Summary of Events and Information	Remarks and references to Appendices
CAMP 56 CAPPY	Feb 21st	—	150 O.R. out on fatigue. Remainder of Battalion in Camp doing permit. Weather still very wet.	P.B.
Do	Feb 22nd	—	150 O.R. on fatigue. Training as usual for rest of Battalion.	P.B.
Do	Feb 23rd	—	As yesterday. Whole Battalion Bath. Battalion would go into support on 24th instead of going direct into front line as previously arranged.	P.B.
Do	Feb 24th	3.30 PM	It appears that numbers in support area have been reduced to have room for details of one of front line Battalions together reduced to leave D Coy behind for the night. Battalion moved off by Platoons at 25 yards interval, where 1/6 GLOSTERS were relieved. Relief complete by 7PM. A Coy in FLAUCOURT. B & C Coys here in less so before. Batn under Bde Brigade Rd. 8 PM. 25th. [B Owing to (2) state of trenches, the following alteration made in system of relief. Bates not to move into front line Def. Scheme into the line, but to stop at least one night in Bde support on Reserve.]	
Brigade Support Trenches E of FLAUCOURT	Feb 25th	6.15 A	Working Parties for R.E. in morning. Battalion ordered to relieve 1/8 WORCESTERS in front line (left from Barleux). Since the Batn last up, practically all trenches have fallen in, or become impassable.	P.B.

WAR DIARY or INTELLIGENCE SUMMARY

Army Form C. 2118.

Place	Date	Hour	Summary of Events and Information	Remarks and references to Appendices
Front line opposite LA MAISONETTE	Feb 25th	—	All movement to & from the Bn by night. A company held [the] WAR RAVINE DEFENCES proper. The LONER ROAD, & COMMIES STEIN. Relief starts at 6.25 pm. SUNK ROAD reached by 10 pm. Dispositions at time same as last relief. Front line with two platoons in front and one in support. Front line Coy - D. Information received that evacuation of line started by enemy 4 pm. FIFTH AVENUE and active bombing between Parties out but enemy shells from 4 to 7 pm. Somewhat [illeg] Enemy trench very [illeg] artillery through the day. [illeg] Enemy trench somewhat.	
Do	Night 25/26	/		
Do	Feb 26th	—	A great deal of artillery activity & harassing fire throughout the night and [illeg] day. Very little movement observed. [illeg] crept down [illeg] & [illeg] [illeg] sniping & [illeg] of [illeg] was taken to [illeg] enemy [illeg].	2nd Lt [illeg] 1535 [illeg] wounded 2nd Lt [illeg]
Do	Night 26/27	—	Further information [illeg] of returned further [illeg] of enemy. A message [illeg] to the [illeg] army live [illeg] site of [illeg] 1.31 at 55.50 where artillery had been wrecking the Lick fighting part A Coy was to try & get into enemy trench at that point & obtain fuller information about FLEETWAY. This was in change of 2nd Lt [illeg] & one [illeg] was [illeg] Wounded first as they were leaving the trench & the [illeg] [illeg] had their [illeg] betrayed to enemy artillery barrage. No [illeg] jap was [illeg] in enemy.	2nd Lt [illeg] [illeg] [illeg] 22[illeg] [illeg] [illeg] [illeg]

WAR DIARY
or
INTELLIGENCE SUMMARY

(Erase heading not required.)

Army Form C. 2118.

Place	Date	Hour	Summary of Events and Information	Remarks and references to Appendices
Front line opposite LA MAISONETTE	Feb 27th		Wire, & forth this fastened & others sent out by other Coys. Front enemy line held by apparently small garrison. An unusually clear day, making movement very difficult & enemy snipers being active against someone going over the top, & two men being hit. The Battalion relieved in the evening by 1/4 R. BERKS Reg.t R. left sectn from Sunk Road at 7pm and war complete by 10.30pm. On relief Battalion moved into Brigade Reserve, being disposed as under. D Coy (3 platoons) N. end of FAUCAUCOURT. A Coy Runent leading N from HERBE COURT. Battalion Battn Hq. SOPHIE TRENCH Relief reported by moon 8pm 27/2/18.	A/B
				735 # MILES 789 PT MARTIN Wounded
Bryant Road SOPHIE TRENCH HERBECOURT	Feb 28th		Quiet day. Men resting after trenches N&L 28 Feb/March 1st D Coy working for R. BERKS	

A. Worrall Lt.Col.
1/4 Ox & Bucks L. Infty

Vol 24

P.24

CONFIDENTIAL

WAR DIARY

OF

1/4th Oxfordshire & Buckinghamshire L.I.

From 1st March to 31st March 1919.

CONFIDENTIAL

Vol. XXIV
of the
WAR DIARY
of the
1/1 Batt" OXFORDSHIRE & BUCKINGHAMSHIRE LIGHT INFANTRY
[145 INF BDE
48TH DIV.]
for
MARCH 1917
VOL XXIII

Army Form C. 2118.

WAR DIARY or INTELLIGENCE SUMMARY

(Erase heading not required.)

Instructions regarding War Diaries and Intelligence Summaries are contained in F. S. Regs., Part II. and the Staff Manual respectively. Title Pages will be prepared in manuscript.

Place	Date	Hour	Summary of Events and Information	Remarks and references to Appendices
BRIGADE RESERVE SOPHIE Trench HERBECOURT	MARCH 1st	11 A.M.	Two enemy aeroplanes flew over our lines proceeding in direction of CAPPY.	
		3 P.M.	One aeroplane flying low came over our lines & proceeded towards CAPPY. It attracted none of our observation batteries. Both aeroplanes were observed to get out. The Bn relieved the 1st ROYAL BERKS in the line. 'D' Coy moved into Reserve Trenches at SUNKEN ROAD — B Coy 7.30 P.M., C Coy 7 P.M., 'D' Coy 8.30 P.M. Trenches with no material movement along over the R.E. relay company by 10.45 P.M. Dispositions taken over as last time, but orders received that there were to be a Strong on Companies in Art-Line. Front line held by two Companies (B on right & A on left) each with two platoons in Art-Line & two in Support. 'C' Coy moved into Support, accommodation being found at STETTIN. New dispositions completed by 5 A.M.	
Bn Front line opposite LA MAISONETTE	MARCH 2nd	4.30 A.M.	Patrol of 1 NCO & 6 men left Q.1.B.50.30 at 4.30 A.M. & proceeded eastwards. Report few movements. Reached enemy wire. Falling in his trenches, but the length of the garrison could not be estimated. Returned to Q.1.B.40.10 at 5.45 A.M.	
		2.45 A.M.	Patrol of 2 NCOs & six men left our trenches at O.1.B.02.72 at 2.45 A.M. & proceeded northwards. On reaching enemy wire they followed it northwards for 150 yards but were fired on & gave (?). Returned 4.20 A.M. Enemy artillery extremely active the whole day. From 9 A.M. to 1.30 P.M. shells came over at the rate of 4 per minute. At 1.45 P.M. the intensity of fire increased & continued until 5.45 A.M. DOUBLEMENT, STETTIN & FAVOIRE receiving special attention. Shells chiefly 4.2's & few 5.9's. 77 m.m.	
		7 A.M.	CAPT. & ADJT. E.E. BRIDGES wounded by bullet in the right arm.	
		11.30 A.M.	A patrol of one N.C.O. & 6 men left our trenches at the junction of BORDER & OSTCHAUSSEE	

Army Form C. 2118.

WAR DIARY
or
INTELLIGENCE SUMMARY

(Erase heading not required.)

Instructions regarding War Diaries and Intelligence Summaries are contained in F. S. Regs., Part II. and the Staff Manual respectively. Title Pages will be prepared in manuscript.

Place	Date	Hour	Summary of Events and Information	Remarks and references to Appendices
Front line opposite LA MAISONETTE	March 3rd		Owing to stormy moonlight patrols obtained no leaving our wire & first in by Maxim fire. Two more attempts were made, but without success. Our artillery activity on the HUN prevented them for going out at a later hour. Work continued on clearing up STETTIN Tr. from ROUEN DUMPES to SONDER. Work suspended last trench made passable. Work continued in Front line. BOUCHERSEN, REMAIN DESTROYED, DOUSEEMONT.	
			Quiet day. Bn relieved by the 4th CLOTIERS. Casualties — 3 O.R.'s in front line & one in support. D Coy relieved by ay by the 6th CLOTIERS. Relay went well, being complete by 10.15 p.m. Two Coys had the journal out on SUNKEN ROAD & on arrival at SOPHIE TRENCH, B, C & D Coys in SOPHIE A Coy in HERBECOURT. Bn H.Q. in by 12.55 A.M.	
SOPHIE Tr. HERBECOURT	March 4		Some snow fell during the morning, half intervals of bright sunshine. Bn. the moved from SOPHIE Trench to brigade reserve, resting & improving accommodation.	
Do	March 5		Little snow during morning. Bn. HQ. moved from SOPHIE Trench to huts in the Priory at point 572 in HERBECOURT – CAPPY ROAD. Working parties of 575 O.R.'s required at night. Orders received later in day reducing the to 200 O.R. This party was also cancelled later, but the fact to stop party from reaching their destination & wasting work.	

Army Form C. 2118.

WAR DIARY
or
INTELLIGENCE SUMMARY
(Erase heading not required.)

Instructions regarding War Diaries and Intelligence Summaries are contained in F. S. Regs., Part II. and the Staff Manual respectively. Title Pages will be prepared in manuscript.

Place	Date	Hour	Summary of Events and Information	Remarks and references to Appendices
SOPHIE Tr. HERBECOURT	MARCH 6	1.30 P.M.	Bn moved to MARLY CAMP to billet. 1st Bdn B" to stay on right at SOPHIE Tr. Half way up to the line.	
MARLY CAMP MARCH HALF	MARCH 7		Order of march :- D. Coy, C. Coy, B. Coy, A. Coy. Passed at SH yds interval from SOPHIE to MARLY moved by Bys. B.H.Q. -- HERBECOURT -- CAPPY to SOPHIE -- FRISKY road. Bn paraded in billets by 4.30 P.M. As we were the only Bn in the Camp there was much more accommodation than when we had three here.	
			The Bn had talks all day.- M.G. details at CAPPY from 10.30 -- 12.30. B. at FRISKY from 2 -- 12.30 P.M. C. Coy at FRISKY from 2 P.M. to 5 P.M. A Coy at MARLY from 2 P.M. -- 3.30 P.M. & B Coy at CAPPY from 3.30 P.M. -- 5 P.M. See than Stronger parts thing forwarded.	
			In the evening the Bn moved back to SOPHIE TRENCH. A & D Coys had men at CAPPY & C Coy at FRISKY. A Coy & B Coy moved up to form supply parts. 13 Coy left CAPPY at 6.10 P.M. & D Coy left FRISKY at 5.30 P.M. to join HQ details. B. left MARLY CAMP at 5.30 P.M. B. & C. Coys -- supply in MARLY TRENCH & SUPPLY Tr. roads. Companies moved by platoons at 300 yds distance. Bn formed at SOPHIE by 8.30 P.M.	
SOPHIE Tr. HERBECOURT	MARCH 8		Preliminary instructions about proposed raid received. Coy Officers & NCOs of B & C Coys went out in the afternoon to view plan of German trenches in type new CAPPY & CAPPY -- CHAIGNOLLES Trs. A & D Coys supplied working parties.	
Do	MARCH 9		B & C Coys went out in the morning to practise plan of attack on ground, as yesterday. A & D Coys supplied working parties.	

2449. Wt. W14957/M90 750,000 1/16 J.B.C. & A. Forms/C.2118/12.

Army Form C. 2118.

WAR DIARY
or
INTELLIGENCE SUMMARY

(Erase heading not required.)

Instructions regarding War Diaries and Intelligence Summaries are contained in F.S. Regs, Part II. and the Staff Manual respectively. Title Pages will be prepared in manuscript.

Place	Date	Hour	Summary of Events and Information	Remarks and references to Appendices
SOPHIE Trench HERBECOURT	MARCH 10	1 A.M.	Working parties supplied by A & D Coys. Detailed orders about raid received. During the morning the C.O. held discussed these orders with the Coy. Commanders of 'B' & 'C' Coys, & all details were settled. The men of 'B' & 'C' Coys paraded getting over was met with wire however made. These arrangements made — a study of intent counts was made however slats bridges across — forward guide efforts &.	
		3.30 A.M.	Orders received that operation would not take place to-night, on owing to the bad visibility it had been impossible to cut enough gaps in the enemy ground. B & C Coys paraded at once & moved up to the enemy ground.	
Do	MARCH 11	10.30 A.M.	The Commanding Officer went to Bgde. Headquarters to discuss plans for again. It was decided that it would take place to-night.	
		2 P.M.	The Commanding Officer held a conference with O's C 'B' & 'C' Coys to discuss plans.	
		3.30 P.M.	Orders received that raid would not take place owing to bad state of trenches & ground.	
		5 A.M.	Preliminary orders received to relieve 1/4 ROYAL BERKS to-night in the line.	
		8 P.M.	Detailed orders about relief received.	
			The Bn moved up to relieve 1/4 ROYAL BERKS. Order of march 'D' Coy, 'C' Coy, 'B' Coy. The trenches was in very bad condition & all movement had to be done over the top. Relief took a long time & was not completed until 2 A.M. the following morning. Dispositions the same on last tour D Coy & B Coy were right front Coy & B Coy were in reserve.	
FRONT LINE opposite LA MAISONNETTE	MARCH 12		Rained hard in the early morning & some of the communication trenches became almost unpassable. 2 snipers fire slightly with 77 mm guns, men kept off during the early morning as our sent lines trenches & forward communications. Two patrols were sent out to examine the enemy's wire. Both patrols reported enemy wire badly damaged in places, but no actual gaps. No enemy working parties were seen. No Man's Land in a very bad	

2449 Wt. W14957/M90 759,000 1/16 J.B.C. & A. Forms/C.2118/12.

WAR DIARY
or
INTELLIGENCE SUMMARY

(Erase heading not required.)

Army Form C. 2118.

Instructions regarding War Diaries and Intelligence Summaries are contained in F.S. Regs., Part II. and the Staff Manual respectively. Title Pages will be prepared in manuscript.

Place	Date	Hour	Summary of Events and Information	Remarks and references to Appendices
			stat.	
		8 P.M.	Whole of Trenches searched & patrols sent out specially reconnoitering enemy information. Orders received that "C" routes be relieved tomorrow night by 9th Manchesters.	
FRONT LINE opposite IN MAISONETTE	March 13	1:15 AM	9th Hull F.E. JONES, E.J.H. MINGER & 42 OR's joined the Bn.	
		1:30 AM	Patrol 1/s one Offr & 2 men left post O1D05.95 at 20.3.44 & not reported badly wounded on return.	
			Patrol 2/s one Offr & 2 men left post O1D05.25 & proceeded down to Commn. trench at O1D05.05 which was found to be occupied. Was repulsed to & returning reached their own lines at 2.50 AM. Patrol returned at 2.50 AM. Two more patrols went out from Coy. "B" to reported mine shaft craters (badly damaged "No-Man's Land") reported the enemy had sentries.	
			Own artillery were fairly active during the day, chiefly on right & on enemy lines. Trench Mortars heavily shelling enemy line.	
		1 P.M.	Enemy fired on support Bn. H.Q. & two Field Guns & 60 rounds relatively but without much effect in Bn MAISONETTE.	
		3:30 AM 6 AM	Enemy again became aggressive on our front opposite registering trenches. Enemy few rounds.	
			Bn relieved by 9th MANCHESTERS. Trenches in very bad state, but owing to rainy weather & heavy frost, relief carried over via TANGN. DESROSSES & by fine Coys in succession. This seemed well to be taken over & completed by 12 Midnight. No Fire caused such as UNKNOWN ROAD. Bn. moved to CAMP 56 & all were present in Camp by 4 AM.	
CAMP 56 CURRY	March 14		Bn. resting. Kit inspection held by O.C. Coys. 2nd Lieut. H JEFFERSON reported to Bn.	
Do	March 15		Inspection of Coys. The Quartermaster visited Coys whilst clothing etc.	

Army Form C. 2118.

WAR DIARY
or
INTELLIGENCE SUMMARY
(Erase heading not required.)

Instructions regarding War Diaries and Intelligence Summaries are contained in F. S. Regs., Part II. and the Staff Manual respectively. Title Pages will be prepared in manuscript.

Place	Date	Hour	Summary of Events and Information	Remarks and references to Appendices
CAMP 56 CAPPY	March 16		Battalion resting & Companies occupied with interior economy. "B" & "C" Coys left at 7.30 by motor lorries to carry out an attack on LA MAISONETTE. Weather fine & Camp becoming drier. A Coy r H.Q details to Baths.	
	17		Attack took place at an early hour & thoroughly successful. Casualties 1 Officer 2/Lt H.F. PEARSON wounded. O.R. 1 killed & 3 wounded. (Full account in Appendix). A & D Coys provided parties for work on roads. "D" Coy had baths at CAP B. Weather much brighter & milder. "B" Coy returned late, having experienced delay & casual overnight at advance by Brigade at night from LA MAISONETTE on way prob. Spirits & spell of their experiences.	2/Lt H.F. PEARSON (Wounded) (H.Q.) 200726 L/Cpl TAYLOR J.S. WOUNDED 200125 Pte PULLIVER H 203907 Pte DAVIES S.H. 203550 Pte SECCOMBE M
	18		No parade - Church Service voluntary. B & C Coys resting during morning & baths at FROISSY in afternoon - Parties for road repair at DIACHES.	
	19		Companies fitting small Box Respirators in Packing. Lecture to Officers by C.O. on Advanced Guards. Weather milder & no other parade. dull & showery.	
	20		Companies being on range at CAPPY & practical A.S.G. Battalion warned to move in afternoon & eventually left CAMP 56 at 3.45 P.M. for PERONNE via ECLUSIER, FRIZE FEUILLERES crossing RIVER SOMME by pontoon bridge at HALLES thence into PERON N/E which bag reached at 7.30 P.M. The route between by Canal had 7 in places very much broken in very good repair on arrival at PERONNE	

Army Form C. 2118.

WAR DIARY
or
INTELLIGENCE SUMMARY

(Erase heading not required.)

Instructions regarding War Diaries and Intelligence Summaries are contained in F. S. Regs., Part II. and the Staff Manual respectively. Title Pages will be prepared in manuscript.

Place	Date	Hour	Summary of Events and Information	Remarks and references to Appendices
PERONNE	MARCH 20		Troops billeted as follows 'B' Coy in a private house, A, C & D Coys in HOSPITAL	
	21		'B' Coy at work on Railway round about. Place in between BOURELLES & OBIGNY & were relieved by A Coy in afternoon. Both Coys proceeded to CARTIGNY & remained there for the night. PERONNE in a very much damaged condition, no building being left whole. The enemy appear to have blown out the front walls of houses causing whole structure to collapse & many fires have added to the general destruction of property. C & D Coys & H.Q. remained in PERONNE for the night.	
CARTIGNY	22	9.0 A.M.	H.Q. & C & D Coys marched to CARTIGNY via DOINGT & COURCELLES & arrived about 10.45 A.M. 'B' Coy formed in neighbourhood of station in S.E. Corner. The men were able to make fires owing to quantity of timber from destroyed buildings. Also the destruction has been so complete & systematic also in PERONNE & all around that has been taken away in trucks. Battalion occupied in working parties filling in mine craters on roads, clearing tracks & removing trees & obstacles etc. Battalion was moved South of WARD's Column	
"	23	5.4 AM	'C' Coy left for BURE & three patrols under orders of O.C. Cavalry operating in the neighbourhood of TINCOURT. Yet by afternoon took up an outpost position in front of TINCOURT and HAMEL. A, B & D Coys are working parties filling in craters & clearing roads of trees etc.	
"	24		D Coy moved to take up an outpost position as follows: - 1 Platoon at BOUCLY, 1 Platoon at HAMELET & BOUCLY, One Platoon of C Coy moved into MARQUAIX & held the village. Enemy burnt in neighbourhood of BOIS DE TINCOURT & MARQUAIX and also RUSSEL Wood.	

WAR DIARY or INTELLIGENCE SUMMARY

Army Form C. 2118.

Place	Date	Hour	Summary of Events and Information	Remarks and references to Appendices
CARTIGNY	24		Been shelled by 4.5" Howitzers & patrol from "D" Coy entered the town & found it deserted. A foot bridge established in the evening. 2nd Lieut "C" Coy were put in MARQUAIX during the evening. Orders were received that "C" & "D" Coys were to be relieved by Cavalry of 5th Cavalry Division. "C" Coy were relieved & the 3 Platoons of "C" Coy & remained Held in CARTIGNY at about midnight. Lt. Scouts & 2/Lt WHITE's Plat. Remained there and returned to CARTIGNY at midnight. HOOD arrived late & half platoon & TINCOURT.	(Wounded) N° 3426 Pte W. N° 15844 N° 9157 L/Sgt N° NVE 7.5
"	25	6 AM	"D" Coy Platoon in front of HAMELET not relieved till next night but at dawn were forced to retire by superior number of the enemy, who advanced & occupied cavalry in some between HAMELET & ROISEL. A patrol moving towards ROISEL were fired on & the Coy, Officer Major was wounded & his orderly killed.	Killed N° 9175 Pte N° 9750 S.M N°9875 2.5M NOSTTO N AM
		11:30 AM	Orders received for Bath to move to TINCOURT. "A" Coy & the own disposition of "D" by 1 pm. "D" Coy & 2 pm. H.Q. details at 2:15 pm. "C" Coy at 2:30 pm. "B" Coy at 3 pm. "B" Coy had been working on road at BUIRE. On arrival one platoon of "B" Coy relieved & moved out.	
		10 PM	MARQUAIX. Patrols sent out by A & B Coys to ascertain whether ROISEL occupied. Both parties were heavily fired on by enemy. Patrols returned & reported ROISEL occupied.	WOUNDED (See appendix)
TINCOURT			& "A" Coy Guards of RIVER COLOGNE.	
	26	6 AM	Patrols again sent out at 6 AM & were again fired on - one man of "A" Coy wounded.	
		10:30 AM	10 R Welsh & 8 R. Warwick. Attack on ROISEL by us. Carried out by A & B Coys.	
HAMEL		6 PM	Attack successful and ROISEL occupied. (See appendix). H.Q. moved to HAMEL as Bde wished to keep Btn - C Coy also moved up to HAMEL. Capt M. EDMUNDS returned to K. Bn.	

Army Form C. 2118.

WAR DIARY
or
INTELLIGENCE SUMMARY
(Erase heading not required.)

Instructions regarding War Diaries and Intelligence Summaries are contained in F. S. Regs., Part II. and the Staff Manual respectively. Title Pages will be prepared in manuscript.

Place	Date	Hour	Summary of Events and Information	Remarks and references to Appendices
HAMEL	March 27	9 A.M.	B: relieved by 1st Bucks B: & went into billets at TINCOURT. Coy Coy recently.	
TINCOURT			First former held. A B. & D. relieved in ROISEL & HARQUAIX - B: of Relief completed by mid day. Remainder employed away & numbers of bugs in billets.	WOUNDED
	28	10 A.M.	Rested & remainder of day. Weather fine on the whole.	2nd Lt 353 90
			2nd Lt W. S. STEELE, 2nd Lt V. S. WILKINS & 2nd Lt PITTS joined the Battalion. Inspection of hay & Coy Commanders & Officers. Cleaning. Coy Commanders	PKE 8t
			C. Coy at work all night digging Cucumber Posts in shifts of half battalion at a time.	
	29	11 A.M.	Battalion under orders to move to BUSSU & C.O. went off to reconnoitre billets & 3 P.M.	
			FC LAY with billeting party at work. Orders to move at 3 P.M.	
		2.55 P.M.	B: ordered to stand fast & takes & drive to HARQUAIX in relief of BUSSU	
MARQUAIX		5.30 P.M.	B: moved by Platoons at 100 to intervals in heavy rain. B: LG very shortly.	WOUNDED
			strung out completed demolition of buildings. All present by 8 P.M. Ours.	2nd Lt 4f96
			Having many to complete demolition of railways. Shells arrived & Cucumber Posts Man MARWSS Z L.G.	
			funny old night there some Bivouacs shells dropping also & Cucumber posts & certain position	
	30	11 A.M.	Conference of Coy Commanders with reference to Bivouacs shelters.	
			Hd day to the Welsh.	
		2.30 P.M.	Commanding Officer & Coy Commanders invited into lunch & armed funters	
			had lunched luncheons. 6 Coys at work on Cucumber Posts during night.	
	31		A few shells fell in "E" end of village on N.C.O. being wounded - Men made during the	
			day as B: had been warned to be prepared to move at 2 P.M. Man did not take place.	
		5.30 P.M.	The Commanding Officer & H/Qr attending into me Officers from each Company and the	
			Scout Officer went off & became country. K.N. & RUSEL.	
			Coys at work on Cucumber Posts from 7.30 - 10.30 P.M.	

W. L. W. Buttrick
Lt. Col. Commanding
1/4 Oxf. & Bucks L.I.

2449 Wt. W14957/M90 750,000 1/16 J.B.C. & A. Forms/C.2118/12.

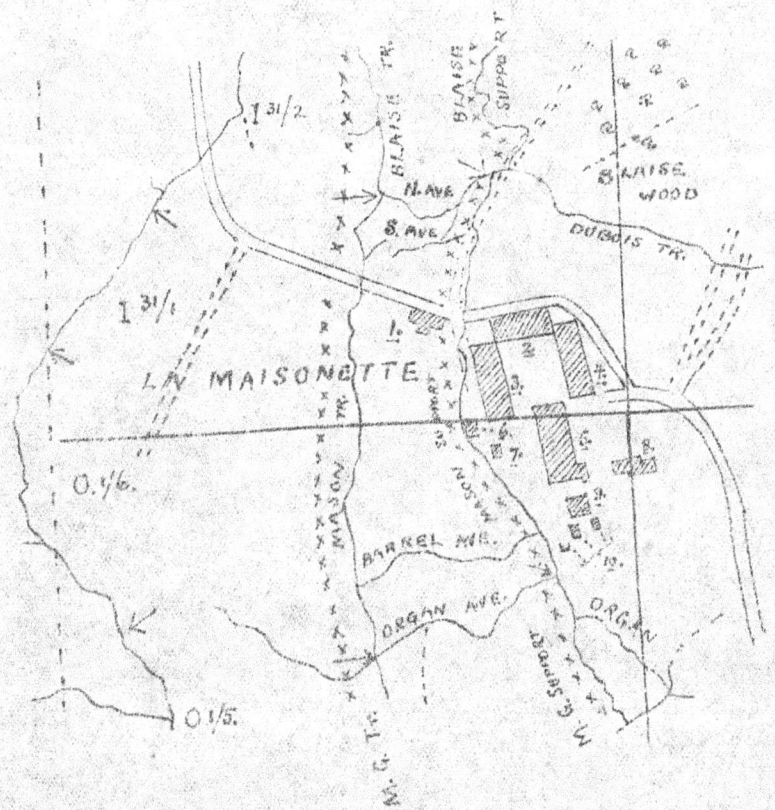

Scale 1/5,000.

WAR DIARY or INTELLIGENCE SUMMARY

Army Form C. 2118

APPENDIX I /5

MARCH 1917

Place	Date	Hour	Summary of Events and Information	Remarks and references to Appendices
PLAN of LA MAISONETTE attached.	March 16	7.30	"B" & "C" left CAMP 56 in motor lorries and conveyed to HERBECOURT. Owing to congestion of traffic on road they were delayed in reaching trenches and in consequence the time for the attack postponed till 2.30 A.M. at which hour the order was given for Companies to form. B Coy left trenches No. 6 Platoon going over first in double section & the remaining Platoons followed. Previous to leaving the trench the enemy artillery shelled the trench and one officer (2.Lt Mt PEARSON) was wounded, 1 O.R. killed & 2 O.R. wounded. The leading Platoon found the German trenches occupied by a Sentry & when some were killed by bombs & others made good their escape – one man was taken prisoner. C. Coy followed B Coy and both proceeded to work down the enemy trenches & reached the U.K. line beyond which they received orders not to go. No enemy were found and patrols were sent out and investigated the ground to the banks of the RIVER SOMME but found no traces of party who escaped from the first line trench. Denny the Coy the position was consolidated – A certain amount of shelling was directed upon the position but without casualties. – The Companies were relieved at about 7 P.M. by the 1/4 GLOUCESTERSHIRE and returned to Camp 56 by F.S. Wagons.	

WAR DIARY or INTELLIGENCE SUMMARY

Army Form C. 2118

APPENDIX II to MARCH 1917.

Place	Date	Hour	Summary of Events and Information	Remarks and references to Appendices
ROISEL	MARCH 26	10.0 A.M.	OPERATIONS in connection with the capture of ROISEL. Disposition of Battalion. A Coy. — 2 Platoons in HAMELET, 2 Platoons in BOUCLY B Coy. — 2 Platoons in MARQUAIX, 2 Platoons in TINCOURT. C & D Coy. — TINCOURT. A Battery of 18 lb. Field Guns & one section of 4.5 Howitzers shelled ROISEL for 30 minutes and heavy MG covered the Barrage & Platoons of A & B Coys. moved towards the objective. The Platoons of A Coy advanced along HAMELET — ROISEL Rd. by sections & were held up by rifle & M.G. fire upon approaching the railway & owing to marshy ground were unable to advance in extended formation so had the embankment of the ROISEL — MONTIGNY branch railway. These Platoons were No. 1 & 4 under 2/Lt. A.E. PEARSON & C.A. BOWMAN. Meanwhile Nos. 5 & 6 Platoons of B Coy moved out of MARQUAIX on high ground N of ROISEL & owing to enemy fire had to advance in extended formation in this line, 2/Lt. A. ALLAN was in command and upon reaching crest of ridge he quickly gained superiority of fire. They & Patrol under Sgt. WIGGINS (which entered) ROISEL and dislodged a M.G. Left that had been firing upon A. Coy. The 2 Platoons of B Coy then followed into ROISEL & made a thorough search of the houses & found it had been completely evacuated by the enemy one prisoner of the 118th I.R. being taken. The 2 Platoons of A Coy were then able to enter the town. Two armoured cars rendered assistance by entering the outskirts of the town on N.W. side and firing on the enemy. Capt. G.A. GREENWELL was able to make good use of an outside gun captured from one of the Armoured Cars by causing it forward with a ration of his Coy to the high ground on the N. side from which effective fire was directed upon the retiring enemy. When the town was in our hands one platoon of A & B Coys. respectively took up Outpost positions on the E. side of the town. A	

WAR DIARY or INTELLIGENCE SUMMARY

Army Form C. 2118

(Erase heading not required.)

Place	Date	Hour	Summary of Events and Information	Remarks and references to Appendices
ROISEL	MARCH 26	4 P.M.	Action of the 145 Infy Bde had two Vickers M.G's in position – Two Platoons of D Coy were recd to reinforce B Coy & then occupied an outpost position on the Ridge on the N side of ROISEL. The remaining 2 Platoons of B Coy were moved up into ROISEL with one of A Coy & occupied support positions during the night. Coy H.Q. in East of Crossroads in ROISEL. 2/Lt A.D. ROWMAN (Commanding A Coy) left one Platoon in HAMELET. The remaining 2 Platoons of D Coy moved into MARQUIX for the night. The enemy shelled ROISEL heavily for about 30 minutes during the afternoon but without causing any casualties. The Coys were relieved at about 10 P.M. by the 1st Bucks Bn & returned to TINCOURT. Casualties Killed. 200505 L/Cpl WANE H.F. B Coy 203284 Pte POLMER C. " 203046 " FOWLER J.H. A Coy 202236 " SOMMERS H. " WOUNDED. 203003 Cpl COCKLIN J.H. B Coy 200667 L/Cpl SALLIS R.W. " 238001 L/Cpl SAUNDERS H.J. " 203939 L/Cpl NASH S.H. B Coy 203657 Pte PARKER W. A Coy 203599 " WILSON R.S. " 207325 " LAMBOURNE H. " 200737 " TARRER A. B Coy 203312 Pte KNIGHT R.M. B Coy 203987 " RANDLE J.T. " 202334 " COX G.W. " 203574 " GROOT C.B. " 208312 " BEA W.A. " 203679 " RILEY H. "	

"Active Operations of 1/4 Bn: 1 Berks Lt Inf: March 1917

March 16th. Two Companies moved at 7.30 pm. by lorries from CAPPY to HERBECOURT for attack on LA MAISONNETTE.

March 17th. Zero at 1.30 am. - postponed to 2.30 am - which not even then allowed time to get into position owing to mud and the one trench board track congested by Batt. the two Companies of the Battalion on our right also using it, also by carrying parties of Battalions holding the line.
Enemy barrage started practically same time as ours at 2.30 am. before Companies were in position" They took cover till it finished, reorganised and went over in originally intended formation - two platoons on the left to form a defensive flank, remainder, three waves on a two platoon front. Opposition slight.
Casualties in enemy's barrage - 1 Officer wounded, Other Ranks 1 Killed and 3 Wounded.
Casualties in advance and afterwards - NIL.
(Note. Our own wire caused more inconvenience than that of enemy and its value up till then seems to have rather been underestimated.)
Patrols pushed out down to SOMME without opposition likewise N.E. behind BIACHES where 143 Bde on our left advanced about 11 am.
2 Companies relieved by 9 pm. by Battalion of 144 Bde. and returned to CAPPY by midnight.

March 20th. Battalion march 3.45 pm from CAPPY and reach PERONNE 7.30 pm. Battalion Transport by different road got in very late owing to missing road in BIACHES, which should have been picketed and wrong roads blocked.

March 21st. Battalion came under command of WARD'S COLUMN - 2 Companies mending road and bridge on way to CARTIGNY where they stopped for night.

March 22nd. Battalion Headquarters and other 2 Companies to CARTIGNY

March 23rd. 5 am. C Coy. went to TINCOURT to be under O.C. Cavalry, took up outpost position TINCOURT and HAMEL with patrols into MARQUAIX which they cleared of enemy's rear post.

March 24th. D Company went up before daylight to hold BOUCLY and HAMELET, C and D holding an outpost line of resistance in front of MARQUAIX and HAMELET, by 6 am. Enemy's patrols in TINCOURT WOOD prevented any approach up to the high ground. About 5 pm group of Battalion Scouts and patrol of Corps Cavalry occupied TINCOURT WOOD which was taken over by 8th Warwicks later in evening.
5 pm. Patrol of D Coy from HAMELET entered ROISEL and found it unoccupied and established post.
6 pm. Squadron 18th Lancers, 5th Cavalry Division took over Outpost Line North of River COLOGNE but on going up to ROISEL were fired upon and returned to MARQUAIX.

March 25th. Post in ROISEL remained till 5 a.m. when enemy re-entered village and drove it back on platoon at HAMELET.
(Note. No relief by Cavalry south of river COLOGNE.)
11.30 a.m. Battalion moved to TINCOURT and took over outpost line again.
10 p.m. Patrols both sides of river met strong opposition from enemy in ROISEL.

March 26th. 10 am to 10.30 am. ROISEL shelled by 18 pdrs, 4'5's, and two 60 pdrs, under cover of which B & A. Coys advanced to attack North and South of river respectively.
11 am. Three platoons of B. Coy advancing widely extended gained outskirts of village. A. Coy held up by M.G. and floods.
11.30 am. Enemy M.G. holding up B. Coy was cleared out

by an Armoured Car and B.Coy cleared the village by 1 pm. enabling A.Coy to enter from South.

3 p.m. Village and position just East consolidated. Casualties. O.R. 4 killed, 14 wounded.

(Note. Squadron of 18th Lancers opperating as Cavalry on either flank - on north side helped greatly in guarding flank and finally siezed high ground N.W. of village. Squadron on south side held up the floods and no help to Infantry.)

4 p.m. 2 troops of Cavalry holding high ground facing VILLERS-FAUCON relieved by 2 platoons D Coy.

6 p.m. Command of line and of Battalion taken over by 145 Brigade from WARD'S COLUMN.

March.27th. Battalion relieved by 1st BUCKS Battalion and returned to TINCOURT.

Apl.3/4. Battalion took over outpost line in front of RONSSOY from 1/8th WORCESTERSHIRE Regt, during night. Active patroling carried during night and following day and night. Enemy located holding Village strongly.

Apl.5th. Battalion attacked RONSSOY at 4.45 a.m. in accordance with Brigade order No.192.
A and B Coys each on a 150 yard front and in four waves forming main strength of attack formed up on a north and south line at head of valley due west of RONSSOY (forming up line, which was previously flagged for each Coy, was eight hundred yards from enemy lines and roughly in our outpost line of resistance.) 2 platoons each of D and C Coy respectfully N and S of this line joined up with 1/5th Glosters attacking from N.W. and 1/4th R.BERKS attacking from S.W. 2 platoons each C and D Coys formed Battalion Reserve at ST.EMILIE.
Battalion H.Qrs. at east end of St.EMILIE with forwarding observing Officer and relay post for messages half way between Battalion H.Q. and objective. Attack was sucessfull The strong post at south west end of RONSSOY gave trouble with M.G's which our Lewis Guns put out of order, after which both Companies pushed through the village till stopped by our own barrage which was short. When this ceased stopped they made good the objective and reformed. One Company and one platoon held the posts 500 yards east of village remainder withdrawn to support positions clear of S.W. corner of village.

(Notes. Enemies barrage was just over and clear of forming up line and caused no casualties. Village had been cleared before enemy had started shelling it. Companies had previous warning on this point.)

P. 25

Vol 2 5

CONFIDENTIAL

WAR DIARY.
of the
1/4 Bn. OXFORDSHIRE & BUCKINGHAM SHIRE LIGHT INF Y
(145 Inf Bde. - 48th Div.)
for
APRIL 1917.

XXIV

WAR DIARY
or
INTELLIGENCE SUMMARY

(Erase heading not required.)

Army Form C. 2118

Place	Date	Hour	Summary of Events and Information	Remarks and references to Appendices
MARQUAIX	APRIL 1		Battalion standing by all day in case move ordered. No orders were received however and work carried on in the evening on Cruciform Posts.	
	2		Battalion at work on Cruciform Posts in morning. Weather has been wet & stormy for past 2 days.	
VILLERS FAUCON	3		Battalion moved to VILLERS FAUCON in evening to relieve 1/8 WORCESTER REGT leaving MARQUAIX at 8.15 P.M. in following order. C. D. A. B. C + D Coys took over positions in outpost line in front of ST EMILIE & VILLERS. A Coy in support to B Coy in reserve at VILLERS. Night found with HQ & 2 Platoons at ST EMILIE. Outposts ordered to maintain active patrolling. D Coy had HQ & 2 Platoons at VILLERS.	
	4	3.30 AM	Patrol from D Coy (left outpost Coy) went out and did not return until shortly mid-day. Patrol had been compelled to shelter in shell hole owing to light becoming too strong on making dash for outpost. 2 were hit. 1 killed & seriously wounded & lain out of Patrols sent out from both outpost Coys were fired on by enemy & outpost positions also shelled. During morning shell burst in dug-out occupied by B Coy with casualties.	Killed 203400 Pte RUSSELL W.E. 1 Died of wounds 203609 Pte CHAPLIN A. (both with A Coy)
		7.0 PM	Barrage by our artillery on enemy positions. Patrols sent out to ascertain whether enemy still in occupation of village, were fired upon by enemy from PELIZE of C Coy and 5 men hit - one man of C Coy audibly killed.	Killed
			Orders were issued for attack to-morrow on RONSSOY in conjunction with 1st Royal Berks Reg. on our right & 1/5 Gloucester Regt on left. A. + B. Coys moved from VILLERS FAUCON to take up position.	
	5	2.30 AM		
		4.15 AM	Attack launched & front successful with comparatively slight casualties. A number of prisoners & 2 M.G.s taken.	Wounded 2nd Lt F.C. HAY (shell casing)
		7. AM	RONSSOY in our hands & position taken up on E side of village. Enemy shelled RONSSOY very heavily but without causing casualties to the Bn as the men were well under cover. Bn relieved in evening when B Coy were about to consolidation of positions continued all day and "B" Coy moved forward & S.M. Weeks	

WAR DIARY or INTELLIGENCE SUMMARY

Army Form C. 2118.

Place	Date	Hour	Summary of Events and Information	Remarks and references to Appendices
	APRIL 5.		OPERATION resulting in capture of PONSSOY, BASSE-BOULOGNE & KEMPIRE in which 1/5 Bn Oxf & Bucks L.I. Infy took part —	
			Disposition of Battalion when in position— A & B Coys formed up in 4 waves each on a front of 150 yards on a N. & S. line on West of Valley. 2nd Lieut W. F. PONSSOY forming main attack against 2 Platoon of D Coy on N & W. the 2nd to maintain touch with 1/5 GLOUCESTER REGT & 2 Platoons of C Coy on S of line to keep touch with 1/4 R. BERKS Regt. Remaining 2 platoons each of C & D Coys at STEENELLE in Bn Reserve. B'n H.Q. at Château at St EMILIE.	
		AM 4.45	Attack commenced at 4.45 A.M. without previous artillery preparation. A & B Coys advanced to within a few yards of objective before being seen, but meeting formidable resistance the enemy sending shellfire many of Barbelamay. 1/5 Oxf. Bucks L.I. met with very successful action with the enemy M.G. and B/5K UPSTONE found very demoralised on arrival in trench owing to the handling of them. During two charges the Huns (B) Coy had reached the village. Captured by 5.38 A.M. Capt. PREENNELL reported that two (B) Coy had reached the village of PONSSOY and by 5.55 A.M. They had worked through the outside leaving superior numbers casualties upon the enemy. Several prisoners taken. At 6 A.M. 2nd Lt A. W. PROCTOR reported A Coy also through & the E end of PONSSOY. Most positions had been taken up on this side — Army HQ and own artillery manage to could not find forward Bn at bottom of enemy field guns were train changing away & Two occupied captured.	
		7 A.M.	The enemy shelled the village very heavily for a considerable time with H.E. but owing to all men being clear of the Buildings no casualties were caused.	

Army Form C. 2118

WAR DIARY
or
INTELLIGENCE SUMMARY
(Erase heading not required.)

Instructions regarding War Diaries and Intelligence Summaries are contained in F.S. Regs., Part II. and the Staff Manual respectively. Title Pages will be prepared in manuscript.

Place	Date	Hour	Summary of Events and Information	Remarks and references to Appendices
VILLERS FAUCON	April 5		Quiet day till about midnight. (Full account in APPENDIX). 2nd Lt. J.E. BOYLE & 2nd Lt. A.E. CREW joined 12 Battalion. 2nd Lt. R.B. WHITE awarded 1st Military Cross.	
	6		Battalion resting. Orders from to move to R.5. Emerald at there were considerable weather still stormy.	
CAMP R.5 (centre)	7		Bn moved to move to CAMP in R.5 following 14th Gloucesters. Moved about 5 P.M. but could not take over till 7 P.M. when relief 12 B: left for the support line. Very little accommodation. Capt R. PICKFORD returned from F.B.	
	8		Sunday. Weather dull at first but clearer up and rest of day was bright & fairly warm. Wesleyan Service at 10 A.M. — Church of England at 7 P.M.	
	9		Snowing very hard & set in lot of snow & hoping for open weather at last. Bn Reserves. For a search with assistance of two Lewis "Rifles" & others, Capt GREENHILL awarded Military Cross. Very cold & equally weather poor. Nothing further owing to were unable to find anyone to inform them & no relievement.	
	10		Work continued on some in front of Gunform Posts E & D in morning A & B in afternoon. Weather cold with snow at times.	
	11		A & B at work on Gunform Posts in morning but were recalled. Remainder of 12th resting in Camp. 2nd Lt. J.D. PICKMAN returned to Bn from Hospital.	
	12		No working parties. Companies at disposal of Coys Commanders. Morning was brightly sunny but changed to previous cold conditions in afternoon. Disposition — C Coy R: Front Coy D Coy left front Coy	
	13		B: relieved 17 Worcesters in evening.	

Army Form C. 2118.

WAR DIARY
or
INTELLIGENCE SUMMARY.
(Erase heading not required.)

Instructions regarding War Diaries and Intelligence Summaries are contained in F.S. Regs., Part II and the Staff Manual respectively. Title pages will be prepared in manuscript.

Place	Date	Hour	Summary of Events and Information	Remarks and references to Appendices
Outpost line in front of RONSSOY	14.		A Coy relieved right front Coy of 1/4 GLOUCESTERS, but were later relieved by Coy F/5 thereby & their area had into support. B Coy in Reserve. Relief complete by 2 P.M. Front held by outposts, left Coy from CROSS post F18c06 to Coys post F25 b 97, right Coy thence to L7 b 78. Night quiet. No casualties.	
Do	15		Quiet day except for desultory hostile artillery fire. Rained continuously the whole day & night. Casualties nil.	
Do	16	3 A.M.	Patrol of 1 N.C.O. & 2 men went out from B Co Front Coy at F18c05 & found trench about 200 yds from our line occupied by enemy. Patrol returned 4.15 P.M. Another patrol of 1 N.C.O. & 2 men went out at F25 D 95 to reconnoitre ground in vicinity of QUENNEMONT FARM, & encountered enemy post 200 yds from our front. Reports enemy holding series of detached posts, posts found pushed out at night. Quiet day. Bn relieved by 1/4 ROYAL BERKS. Relief complete by 12 Midnight.	
Camp S/E EMILIE	16		Camp in railway cutting. Owing to hard work up the previous afternoon suffered accommodation found. Coys carried out inspections. Fine morning changing to rain in afternoon. C Coy left at 6 P.M. & went into support to 1/4 ROYAL BERKS in TONE WOOD.	
Do	17		A quiet day but ordered to be west most of the morning. Relieved 1/4 ROYAL BERKS in evening - Disposition - A front Coy - A left front Coy. C - D in support - Relief complete about 2 A.M. Same front as when B A was took in support there.	
Outpost line in front of RONSSOY	18		A patrol of 4 by invalid 2/Lt J.E. PEARSON under 2/Lt GUILLEMONT made & brought. GUILLEMONT magn & fences in & to strong Rifles. Endeavoured to an attack on the farm & night by B Coys artillery fired on farm in afternoon which resulted in retaliation but no casualties were caused. Plan for attack continuing morning & eventually put off about ½ an hour before time enemy. Fired at to bed. Quiet night but some crisis momental. C Coy Rt Front Coy. D Coy 1/Lt Front Coy	

Army Form C. 2118.

Instructions regarding War Diaries and Intelligence
Summaries are contained in F. S. Regs., Part II.
and the Staff Manual respectively. Title pages
will be prepared in manuscript.

WAR DIARY
or
INTELLIGENCE SUMMARY.

(Erase heading not required.)

Place	Date	Hour	Summary of Events and Information	Remarks and references to Appendices
	APRIL 19		Patrol of A Cy sent out again reported FILLEMONT FARM strongly held & M.G's on edge in front of it. Orders received that D Cy should make the attack the evening 25 7.30 p.m. "C" Cy sent 5.40 messaged copy of their orders. Schedule of R.E & C/s POTAISUSSEX Bty was also to assist D Cy to consolidate when taken. Artillery preparation on afternoon — B" to be relieved by 18 MIDDLESEX 25th Manchesters consulted.	
		7.30 p.m.	D Cy in position two lines with bombers interval between. Leaders pivoted on front platoon forward movement. As one side swung the flank pile R10 FILLEMONT FARM. Very few Germans in it but M.Gs & snipers in adjacent trenches & from the adjacent shell holes hampered the advance. Bombers kept moving up the remains of the sunken road. Opposition became gradually weaker & soon & [...] Left flank platoon & [...] able to [...] though it [...] as soon as [...] no advance from FARM to the ridge & held. The position was secured but [...] and more strongly held. Sentry posts R14 & the British Barrier along the road put in. A Cy moved considerably forward by 12 [...] were & ready at one platoon 3 R.E. Div Dumps NULLED C.R. (killed) 3 missing & 18 wounded.	CASUALTIES KILLED 1 D & O WOUNDED O.R. — 7 MISSING 3 O.R.
HAMEL	20	7.15	Upon with a word of appreciation of D Cy's work [...] (see POISEL & NAROEUX) Relief performed R. S. ENGITIE came. 1st line reinforce [—] three packs in from trenches to rear (munich) & M W.Y.22 were also apt & came up late. D Cy were amongst from ST ENGITIE we on 98, who were 2 Platoons of A Coy & tried by unawathed shelters as about 7.30 a.m.	
	21		Afternoon. D Cy were much improved in the situation altogether new to them. & the BM. reported the attack as [...] Returned to the 24 & 17 O 8 (in information) who accrued. 2 Lt A ALLAN evacuated to N Military Corps of A Balks most of day. Few much approved & twenty second which gave to the 1/3 O.R. us A.O	
	22		C.O.O. pair on the [...] [...] Conference held at [...] [...]	
			Before relief was received by [...] 1/4 L.O.C. Inspection will place at 3.30 PM C Pinnell off [...] was necessary [...] [...] [...] to concern. Everything moving & when special [...] [...]	

A 5834 Wt. W4973/M687 750,000 8/16 D. D. & L. Ltd. Forms/C.2118/13

WAR DIARY or INTELLIGENCE SUMMARY

Army Form C. 2118.

Place	Date	Hour	Summary of Events and Information	Remarks and references to Appendices
HAMEL	22		Living in the Reserve tr. The B.O.C. supervised himself day that being minor at B'.& - 2 rdrs. of per ards during past few weeks. Weather must unpleasant - heavy/heavy at night.	
	23		Companies getting in on company movement. B' in reserve with para available to M.C. O's officers. C Coy sent up bombing parties to bombs all day. Platoon 2 B' of D'ebb's corps at 2 P.M. for an sent under O.C. V Battalion seemed rather an the an 1 P.M. to assemble in rest Bde called upon to support own Bde had been making an attack on VIAZERMONT FARM P.M.	
	24		Battalion standing by in billets until two am. Small working parties from B'y	
	25	3 A.M.	Battalion moved to R.5 entrail to be in readiness for attack upon Hill 266 were making an assault upon GUILLEMONT FARM at dawn. The attack & any French arrangement orders were received for B'y to relieve 5s HAMIEL on relief of Battn. and expected till tomorrow. March back rather trying animals had sufficiency for two successive nights. Battn reached about 10.30 AM & rest from 11 & afternoon standing nearly to relief.	
		4.30 P.M.	Orders received for B'y to relieve 8th WORCESTERS 9/10 S.W. support B's 4 to more at once. B' moved at 6.15 P.M. and relief complete at 10.30 P.M. Disposition A+D Coys in reserve at F.2.5.a. C Coy 2 Platoons in TRONE WOOD & 2 platoons at "Coy h.qrs" (F.2.9.c.) B Coy & H.Q. at F/1.27.a. The right was firm from — [sketch] forty yards. B.	
In support position about F.2.7.	26		A quiet day with a little shelling/shelling. B + C Coys at work during morning on Arrowform Posts in "Baron Line" at about F.2.2 & 2.3. Transport & Q.M. stores arrived at R.10 en route to day. A Coy occupied & manned M.G's at QUECHETTES WOOD & Baron/Roadway F.17 a & c. R. Berks Regt: were re-establish astronaut posts in N. of GUILLEMONT FARM early afternoon. The Off: returned from C.O's conference the evening.	
	27		A fresh day. Major SCHOMBERG left B'y at 9.30 P.M. as good board line. Relief complete about mid-night. Dispositions - relieved by R. BERKS Reg'y at 9.30 P.M. as good board line. Relief complete about mid-night. Dispositions - A Coy 2 Platoons in relief line or left & 2 Platoons in support at QUECHETTES WOOD - B Coy 2 Platoons in line in centre & 2 in support at sunken road - C Coy in GUILLEMONT FARM - D Coy 2 Platoons in line in support at sunken road & H.Q. in gun pit. Front line extended from F.22 & 6.1.a. at F.2.2 & 6.1.a.	F.18.a & F.2.9.c.

Army Form C. 2118.

WAR DIARY
or
INTELLIGENCE SUMMARY.
(Erase heading not required.)

Instructions regarding War Diaries and Intelligence Summaries are contained in F. S. Regs., Part II. and the Staff Manual respectively. Title pages will be prepared in manuscript.

Place	Date	Hour	Summary of Events and Information	Remarks and references to Appendices
In outpost line about GILLEMONT FARM.	April 28		Nothing of importance occurred during day or night - Enemy artillery more being active - Weather fine. At night Coys. at work improving positions & number cover. 2/?	
	29		Quiet all day. B". relieved by 8". WORCESTERS in evening without incident & returned to Camp at R. 5 central by midnight. A good times without any casualties being incurred.	
	30.		Beautifully sunny day. B". moved to billets at HAMEL at 2 P.M. & in the following order M.B. C. D. Gun renting for remainder of the day. All are immensely pleased with the prospect of good rest & look forward to some fine weather & food filled.	

NOTE MAP REFERENCES - All references are to Sheet 62 & N.E. F.&. 3. a. Scale 20,000

The position consolidated was approximately upon the line F.22.c.3.4. to F.22.c.7.4.
& also F.22 & 79 there by A Coy & 1 Platoon of B Coy.
The remaining Platoons of C & B Coys + 1 Platoon of D Coy were withdrawn to
Ste MARIE.
The Bn was relieved in the evening by the 1st R. BERKS REGT relieving to
billets at VILLERS FAUCON.

Our casualties were comparatively slight & were as follows.

KILLED.   7 O.R.
          2. Lt F.C. LAY.
WOUNDED   23. O.R.

Army Form C. 2118.

WAR DIARY
or
~~INTELLIGENCE~~ SUMMARY.
(Erase heading not required.)

Vol 26

CONFIDENTIAL.

WAR DIARY

OF THE

1/4 Bⁿ OXFORDSHIRE AND BUCKINGHAMSHIRE LIGHT INFᵀʳʸ

(145ᵗʰ Inf. Bde. — 48ᵗʰ Div.)

MAY 1917.

XXV

Army Form C. 2118.

WAR DIARY
or
INTELLIGENCE SUMMARY.
(Erase heading not required.)

Instructions regarding War Diaries and Intelligence Summaries are contained in F. S. Regs., Part II. and the Staff Manual respectively. Title pages will be prepared in manuscript.

Place	Date	Hour	Summary of Events and Information	Remarks and references to Appendices
HAMEL	MAY 1		Battalion resting - Baths at TINCOURT - Q.M. issued new clothing to Companies following working parties formed - A, B, & D Coy in turn at work on road between TINCOURT & MARQUAIX - C Coy provided party of 50 to work on flooded pontoon of BOUCLY - TINCOURT Rd - Weather continues to be excellent.	
CAMP at DOINGT	2		Battalion moved to CAMP at DOIGNT at 2 P.M. Order of March A, HQ Details B, C, & D Coy's. Rather hot march but now all rested Camp in fair condition. 2/Lt. W.J.L. WALLACE joined Battalion Company worked Company arrangements during morning - In afternoon Camp shifted to a new site near COLOGNE RIVER.	
	3		A & B Coys on working parties - C & D Coys on Company arrangements.	
	4		C & D Coys on working parties - A & B Coys under Company arrangements - Company Commanders attended wire cutting demonstration by Bertha in afternoon.	
	5		Sunday - Church Service at 11:30 A.M. Day spent in recreation - 2/Lt. J.L. MACKAY joined Battn the CO left the Company on leave Company under Company arrangements.	
	6		Raining nearly all day - Not much to come from available in Cubs & Company Lectures.	
	7			
	8		A & B on working parties at TINCOURT - BURK on roads. C & D training in morning. A party of 80 had reopens for C & D Coys at Coal dump just to took at 2.35 P.M. & here that camp moved from 7.30 P.M.	

WAR DIARY or INTELLIGENCE SUMMARY.

Army Form C. 2118.

Place	Date	Hour	Summary of Events and Information	Remarks and references to Appendices
CAMP at DOIGNT	MAY 10		Companies continued training - C & D. Coy had Mantles & clothing disinfected at P.P.O. VMS. Heavy rain in evening.	
	11		Training programme continued. Returns received that Bn. moves to-morrow.	
COMBLES AREA	12	6.30 AM	Bullis left Camp - Order of march A, B, C & D Coys. Route PERONNE CLERY, MAUREPAS to COMBLES area. March rather trying owing to heat & absence of breeze & several checks from time to time. Destination was reached about 12 noon. Accommodation consisted of bivouacs & shelters in bank. Rather dirty. Men rested for remainder of day.	
BEAULENCOURT	13	4.45 AM	An early start. It became hot all the march to-day. Considered about 20 miles FREGICOURT SAILLY-SAILLISEL, LE TRANSLOY to Camp N.E. of BEAULENCOURT. Arrived in Camp at 8 A.M. & found very ample accommodation more in fact than we have seen last senior on entered to SOMME. Reliques Camp for remainder of day and as few energetic people went into BAPAUME.	
	14		Orders received that Bn. to relieve 6th LINCOLN REGT in support of B! From 3! Bn. left Camp at 5.30 in following order C.D. & H.Q. Coys. The parks of trill lorries were known conveyed to VELU by lorry which were a considerable relief & like were as heavy thunderstorms during afternoon had made things very heavy. B. & A. Coys made up before reaching VELU & on 9 P.M. Guides from Lincolns met parties	MAP REF.
SUPPORT POSITION about HERMIES			Position - Disposition - H.Q. & C & D. Coys on bank at J.34.d. A. Coy at J.36.d. & B. Coy at J.39.a. Accommodation almost entirely consists of shelters in banks & dugouts suitable for fire than for weather 10th Corps unable to Coys fairly comfortable Relief Complete about 1 A.M.	57. C.N.E. 1/20,000

WAR DIARY or INTELLIGENCE SUMMARY

Army Form C. 2118.

Place	Date	Hour	Summary of Events and Information	Remarks and references to Appendices
Support position about HERMIES	MAY 15.		A very quiet day with scarcely any artillery activity. Coys spent day improving shelters etc. Working parties as follows (at night) A. & B. at work on reference posts N, 4 & 2. HERMIES, C. & D. Coy. carrying parties for R.E. B/Pt. found Bath. Weather changed & became dull during latter part of day.	Capts L.W.
	16		Very quiet day again. Rain commenced about noon & continued for remainder of day. Nothing of interest occurred.	
	17.		Very quiet day again. Weather dull but fine. Enemy Bns. Intensive quiet.	
	18th		The HAYRINCOURT Road Feb.3. Bn relieved 1/4 R.BERKS. in line. Disposition Reng. C. Coy, L. Coy, B. Coy. Butts Coy A. Coy, D.Coy. in reserve. Relief complete 11 pm 19th inst.	
Out Post Line N.E. of HERMIES	19		Weather fine. Comparatively quiet except for desultory enemy shelling. One of our planes came down in flames at 4:15 p.m. No casualties during march here.	
	20		Fine day. Enemy artillery a little more active. A patrol under 2/Lt. BOYLE morning N.O.R. left to reconnoitre Gaps at K14.d.4 & 7.K.14.b.23 & report if changed. At enemy party of 30 were working on trench of Sub party of som 2nd gap. The patrol without suffering any casualties. At 7 p.m. demonstration was carried out in conjunction with 4/5 on enemy trenches on E. side of canal. The operation was truly successful. A patrol consisting of 2/Lt. PENROSE & 3 O.R. left our line to reconnoitre the gnmd. in front of SPOIL HEAP K20. central. They located an enemy post which is why further south where they immediately walked into an enemy post. Laming.Q. rapid rifle fire they withdrew, coming to the challenge. They were sharply fired upon by rifle & M.G. rapid they withdrew running& several minutes, were keenly bombed. The patrol attempted to our line. Casualties. 1 missing. A special patrol consisting of 2/Lt TOWNSEND & 26 O.R. was sent out from	
HERMIES	21.		my B/Pt. to establish a post outside the enemy Knife head at K.26 central	

A 5834. Wt. W4973/M687 750,000 8/16 D.D. & L Ltd. Forms/C.2118/13.

WAR DIARY or INTELLIGENCE SUMMARY

(Erase heading not required.)

Army Form C. 2118.

Place	Date	Hour	Summary of Events and Information	Remarks and references to Appendices
OUTPOST LINE N.E. of HERMIES	21		They proceeded in two waves but owing to darkness experienced difficulty in keeping touch. In addition party who had been South of 31 in front of COPSE RED in which several men fell. They advanced previously located enemy posts S. of COPSE from which was opened machine gun & rifle fire. They charged objective who from bayoneting certain men of the enemy C.O.'s & S.M. managed to proceed to them this Bn did return who refused to come out & attempted to get away. Three of the wounded. During this movement 2/Lt BARNARD although wounded himself. When he saw Lt. AKERMAN how gallant division were cleared & attained objective these fatigues eventually compelled by weight of numbers to retire. Casualties 2 KILLED 1 WOUNDED 1 MISSING. Total 4 killed 32 Lows 3 KILLED 2 WOUNDED 1 MISSING	
	22		Enemy artillery active. Weather warm. Began to turn cooler in evening intermittently throughout the day & night. Fighting gas shells were used by enemy 2a.m. to 8 a.m. the entire wood from DUBLIN this being unknown to us to which patrol composed of 1 N.C.O. & 6 men to reconnoitre dying nature of Ground. A patrol of 1 N.C.O. & 6 men who to work patrol of 2 sections 1 N.C.O. to be made in passing tour to men three N.C.O.s & 9 men. An expedition by wire & ravine weary that this was the difficulty owing to this DUBLIN to be sent to COPSE RAMILIES.	
	23		Enemy quiet. Began in morning. Reconnaissance dominated by 2/Lt MARTIN was changed before enemy RAMILIES COPSE, very light used by the enemy. Marked in returning after 7.30 from own lines of morning was enclosed at daybreak & kept up. Advanced to COPSE NOVON after 4 hour since. Bombardment of BEAUMOND N. RAYAVIS 37	
	24		Carried out and exercises with T.M. Dispositions again to-day and wreck of DUBLIN & D Coy. Batallion relieved by 1/LT BUCKS. By B Coy & C Coy of BEAUMONT. B Coy especially stood up. Day at DEMICOURT. D Coy	
NIGHT OF 24-25			at DOIGNES & COY AT BEAUMETZ. These who took over supply at DEMICOURT monument. I hot allowed during day great difficulty experienced. No dead examination available. No men killed by enemy shells.	

D Coy thirty quiet except for enemy bombardment of BEAUMONT N. Rayavis 37. D Coy plough Benelli Rt. 3/Lt.s RAIL completed at 3 a.m. the working party to be gun advanced book of R. 311. Buses were to overlap. While doing so out of men were killed by German shell around carving

WAR DIARY or INTELLIGENCE SUMMARY

Army Form C. 2118.

Place	Date	Hour	Summary of Events and Information	Remarks and references to Appendices
BEAUMETZ	25		Quiet day in trenches. Weather warm. There were had this Sunday service.	
	26		Morning. One D Coy ambush search party to look for body of man killed or missing who was unsuccessful. Another beautiful day. Men engaged in cleaning up from last night's strafe during day. At 9.30 p.m. C Coy opened up with heavy half-hourly to O.P. D Coy again sent out search party. Logan was in reliefs of O.P. and this morning reviewed the only one of a man at the York's Regt. B Coy spent most of the night acquiring distribution on attack all with rest of time at the lines. Relief was completed by 12.35 am.	
	27		2nd Lt EARLY returned from month's leave. Another beautiful day. Owing to being the centre with the rest front, also are with both coys. Alert to Old Trenches. Rel. at front line. Battalion moved into line at A@E to B to O moved in reserves. Reorders. D Coy learned this evening to have new Defence Plan completed. 27th & 28th inst. Firing party of 3 LT/NCO OP was found by A Coy to work under RE. The General Coy sling work with 1 office 8 men.	
	28		Glorious morning gas shout woken up at 1.0 & moving to entrenched end REL.	
NIGHT OF 28-29		Y day continuing enabling Lt. Duet of Brigade schools. @ back from Right Battalion relieved Mr R. BERRIS in Rt. Duet of Brigade schools. @ back from Right Company C Coy Centre company. B left company. A Coy Ensure Coy training 3 platoons & kept 2 in support. Support @ Coy. D Coy was very quick forms and by from enemy firing from front to front. Gas alarm again for 2.0 min. Battalion	
	29		HQ in a mined dugout. S.Q. Depot. Arthur was very hot too hot. Gas released at last every body made to get all gas masks on. Most ½ minute after alarm from Rachel Huns. Exceedingly serious gas Rel. and complete, another day. Gen sent orders his aunt returned Reg. Duce. Therefore a day complement completely admirable. S:B: Moving about in Battle trenches. A squad consisting 2nd Lt TETLEY 15 men left to assemble round or near. They secured hired something bad. No action took place again stormed early City, & N.C.C. A and made around 2 primes. 2nd Lt Wolf ESPORY to back arrayed during entering Pat. had experience of work where on Rear of Down &. Lt of Pigeons & not well evident. Wanted for 3 Brers were able to him away. Field Flares RD.etc. return to say my rifles. No answer was accomplished on party. Return. by Allies. the Cpt. Ind Bgy Chipring for hour. Auts anxious Cpt. Caking from the hole day, each with addition to support in stores. By sub. 2 pt. PROCTER goes to hospital	

A 5834 Wt. W4973/M687 750,000 8/16 D.D. & L. Ltd. Forms/C.2118/13

WAR DIARY
or
INTELLIGENCE SUMMARY.
(Erase heading not required.)

Army Form C. 2118.

Place	Date	Hour	Summary of Events and Information	Remarks and references to Appendices
	30		Fine weather. Quiet day. A patrol under 2nd Lt Murray holding 20 O.R. T.L.G. left camp at 7pm and took up observable position 78 & TP. Graph B.16.d.9.4 & opened rapid rifle & L.G. fire at the enemy but the enemy had retired before it could open fire. Enemy strength 42. Patrol returned to camp 4KSP 20C3. R.16 to break up early tomorrow for H Sqn 4KSP 30A3. T.16 to break up on arrival T.4th. R.16 T.R.S. T.18 to be sent 4KSP to R.16 T.P.S T.18 to now be relieved by R.1B & R.2B respectively & hereafter R.1B moving to R.16 T.R.S. based returned without noticing a atin amnition or ration escalier.	
	31.		A fair cool day. Orders rec'd: Hardly any enemy activity. Patrol consisting of 2nd Lt Murray 2½ OR T.L.G. left 4KSP R16.B35 7 10:53 and took up observation post at OR R.11.B.93 determined to mount gun into TP.D CC TP 5"45. No shots were fired in the area followed. Kamaship at 10. TP gun were posted on my twice. The L.G. then opened fire at 2004 rang at distance of a other officer were observed approaching on the first post. The L.G. again opened fire on enemy & two min after were dispersed. At about the same & after open the patrol & two swore in T.P.S. the position being very favoured & now decided to withdraw this was carried out by patrol creeping out Camel Nullah OR R.12 C0.1. Weyned 20.3 & seemed patrol consisting of 2nd Lt Mahon 11. 24 OR ra LG Cert R.12 a.l.r.s. 10 reconitre road through K.14.a. They proceeded without opposition until within 300% 7 some function at K.14.q.a.s where they were fired upon by an enemy post presumably at some function on the post continuing to advance & on retiring the enemy could now in the direction of these huts. The patrol returned at 8.45am w/out any casualties.	

Ref to above SHEET 34º NE Zone

Pickford
J. Mayor
1/c Oxford Bucks Light Inf.

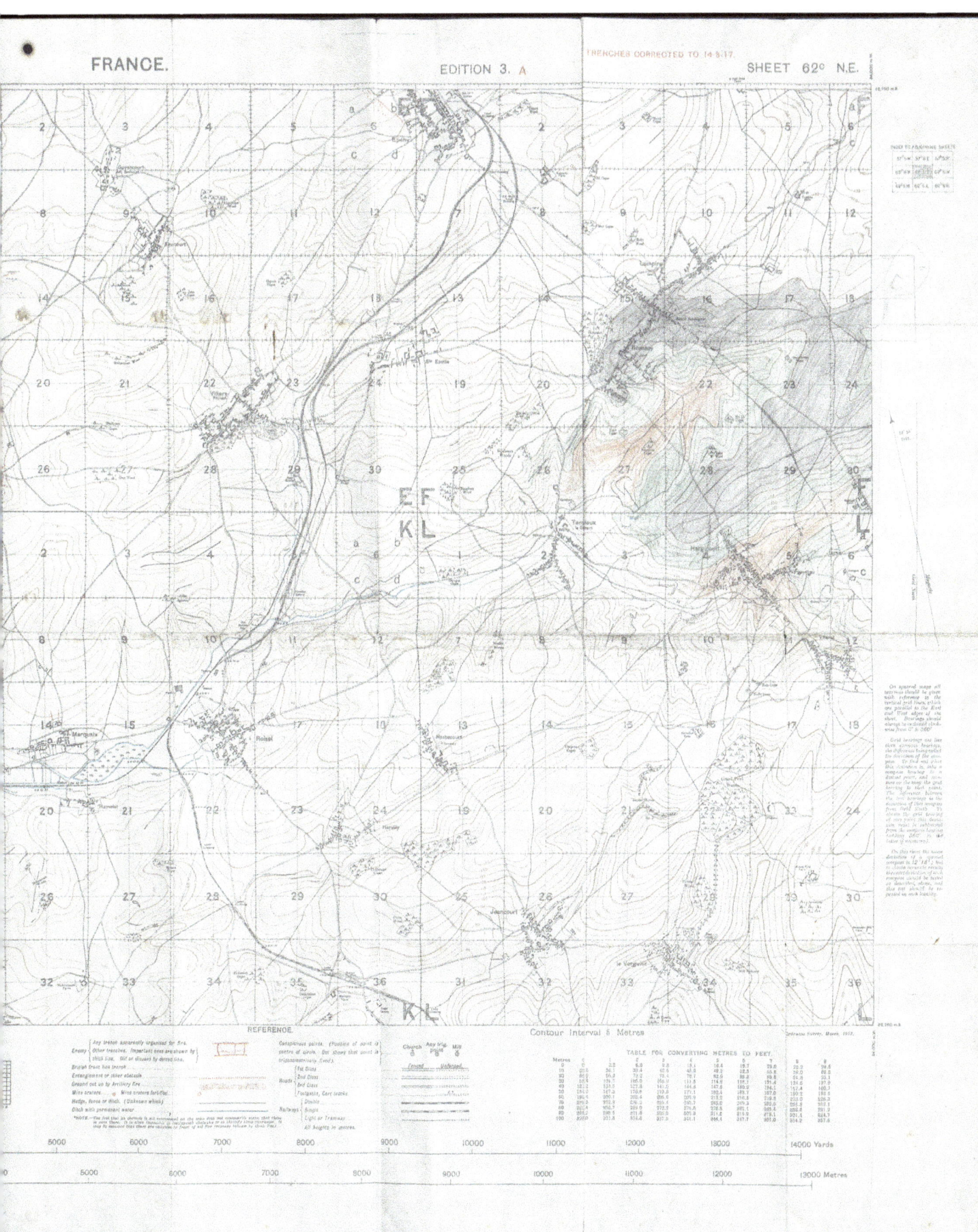

GLOSSARY.

Abbaye, Abbⁿ	Abbey
Abreuvoir, Abʳ	Watering-place
Abri de déosssion	Cyclone shelter
Aciérie	Steel works
Aiguilles	Points (Ry.)
Allée	Alley, Narrow road
Ancien, or, Ancⁿ	Old
Aqueduc	Aqueduct
Arbre	Tree
,, éventail	fan-shaped
,, décharné	bare
,, fourchu	forked
,, isolé	isolated
,, penché	leaning
Arbrisseau	Small tree
Arc	Arch
Ardoisière, Ardⁿ	Slate quarry
Arrêt	Halt
Asile	Asylum
,, des aliénés	Lunatic asylum
,, d....	
,, des pauvres	
de refuge	Asylum
Auberge, Aubⁿ	Inn
Aune	Alder-tree
Bac	Ferry
,, à traille	
Bains	Baths
Place aux bains	Bathing place
Ballon	Beacon, Bocoe
Banc de sable	Sand-bank
,, vase	Mud-bank
Baraque	Hut
Barrage	Dam
Barrière	Gate, Bills
(Machine à) Bascule	Weigh-bridge
Bassin	Dock, Pond
,, d'échouage	Tidal dock
Bassin de radoub	Dry dock
Bateau pharo	Light-ship
Blanchisserie	Laundry
B.M. (borne militaire)	Mile stone
Bⁿ (borne kilométrique)	
Boulangerie, Fabʳ de boulons	Bolt Factory
Bouée	Buoy
Brasserie, Brasⁿ	Brewery
Briqueterie, Briqⁿ	Brickfield
Brise lames	Breakwater
Bureau de poste	Post office
,, de douane	Custom house
Butte	Butt, Mound
Cabane	Hut
Cabaret, Cabⁿ	Inn
Câble sous-marin	Submarine cable
Calvaire, Calvⁿ	Calvary
Canal de dessèchement	Drainage canal
Creul d'irrigation	Irrigation canal
Fabʳ de caoutchouc	Rubber factory
Carrière, Carrⁿ	Quarry
,, de gravier	Gravel-pit
Caserne	Barracks
Champ de courses	Race course
,, manoeuvres	Drill-ground
,, tir	Rifle range
Chantier	Building yard
,, Ship yard
,, Dock yard
Chantier de construction	Slip way
Chapelle, Chⁿ	Chapel
Charbonnage	Colliery
Château d'eau	Water tower
Chaussée	Causeway
,, Highway
Chemin de fer	Railway
Cheminée, Chⁿ	Chimney
Chêne	Oak tree
Cimetière, Cimⁿ	Cemetery
Clocher	Belfry
Clouterie	Nail factory
Colombier	Dove-cot

Corⁿ	Workmen's dwellings
Cour des marchandises	Goods yard
Couvent	Convent
Crassier	Slag heap
Croix	Cross
Docks	Inner dock
Démoli - e	Destroyed
Détruit - e, Détⁿ	
Déversoir	Weir
Digue	Dyke, causeway
Distillerie, Distⁿ	Distillery
Douane	
Bureau de douane	Custom-house
Entrepôt de douane	Custom warehouse
Dynamitière, Dynamⁿ	Dynamite magazine
Dynamitisme	Dynamite factory
Écluse	Sluice, Lock
Éclusette, Eclⁿ	
École	School
Écurie	Stable
Église	Church
Émaillerie	Enamel works
Embarcadère, Embⁿ	Landing-place
Estaminet, Estamⁿ	Inn
Étang	Pond
Fabrique, Fabʳ	Factory
Fabʳ de produits chimiques	Chemical works
Fabʳ de faïence	Pottery
Faïencerie	
Ferme, Fⁿ	Farm
Filature, Filⁿ	Spinning mill
Fonderie, Fondⁿ	Foundry
Fontaine, Fontⁿ	Spring, fountain
Forêt	Forest
Forme de radoub	Dry dock
Forge	Smithy
Fosse	Mine Pit
Fossé	Moat, Ditch
Four	Kiln
,, à chaux	Lime-kiln

Four à coke	Coke oven
Ganterie	Glove factory
Gare	Station
Garenne	Warren
Garnison	Garrison
Gendarmerie	Gendarmes
Glacerie	Mirror factory
Fabʳ de glaces	
Glacière	Ice factory
Urne	Urne
Gué	Ford
Guérite	Sentry-box, Turret
,, à signaux	Signal-box (Ry.)
Halte	Halt
Hangar	Shed, Hangar
Hôpital	Hospital
Hôtel-de-Ville	Town hall
Houillère	Colliery
Huilerie	Oil factory
Imprimerie, Impⁿ	Printing works
Jetée	Pier
Laminerie	Rolling mills
Ligne de haute mer	High water mark
Laisse de basse marée	Low
Maison Forestière / Mⁿ Fⁿ	Forester's house
Malterie	Malt-house
Marbrerie	Marble works
Marais	Marsh
Marais salant	Saltern, Salt marsh
Marché	Market
Mare	Pool
Meule	Rick
Minière	Mine
Monastère	Monastery
Moulin, Mⁿ	Mill
,, à vapeur	Steam mill
Mur	Wall
,, crénelé	Loop-holed wall

Nacelle	Ferry
Orme	Elm
Orphelinat	Orphanage
Ossuaire	Ossuaire
Ouvrage	Port
Ouvrage hydraulique	Water works
Papeterie	Paper-mill
Parc	Park, yard
,, aéronautique	Aviation ground
,, à charbon	Coal yard
,, à pétrole	Petrol store
Passage à niveau P.N.	Level crossing
Passerelle, Pasⁿ	Foot-bridge
Pépinière	Nursery-garden
Peuplier	Poplar tree
Phare	Light-house
Pilier, Pⁿ	Post
Plaine d'exercice	Drill ground
Pompe	Pump
Ponceau	Culvert
Pont	Bridge
,, levis	Drawbridge
Poste de garde	Coast-guard
Station côte	station
Poteau Pⁿ	Post
Poterie	Pottery
Poudrière, Poudⁿ	Powder magazine
Magasin à poudre	
Prise d'eau	Water supply
Puits	Pit-head, Shaft, Well
,, artesien	Artesian well
,, d'avoyage ventilation	Ventilating shaft
,, de sondage	Boring
Quai	Quay, Platform
,, aux bestiaux	Cattle platform
,, aux marchandises	Goods platform
Raccordement	Junction
Raffinerie	Refinery
,, de sucre	Sugar refinery
Râperie	Beet-root factory

Army Form C. 2118.

WAR DIARY
or
INTELLIGENCE SUMMARY.
(Erase heading not required.)

CONFIDENTIAL

WAR DIARY
of the
1/4 Bⁿ OXFORDSHIRE & BUCKINGHAMSHIRE LIGHT INFTY
(145 Inf Bde — 48ᵀᴴ DIV)
for
JUNE 1917

XXVI

WAR DIARY or INTELLIGENCE SUMMARY

Army Form C. 2118.

(Erase heading not required.)

Place	Date	Hour	Summary of Events and Information	Remarks and references to Appendices
OUTPOST LINE EAST OF DERNANCOURT	1		A fine cool day. Enemy very quiet. Observed an object emerging from 1.0 improved m.g. at 11.0 pm. 2nd Lt MACKAY + 2 om. went out in camouflage suits at 6.0 pm to obtain an identification from the dead Bosche killed by his patrol the night previous, but a party of the enemy forestalled him. Made rumours the hostile were he rescued from was carried out on his defences to flak post. Was dug 400 ms head of P.16	
	2		Weather continues to be fine. 2nd Lt M°KAY guns to hospital. Gas was discharged successfully at 12.30+1.30 am. Patrols sent out to R.16 in. By 8 m. & 8 R m KAY met at M-29-d-3-1 KAY wounded. Patrol wounded by by 2nd Lt BATTS at M-29-d-3-1 Patrol mounted by 2nd Lt BATTES at M-29-d-3-1 B OR R B CAP R B Petrol claimed ? early observed 33 or more of the enemy. Patrol reach to investigate the dead turned safely.	
	3	NIGHT OF 3+4	Peaceful summery day. Enemy very quiet. Battalion relieved by 1st R'S BERKS musketeers - who formed at VELU WOOD Rel. at 3.15 am. 4th BUFFS B.H.Q. + mop. bks. Enemy observed in small numbers at various points. Surrendering. Went arms for B Coy - Mr Hurst, Mr JONES, Mr AUBYN & Lt ENDOR returned from BEC	
CAMP IN VELU WOOD	4		Another fine summery day. Men packed up for ... Rec Lt ENDOR attached to Pop Bn Left camp but BOYCE sent to hospital... by sickness. 35 ORs + 4 CORs moved to R.H. Kildare at 0.6.5.9.9 m... at 8.0 am of A.B. were inspected The following day at 2.0 pm. marched the Lor, gave the ...	
	5		At 3.30 pm on 4th inst. Oneth gave march: Men have acquired badly Feeling by night...	
CAMP AT O.6.6.9.9	6		A fine day. 2nd LT GARLICK 15 OR D. Coy. & R left ... on early... An early parade drill + smoke helmet... at 8.30am day of right strictly. Lt Col R STEPHENS arrived & assumed command of Bn. Parade from 9.13 noon drill+ Lewis Gun training for coys.	

WAR DIARY or INTELLIGENCE SUMMARY

Army Form C. 2118.

Place	Date	Hour	Summary of Events and Information	Remarks and references to Appendices
CAMP P4	7		[illegible handwritten entry]	
06.6.9.9	8		Rather dull morning. [illegible]	
	9	Night 9/10 9.10	Raining all day. [illegible] Bn relieved 2nd Lt Wilson B.COMP — BORDER to hospital 13 Battalion relieved the 1st R. BERKS in the C.H. Sector. Relief completed by 2.30 a.m. B Coy, A Coy & D Coy in outpost line & C Coy in reserve. GREENWELL acts as battery for battalion. Relief completed by 9.15 p.m.	
OUTPOST LINE EAST OF DERNICOURT	10		[illegible handwritten entry about patrols and operations]	
	11		Still fine. A small operation was arranged for the day. A patrol consisting of 2nd Lt TOWNSEND & 20 O.R. T.S. left Greenwich the expected post of K.1.d.7.k.2.c. & was found to be held but not in strength. The patrol returned without casualties. A 2nd patrol consisting of 2 with Powell & Oth 7.5. left K.1.d.o.s. to reconnoitre ground in K.T.G. An enemy party of 3 were seen but no further signs of Boche occupation. Patrol returned without casualties.	
	12		2nd Lt TOWNSEND & party were out during the day. Patrol located enemy MG posts at K.T.A. & K.1.B.W. & was again approaching but the wire belts & K.T.A. when 2nd Lt WHITE and 2 NCOs & 7 OR. were met with heavy fire. 2nd Lt WHITE was wounded & the party had to withdraw covered by rifle fire. Raid resulted in 1 OR. killed & 6 others wounded including 2nd Lt WHITE. Enemy losses were heard but by our observation patrols. Patrol led by 2nd Lt COCHRANE found two M.G.s & had arranged to take these on the night of 12-13 but book was not ready.	
	13		Another fine day. A patrol consisting of 2nd Lt MATTHEWS & 7 O.R. [illegible] went out at 2 a.m. & 20 O.R. T.S. under 2nd Lt WINDLAE B was entrusted as to act as a covering party to the front of the village. The M.G. at K.1.d.6.x1. was not found by our patrol. The enemy swept the ground with M.G. fire causing a number of casualties our party returning safely at 4 a.m. [illegible]	

Army Form C. 2118.

WAR DIARY
or
INTELLIGENCE SUMMARY.
(Erase heading not required.)

Instructions regarding War Diaries and Intelligence Summaries are contained in F. S. Regs., Part II. and the Staff Manual respectively. Title pages will be prepared in manuscript.

Place	Date	Hour	Summary of Events and Information	Remarks and references to Appendices
OUTPOST LINE EAST OF DEMICOURT	14		Comparatively quiet. An attempt to take place on the night of 14-15 with the object of inflicting 2 losses and to get in an N.R. at T/26 to 7 [?]. Inhabitants, Debris etc. 3 companies contributed to the party. Company of "A" Boys who went up to [illegible] by [illegible] party 2 platoons of "C" Boys ["B"?] block and took the 1st [illegible] Flank [illegible]. 1 platoon of "A" Boys in reserve [illegible]. 1 section of "A" Boys in reserve at 20 [illegible]. 1/30 AM up [illegible] After a little [illegible] they had [illegible] all [illegible] they retired. No prisoners were taken. Our [illegible] were [illegible] to the enemy's Front line and we [illegible] in the [illegible] of [illegible].	
	15	Night of 15-16	Nothing doing. Enemy very quiet. Night [illegible] and [illegible] at 30 Jan. By Lt. R. BERKS. Thanks of CO. Surprise battalion at Ribecourt. "B" "D" & "C" [illegible] at DOIGNIES & BEAUMETZ. Two [?] by rail. Complete 3-15 and 10 and.	
T.20.C.84.	16		Line healthy, still conforming [?]. Re-organization. All ranks 1stBn too this barrier was 2/Lt B/K don't [illegible]. [illegible] being done behind the [illegible]. New working [illegible] Lt SCOTT [illegible] home England, [illegible] country efficient. Still very hot, bed [illegible] inclement [illegible] 2/Lt BUTTON leaving home [illegible].	
	17		Still very hot. Col [illegible] interview [illegible] Hospital.	
	18		[illegible] Company [illegible] in tonight. B/D Coys going into four support Coys night. C Coy W.H. [illegible] to Bn HQ	
	19		Baths at VELU for "C" Coy [illegible] for the first time for 2 weeks. The weather has been [illegible] [illegible]	

WAR DIARY
or
INTELLIGENCE SUMMARY.

Army Form C. 2118.

(Erase heading not required.)

Place	Date	Hour	Summary of Events and Information	Remarks and references to Appendices
T.20.c.8.4.	20		Enemy artillery more active today. N.W. of Bn. HQ. shelled heavily 2nd Lt. R.33.2. from Rainbow England	
	21	Night of 21/22 9.22	Mostly Grey Heavy thunderstorm about 3.0 p.m. Relief 1/5 BERKS in left Sub. Section. 2nd Lt. Rickards & Coy left Coy & Coy support any Bery. Relief complete 1-30am 22 inst.	
OUTPOST LINE	22		Nothing of importance during the day. Rt. night a relief connecting of 2nd Lt. MEADES & 15 O.R. to reconnoitre pits in T2.92. & T2.96.t. They also in their objective without opposition but found no signs of enemy. Patrol returned safely. A 2nd Patrol Lt. R13 to reconnoitre No.4 & No.5 mining shafts T9.a.7.6. no lines of enemy Oss anywhere Patrol returned early	
No. OF DEMICOURT	23		Little enemy activity. A Patrol consisting of 2nd Lt BURTON 36 O.R. 079 left R.13 to reconnoitre enemy through T9.a.7.K.14 & No signs of enemy. Enemy exposition was found at Point 188 Patrol returned Safely. 2nd Lt TETLEY 36 O.R. T9. L/c R.13. Lt. R.13 to reconnoitre Position in No pits at - R.2.89.s. found a much patrol East. Patrol engaged rifle also without opposition no enemy seen by 2nd patrol. Patrol returned safely.	
	24		Our Patrons were active today. 2nd Lt. JONES 2nd Lt. TOWNSEND 2nd Lt WHITE & E. BARRIS & R.9. Signallers & Runners Reported Against emanating of 2nd OR ENC 27, R.79 left R.13 to reconnoitre DEMICOURT — RAINCOURT ROADS. Their object was to obtain any information we could of the Patrol returned Safely. Another patrol consisting of 2nd Lt. MICH, M.C. & 11 L/s L 22 & sentry rifle pits in T.2.e.b.5 ammunition dump Which was pushed out how Can Point in a Northerly direction. Infra, no enemy were encountered. The patrol returned safely. 10 prisoners in another one at N.Y. E. Bombarded Such. A Patrol left Ky Outpost consisting of 2nd Lt TETLEY	
	25		2 W.O.R.T.5 & men but T.2.c.6.5. No Diary of enemy were seen except retiring ground in T.2.O.6.5. No Diary of enemy returned Safely.	

WAR DIARY
or
INTELLIGENCE SUMMARY.

(Erase heading not required.)

Army Form C. 2118.

Place	Date	Hour	Summary of Events and Information	Remarks and references to Appendices
OUTPOST LINE NE OF DEMICOURT	27		A 2nd Patrol consisting of 2nd Lt CREW & Cpl R19 Cpl R13 & 2 reconnoitre toward K14.a. No additional information to that already known was obtained. The patrol returned safely. Another patrol (2nd Lt MILLS & 2nd Lt BONNEY & 3 men) went out with R.G.A. 2 to reconnoitre road near K14b. No enemy activity was encountered. The patrol returned safely. A patrol consisting of 2nd Lt BRIBBE & Cpl R.L.S. & Cpl R.K.Y. went to reconnoitre ground NW & W. Sign of several enemy occupations found.	
	27		Night of 27/28 Battalion relieved by 1/4th R BERKS proceeded to Camps no 0t 6 which complete by about 1.10 am 28.	
	28		Bn resting. Fine day.	
Camp OG	29		Bn bathed at VELU. Armourer Sgt inspected rifles. A + D Coy + H.Q details fired on 30 yds range VELU WOOD.	
"	30		B + C Coys fired on range during morning. Very wet during morning & afternoon. Bn relieved 1/4 ROYAL BERKS front coy, supt coy moving off at 9.45 PM. Dispositions: D Coy Right Front Coy, B Coy Left Front Coy, C Coy Reserve Coy with Bn HQ, A Coy Reserve Coy, DOIGNES. The night was very dark & the confusion was during	

Army Form C. 2118.

WAR DIARY
or
INTELLIGENCE SUMMARY.
(Erase heading not required.)

Place	Date	Hour	Summary of Events and Information	Remarks and references to Appendices
			the day had made the tracks very heavy. Relief went well & was complete by 1.5 A.M.	
			R Stephens Lt. Col. Commanding 1/4 Ox & Bucks L Inft	

Copy No. 9

SECRET. 1/4th. Batt. Oxf. & Bucks. Lt. Infty.

Operation Order No. 101. 12.6.17.

Reference:- HERMIES Sht. Ed 1.A. 1/10000

INFORMATION.

1. The enemy is reported to be holding a line of rifle pits running from K.2.a.5.4. to K.2.a.3.9., K.2.c.2.9. to K.1.d.7.6. A second enemy line is reported running from K.2.c.8.0. to K.2.c.6.3.

DECISION

2. These posts will be raided tomorrow night
   (a) to find out if enemy is digging assembly trenches for an attack.
   (b) to obtain identification.

INSTRUCTIONS.

3. On night 13/14th a raid will be carried out by A and C Coys under the command of Capt. M. EDWARDS.
   First objective:- Line of Rifle Pits from K.2.a.5.4. to K.1.d.7.6. will be captured by C Coy.
   Second Objective:- Line of Rifle Pits extending from K.2.c.8.0. to K.2.c.6.3. will be captured by 2 Platoons of A Company.
   The remaining two Platoons of A Coy will be in Support and will take up position about K.7.b.8.5.
4. One Company 1/BUCKS Batt. will be in Brigade Reserve in Sunken Road K.7.c. at ZERO minus one hour.
5. Artillery Barrage will be as under:-
   ZERO to ZERO plus 5   - First Objective.
   ZERO plus 5 to ZERO plus 15 - Second Objective.
   ZERO plus 15 to ZERO plus 20 - Box Barrage on 2nd Objective.
   ZERO plus 20 to ZERO plus 25 - Second Objective.
   ZERO plus 25   - Barrage will die away.
6. Signal Station will be established at Listening Post K.7.d.2.7. and telephonic communication arranged (through) Support Coy. at K.7.b.8.5.
7. Advanced Battalion Head Quarters and Advanced Aid Post will be in SUNKEN ROAD K.7.c.2.5.
8. Dress - Belt, pouches, braces and sidearms, shrapnel helmets without visors, P.H. Helmets and Small Box Respirator.
9. The Countersign will be COWLEY.
10. ZERO hour will be notified later.

REPORTS.

11. Reports to Advanced Battalion Head Quarters.

12. ACKNOWLEDGE.

Issued at 5.15 pm.   Copies 1 - 2   H.Q. 145 Bde.
                            3   O.C. A Coy.
                            4   O.C. B Coy.
                            5   O.C. C Coy.
                            6   O.C. D Coy.
                            7   Intelligence Officer.
                          8 - 10   Retained.

W. Enoch Lt. & Adjt
1/4 Oxf. & Bucks L.In.

WK 28

P. 25

CONFIDENTIAL

WAR DIARY

of

1/4th Bn. OXFORDSHIRE & BUCKINGHAMSHIRE LIGHT INFTY

VOLUME XXVII

From 1st July 1917 to 31st July 1917

2nd August 1917

WAR DIARY or INTELLIGENCE SUMMARY.

Army Form C. 2118.

Place	Date	Hour	Summary of Events and Information	Remarks and references to Appendices
OUTPOST LINE N.E. of DEMICOURT	1		Nothing of importance occurred during day. Enemy aeroplanes of the 13 KINGS LIVERPOOL inspected tent lines preparing to trekking over.	
	2		Bn preparing for relief by 13 KINGS LIVERPOOL. 48 Bn. HQ received by 3rd Div Relief officer fellows. Bn was put on march to PREMICOURT tock Company arriving at 4.30 ay 3rd. HQ re reentering into received for 5th ARMY. 1 Officer & say T.N.C.O. per body both left & retired to the line of the rear received day in camps Rifle got ay tiff muscles needing.	
	3		Bn moving to BIHUCOURT at 4.30 bn order of march A.B.T&C.D. men march very muddy (due to long period in line) so men fell out short march. Only 6 miles Arriv at BIHUCOURT 4.15 pm Officers & rank & men in tents. Transport returns to nearest Ordnance Officer T.N60 left behind to form Companies as 2 horse light turnouts men whe serve in line kicked to have their Transport in the evening by T.N4 & by T6s	
BIHUCOURT	4		C.O. rrH.Q. proceed by Car to a Divisional Conference at HUNNICOURT. Bn move to BAILLEULMONT at 6.30 pm away of march B. & D. Nator Perious in command. Distance 13 miles. New march obediently my one casualty. Everybody pleased to the Saint Bair of Baillelcon again. Great enthusiasm aroused by the sight of an extensive Bn arrive at 10.15 pm All ranks Comfortably housed.	
BAILLEULMONT	6		Occupied of recruiting ammunition. On above 2 horses by Carts. Rest of time spent in engaging number Nator Pickers given to 6 hours during day.	Spotting cut & sent in command.
	7		Training carried on as in S.S143 with observed attacks arranged by Bns.	

Capt HALL M. BURNS Lieut 20th Command

Army Form C. 2118.

WAR DIARY
or
INTELLIGENCE SUMMARY.
(Erase heading not required.)

Instructions regarding War Diaries and Intelligence Summaries are contained in F.S. Regs., Part II. and the Staff Manual respectively. Title pages will be prepared in manuscript.

Place	Date	Hour	Summary of Events and Information	Remarks and references to Appendices
BAILEULMONT	8		This being Sunday day's work had been received but Divicion Pile Employers temporary Commence an endeavour to make people more employers Service were held at BOURECOURT by Cpl E.T. NONCONFORMISTS in Reveillon Hut. BAILEULMONT MORNING & EVENING Capt HALL gave to VIII Corps behind our 4th stage service.	
	9		Batt Orders. Bn paraded at 4.45 am & marched to BISHVILLIERS to BOIS kept tracking. Start operations at 5.0 am. Detrain finished about 4.0 pm got back at 4.15 pm	
	10		Morn training. The VARIETIES gave a concert in Recreation hut at 6 pm.	
	11		The usual training was carried out. Reviews show were arranged for the evening.	
	12		Company training. 2nd Lt GIBSON & 2nd Lt RUATRIDGE 2nd Lt SIMPSON reported from England. 2nd Brigade devised to all officers of the Brigade a Lecture on the probable duration of the Wireless & Rocket practice was also carried out. In the evening another Cinema film was given.	
	13		Bn training. The weather during our stay here has been excellent. Capt HALL return from some type treat to H/Burs Platoon training. Bn staff had ride to HANNES CAMP to BIS Conference.	
	14		MAJOR LLOYD BAKER arrives to take over From command of	
	15		Most perfect than Earl. Sunday arrives at BOURECOURT & no Revercton hut. Lt MACKENZIE 2nd Lt WHITE go to BIS H.Q. to view plans & sketch form the forthcoming operation	

Army Form C. 2118.

WAR DIARY
or
INTELLIGENCE SUMMARY.
(Erase heading not required.)

Instructions regarding War Diaries and Intelligence Summaries are contained in F. S. Regs., Part II. and the Staff Manual respectively. Title pages will be prepared in manuscript.

Place	Date	Hour	Summary of Events and Information	Remarks and references to Appendices
BAILLEUMONT	16		Companies on the usual training. C.O.'s conference at Bde HQ. Weather not quite so good today.	
	17		Bn. Orders Bn parade 4.45 am. orders to HANNESCAMP have been received. Preliminary operation orders received yesterday. Regt HQ to know which of the Companies is ready about 8.30 pm. New RSM & 2 musketry course men arriving at 10.15 pm. The news appears to be somewhat improved conditions. Lines after dark 1 town & any event.	
	18		Coys were on Charing an return trip 10 am - 2 pm. The worst of trainings 2nd LT BENSON 1/1 BUCKS Bn. home from ENGLAND today with 2 men on two days leave. Steady rain most of day. Orders being awaited.	
	19		By evening orders to move arrived, not issued at once as no ?	
	20		Platoon in the YPRES Salient. Platoon travelled from 9.0 am to 12.30 noon.	
	21	NIGHT 21st-22nd	Bn arrived at 12.30 pm. Leaves time for MEO in the afternoon. Order to proceed from no Companies leaving Bn moved off at 12.30 am in order for MONDICOURT (entraining station) they arrived directly before	
	22		4.30 am train up in a full three trucks. Everything worked very smoothly this men all entrained by about 4.15. The train leaving at 4.35 am just 2 minutes behind schedule times. The journey was uneventful and comparatively speedy we were held up for about 2½ hours in turn HAZEBROUCK which the congestion of traffic otherwise the day demanded. We detained at GODEWAERSVELDE - Debussed 3.0 am & marched to HOUTKERQUE at 6.0 pm the morning but at very dusty but in two long arc arrived at 9.0 pm then we took	

WAR DIARY or INTELLIGENCE SUMMARY.

Army Form C. 2118.

Place	Date	Hour	Summary of Events and Information	Remarks and references to Appendices
HOUTKERQUE	22		Most of the officers on bicycle reconnaissance for new rest quarters and at BAILLEULMONT	
	23		In training. Continues as disposed of before. Inspection of the Company equipment about to very battn. The village has no flying covers huts. There is no cover – every available house adequately filled as it is used.	
	24		Training for Companies as disposed. Weather chops that keeps the training continues. Brigade inspected during week marked by higher Generals. MAJOR GENERAL MAASE commanding XIV Corps & Coy having a meeting as before. In the evening we stopped the	
	25		6th Oct Brock billets went to WATOU at rathel – Cpt. Dry Ban Tanning. Brigadier called there. Many him would ex- dict inspected road 6 p.m. Saw no men neither of us stopped.	
	26		Great efforts were made to again	
	27		Still training. Train critic, taken entraining through no work only take go by the train. The Coney went the a BR W ogee included again by Brigadier, then time great satisfaction. Roots marching in divisional No 3 Platoon inspected by the Brigadier in fighting order. Turned out very satisfactorily.	
	28		2nd Lt MCKAY rejoin from Hospital	
	29		Sunday. Attack of bigger spring a nest for the known known of battle. Attack to victory. Hands and all arrived out- clearly	

Army Form C. 2118.

WAR DIARY
or
INTELLIGENCE SUMMARY.
(Erase heading not required.)

Place	Date	Hour	Summary of Events and Information	Remarks and references to Appendices
HOUTKERQUE	30		Bn. preparing for move to camp tonight. Moved to camp in the L.3. Central 3 miles W. of ST JAN TER BIEZEN. Arriving at 1.30 am. 31/8. Fine	
Camp 3 miles W. of ST JAN TER BIEZEN	31		Church march D.A.B. & Coys arriving at 1.30 am 31/8. Fine. accommodation for men good. Officers fair. situation of bivouac very bad, no drainage system. Laboured all day in improving Lighting having for companies. The R.S.M. states that morning fatigue men ate inspection taken. Showery day. Continuous rain. Steady rain during night.	
			Maps Ref. FRANCE Sheet 27B Kem. sh. 16 1/40000 Sh. 28 1/40000	
			BELGIUM Sh. 27	
			FRANCE sh. 27 1/20000 from 6th Aug. sh. 27B 2.a.2 from 30th Aug.	

R. Stephen
Lt. Col.
Commanding
1st Bn Norfolk Regiment

Army Form C. 2118.

WAR DIARY
or
INTELLIGENCE SUMMARY.
(Erase heading not required.)

CONFIDENTIAL

WAR DIARY

OF THE

1/4 Bn OXFORDSHIRE & BUCKINGHAMSHIRE Lt. INFTY

(145 INF. BDE — 48 DIV)

AUGUST 1917

XXVII

Army Form C. 2118.

WAR DIARY
or
INTELLIGENCE SUMMARY.
(Erase heading not required.)

Instructions regarding War Diaries and Intelligence Summaries are contained in F. S. Regs., Part II. and the Staff Manual respectively. Title pages will be prepared in manuscript.

Place	Date	Hour	Summary of Events and Information	Remarks and references to Appendices
CAMP Y ST. JAN TER BIEZEN	Aug 1		A dull wet day. Companies at disposal of company commanders. Gas drill anti-gas Lewis gun drill and lectures. O.C. Companies but miniature range on camp and one camp front only field firing removed.	
	2		Weather continued wet. Indoor training as yesterday. Details of organization for action considered. Covering party of 360 O.R. to being in wounded from the battlefield sent up at 6 am under Lt T.C.R Gamlen to drawing station on canal bank at 625.d. None of the battle indicated the operations delayed by rain.	REF. BELGIUM 2ʳᵈ W.W. 1/40 6 A
	3	9.30AM	Further training under company commanders. Weather slightly improved. Senior officers and company commanders attended a lecture in Poperinghe by Lt.Gen. Ivor Maxse, Comdg. Comm. and others, took up 41ᵗʰ Div. Orders for a move forward by brigade.	
	4	11.30AM	Brigade moved to Dambre Camp B27d N3. the Bn. was dressed at 11.30 a.m. Orders of march A.H.C. with A.B.C.D. Ruts to Poperinghe Poperinghe - Ypres Rd. Plank rd. H.F.63515 - 73615 W. of Vlamertinghe and along Elverdinghe Rd. Arrived 3.30 P.M.	
DAMBRE CAMP			Found extremely pitiful and camp unimproved. Party always. A sunny day with occasional showers.	

WAR DIARY or INTELLIGENCE SUMMARY

Army Form C. 2118.

Place	Date	Hour	Summary of Events and Information	Remarks and references to Appendices
D'AMBRE CAMP	5		Early part of day quiet. B. gave orders to move not	BELGIUM 2.T.N.19. Edn. 6.A.
		7.30 P.M.	of of 39th Div. Battalion moved off at 7.30 P.M. Order H.Q, A & C.D, 3 platoons at 5 minute interval. Route — VLAMERTINGHE	
STEENBEEK — KITCHENER'S WOOD			to I.16.1.4. SALVATION CORNER, road to support Bridge 2A, trench board track to KITCHENER'S WOOD. Took over front line along STEENBEEK C.11.8. 7.2 & C.11.8.1.0 from 5th Bn. ROYAL HIGHLANDERS. 6th Bn. CAMBRIDGESHIRE REGT. and 4th Bn. ROYAL HIGHLANDERS. [Ref. PILCKEM 1/10.000 Edn.] Several casualties sustained going in. Killed 2/Lt. R.H. WHITE, M.C., + Regtl. Sgt-Major R. LANE. The latter had been with battalion since 1914. Gassed, wounded Lt. W.H. ENOCH, adjutant.	PILCKEM 1/10.000 Edn. N.
	6	1. A.M.	Relief reports complete at 1 a.m. Dispositions A & B in front companies respectively. C & D in support. Forming Keloing, platoon at ADM'S FARM & in CANOE TRENCH, latter numerously detailed in THE BUND area, one coy. situation was ALBERTA FARM & CANOPUS TRENCHES. B & Q in CANOE TRENCH at C.10.d.6.5. 1/4th ROYAL BERKS in reserve in CANADIAN CALF & CAPTAIN TRENCHES. Battalion and shells continuous during day. Coy. many casualties. 2/Lt. J.E. BOYLE among adjutants duties.	
		11 am		
	7	3-5 P.M.	Front support platoons at ADAM'S FARM heavily shelled, also H.Q. Front line severely bombarded from 9-10 P.M. Coy. commanders conferred.	
		9 P.M.	Our artillery retaliated effectively. Relieved by 1/4th ROYAL BERKS. Battalion going into reserve in their position. Day casualties 8 N.C.O.'s & men; killed 2/Lt. H.E. GIBSON, wounded. Lt. Col. ROBERT STEPHENS, commanding officer. 7/2/17.	
			J.A.S. McLEAN.	

Army Form C. 2118.

WAR DIARY
or
INTELLIGENCE SUMMARY.
(Erase heading not required.)

Instructions regarding War Diaries and Intelligence Summaries are contained in F. S. Regs., Part II. and the Staff Manual respectively. Title pages will be prepared in manuscript.

Place	Date Aug	Hour	Summary of Events and Information	Remarks and references to Appendices
O.G.1	8	4:30 AM	Relief carried out by [illegible] Brigade. Foggy morning, bright and sunny later until 6 P.M. Intervals [illegible] shells [illegible] with H.E. [illegible] shells during day & D Company suffered casualties. Relieved early evening by 1/6 R. GLOUCEST-	
DAMBRE CAMP		7 P.M.	-ERSHIRE REGT. Returned to DAMBRE CAMP in [illegible]. 1/4 R. GLOUCEST [illegible] for sim. Casualties for 3 days: Killed, 2 LT. R.A. WHITE. M.C. 2 LT. H.E. GIBSON. O.R. 17, wounded LT-COL. R. STEPHENS, LT. W.H. ENOCH, 2 LT. T.A.S. MACLEAY. O.R. 57. Missing O.R. 4.	
	9		LT-COL. A.T.M. BARTLETT returned & commanded the Battalion. Intn. received for attack by 1/145 INF. BDE on Menin front. Aggressive day.	
	10		Light training by Coys. Conference of Commanding officers. [illegible] Menin attack cancelled by reason of [illegible] of our M.G.O.A. A the history of [illegible] [illegible] A Soc. Bright warm day.	BELGIAN 27 N.W. E.3.0. 6.4.
	11		Light company training continued. Officers recce of [illegible] to [illegible] received from [illegible]. Detachment found funeral [illegible]. [illegible] [illegible]. Commander C of 273 M.G. Bn. from [illegible]. DAMBRE CAMP inspected. Battalion practice at [illegible] MEN.	
	12		Sunday, an ordinary day of Rest. Parad Church service with 1/4 R. ROYAL BERKSHIRE REGT. C.R.A. explains artillery arrangements for attack at D3 on N.47 officers of brigade, Army corps & divisional staff to be present.	
	13	Fair	[illegible] through KITCHENERS WOOD to REGINA CROSS and [illegible] [illegible] Battalion paraded at 7 P.M. for attack against bridge. Proceed on [illegible] [illegible] [illegible] hours, [illegible] [illegible] [illegible] canal. Chinese attack for [illegible] [illegible] [illegible] [illegible] [illegible] [illegible]	POST-LEFLABLE 11.0. 0.0 E 34. 1.

A.5834 Wt. W4973/M1687 750,000 8/16 D. D. & L. Ltd. Forms/C.2118/13

Army Form C. 2118.

WAR DIARY
or
INTELLIGENCE SUMMARY.
(Erase heading not required.)

Instructions regarding War Diaries and Intelligence Summaries are contained in F. S. Regs., Part II. and the Staff Manual respectively. Title pages will be prepared in manuscript.

Place	Date Aug	Hour	Summary of Events and Information	Remarks and references to Appendices
DAMBRE CAMP	13		A few H.V. shells fell near the camp in evening and night.	
	14		Relieved by brigade of attack practice. More details included. Weather warm and sultry with rain at Conclusion. Time 9 P.M. to 12.30 P.M. Brigade conference for company commanders at 2.30 P.M. More details follow. war in afternoon. One four observation balloons east of camp brought down in flames by an E.A. Final operation preparations. Rain again overnight.	BELGIUM 28 N.W. 1, 20, 10.0 Edn. 6.A.
	15		Move to REIGERSBURG CAMP — H 6a — at 10.30 A.M. Order of march: C.D.H.Q., A, B Companies. Rested until 10.15 P.M. Air patrol in afternoon above one. One of our aeroplanes falling in the canal. At 10.15 P.M. moved off, in some cases, by	
ALBERTA FARM		10.15 P.M.	trench board tracks to CANAL d'YSER, crossing at BRIDGE 3. Companies proceeded by similar tracks [INFANTRY ROUTE 4, N 10.0.10, Edn.1] where two sight companies turned to right along road thirty trench board track to ALBERTA FARM. Left Companies continued N.E. on a country running through KITCHENERS Wood. Battalion Headquarters went to ALBERTA FARM.	
STEENBEEK	16	4 A.M.	At 4 am all companies reported in position on assembly and dissection tapes laid W. of STEENBEEK, in accordance with brigade orders. Dispositions: C company on right and D on left forming two leading waves, behind them A and B companies respectively forming third and fourth waves. Each were in two lines. On right flank 1/5 BUCKS R: on left, 11TH BN MANCHESTER REGT of INF. BDE 34. Four objectives assigned, first, strong points W. of ST JULIEN — LANGEMARCK road; second, LANGEMARCK — WINNIPEG road	

(A7093) Wt. W12839/M1293. 75,000. 1/17. D. D. & L., Ltd. Forms/C2118/14.

WAR DIARY
or
INTELLIGENCE SUMMARY.
(Erase heading not required.)

Army Form C. 2118.

Place	Date	Hour	Summary of Events and Information	Remarks and references to Appendices
	16 Oct 19		between C.6.b.5.1 and C.6.c.4.9; third LANGEMARCK barrack system between C.6.a.9.4. and C.6.b.9.7; fourth outtrust line from latter point to HÜBNER FARM. Two tanks to cooperate in attacking strong point, & with barrage & in rear of infantry in action.	POELCAPELLE 1/10.00 S.M.
		4.45 A.M.	The attack started promptly at 4.45 A.M. over new advance being rather unsteady in barrage. Little opposition beyond slight rifle fire on our right, until firm wave had advanced 200 yards E of STEENBEEK when it came under effective machine gun fire from MON DU HIBOU and right front. Reinforced by rear waves, advance continued until storm about 100 yards Sow of a line through MON DU HIBOU and TRIANGLE FARM badly mauled by heavy machine gun and rifle fire, proceeded by a strong counter attack the advance continued then for which our losses & random over the 12. Most of the twelve Company officers became casualties in attempting to get forward. We settled down to hold the ground gained on a line C.5.d.9.1. to C.12.a.4.9. Attack on right and immediate left front all up, both that of proposed advance half. The Company on right settled attacking us also against A.11.5.R.T. & STEENBEEK. It was decided with particular caution to gain objectives during night and dawn.	
MON DU HIBOU		7.30 P.M.	Peak arrived with some shot, ammo, his command easily but relieved of advance by LT. R.E. parties at standstill. at 7.30 P.M. a component of 1/4 Bn WORCESTERSHIRE REGT. in reserve attacked MON DU HIBOU & failed to capture it.	

Army Form C. 2118.

WAR DIARY
or
INTELLIGENCE SUMMARY.
(Erase heading not required.)

Instructions regarding War Diaries and Intelligence Summaries are contained in F. S. Regs., Part II. and the Staff Manual respectively. Title pages will be prepared in manuscript.

Place	Date Aug	Hour	Summary of Events and Information	Remarks and references to Appendices
MON DU HIBOU	17	2.30 A.M.	Another company of <?> battalion started at 2.30 A.M. joined a company for <?> was handed out shutting in close in front. We arrived on 6th holding a line of shell holes front line on boring enemy. Shelling was lt. E. of STEENBEEK between the stream W. of it and on ALBERTA FARM and track to St. John, one relief by 1/4th WORCESTERS. Relieving battalion in position shortly after midnight. Many of our later getting out. Proceeded to REIGERSBURG CAMP. Moved on to REIGERSBURG CAMP, arriving to DAMBRE CAMP. Nominal casualties stated. They were, Killed, 5 officers — 2 LT. A.S. WOTHERSPOON, 2 LT. H.H. JEFFERSON, 2 LT. F.E. JONES M.C., 2 LT. C.H. BOWMAN, 2 LT. A.F. SALMON — O.R. 60; Missing O.R. 4; Wounded officers — 5, 2 LT. A.E. CREW, 2 LT. J.H. EARLY, 2 LT. E.C.H. WINGER, 2 LT. D.E. COCHRANE, 2 LT. JOHN SWATRIDGE, O.R. 100. A/Company Commanders had lost early casualties.	About report BELGIUM MAP 5 T.N.W. ENL. 6A
DAMBRE CAMP	18			
	19		Acting being 1st Sunday joint church services with 1/4th ROYAL BERKS. At close MAJOR-GENERAL SIR ROBERT FANSHAWE who attended with BRIG-GEN. DONALD WATTS addressed the two battalions expressing in complimentary "for still boldly holding on" when went to dinner.	
	20		Our second line battalion came into camp right. Inspection of equipment both for preparation of company. LT. G. D.B. GAMLEN become adjutant. 2/LT. J.E. ROYLE takes command of A Company.	

(A7092) Wt. W12839/M1293. 75,000. 1/17. D. D. & L., Ltd. Forms/C.2118/14.

Army Form C. 2118.

WAR DIARY
or
INTELLIGENCE SUMMARY.
(Erase heading not required.)

Instructions regarding War Diaries and Intelligence Summaries are contained in F. S. Regs., Part II. and the Staff Manual respectively. Title pages will be prepared in manuscript.

Place	Date	Hour	Summary of Events and Information	Remarks and references to Appendices
AMBRE CAMP	21		General inspection followed by companies. General parade of 4 O.R. under 2/Lt E. MACKAY went into field of fire and established north of canal. Machine gun at station.	
	22		Three officers and 3 NCOs proceeded with a brigade party to reconnoitre intense bombardment attack on strong enemy entrenchments. Reconn. training as before. 2/Lt GUENY, 12 ards W. of ST OMER. Reconn. training as before.	HAZEBROUCK S.A. Appendix Env. 2
	23		Company training and practice attack on advanced trenches. Conference of officers. Reports sent in for probable operations until assembly point. Lewis gun camp. 2/Lt F.W.H. CAUDWELL join.	
	24	5-7 AM	Training by companies continued. Officers' Mess training planned. Ammunition approach to MONT du HIBOU and examined ground. Approach of prospective situation. Conference of officers.	
	25		Our task for an attack on 27 int neutral. Orders in full. Conference and preparation. Light training.	
	26	3.30 P.M.	Church service at 10.30 A.M. Move at 3.30 P.M. of dispersed billets in canal bank EAST between BRIDGES 2B and 4 – C.19.D. RUE BATH Rd & REIGERSBURG CAMP. Took hard tack as on 15th int. Brigade H.Q., A, B, C, D companies. Very comfortable. Training carrying out.	BELGIUM 2 & 7 A.M. Appendix Env. 68
CANAL d'YSER	27	1.55 P.M.	Final preparations in assembly. Moved at 1.55 P.M. — Zero hour — from canal bank by INFANTRY ROUTE 4, in accordance with ORDER No 245 of 14.5	

(A7092). Wt W12859/M1293. 75,000. 1/17. D.D. & L., Ltd. Forms/C.2118/14.

WAR DIARY or INTELLIGENCE SUMMARY

Army Form C. 2118.

Place	Date	Hour	Summary of Events and Information	Remarks and references to Appendices
THE TRIANGLE	27 Aug		INF. BDE. to which the Battalion should come into support to the attacking battalions — 1/7th and 1/8th WORCESTERS — of 144 INF. BDE. between Zero plus 3 and Zero plus 4 hours occupying their assembly positions in the TRIANGLE — C.6.c. — and known out of fighting until they had attained objective, E. of LANGEMARCK line. Then to advance through to take up line through FORT COTTAGE and HÜBNER FARM to STROPPE FARM. Reached assembly area soon after 4 P.M. with very few casualties although passing through a hostile barrage rather over 700 to 800 yards.	POELCAPELLE 1:10,000 E.D.N.1.
		5 P.M.	At 5 P.M. Lead Company reported in position or digging in. Disposition. Right front, A Company; centre, B; left, C; support, D Company. Battalion Headquarters in concrete blockhouse N.E. of MON DU HIBOU.	
		6 P.M.	About 6 P.M. the 1/1st BUCKS. Bn. came into support and close to our front companies.	
SPRINGFIELD		5 P.M.	Attacking battalions reported on our right, that advance was held up by SPRINGFIELD in sight of our battalions area. Captured at 6.30 P.M. with cooperation of a "tank". Concrete building in vicinity of VANCOUVER falling later. Withstood known Infantry attack with WARWICKSHIRE REGT. on right and 2nd WEST YORKSHIRE REGT. on left, later with 1/4th BN. ROYAL BERKS on right.	
	28		After bright morning afternoon was still and showery. Mist rain fell from 5 P.M. to dusk. Night chilly with rising wind. Ground very heavy. Relieved both battalions of WORCESTERSHIRE REGT. soon after midnight in their advanced position. Failed to find until after being previously grouped then took over from them. A patrol of 4 O.R. under 2/Lt.	

Army Form C. 2118.

WAR DIARY
or
INTELLIGENCE SUMMARY.
(Erase heading not required.)

Instructions regarding War Diaries and Intelligence Summaries are contained in F. S. Regs., Part II. and the Staff Manual respectively. Title pages will be prepared in manuscript.

Place	Date Aug	Hour	Summary of Events and Information	Remarks and references to Appendices
VANCOUVER	28		W.S. TETLEY left outer company and advanced to reconnoitre Blockhouse. Reported 4 further E. than shewn on map. Our line now had nearly due E. running from C.12.b.40.75 to cross road at C.6.a.15.10 and in a slight westerly curving to C.6.b.10.E. Morning dull with strong chilly wind. Enemy artillery quiet except for spasmodic shelling of E. side of THE TRIANGLE.	
		10.15 P.M.	At 10.15 P.M. relief by 3 companies of 2/17th Bn LONDON REGT began.	
	29.	4.50 A.M.	All companies relieved and going out by 2 a.m. Last half battalion completed at 4.50 a.m. On battalion headquarters was killing at NOV DU H.30.V by enemy artillery fire, what drew communication trench, and a new down horses along STEENBEEK. Arrived at REIGERSBURG CAMP for breakfast and rest. At 10.45 A.M. marched by RATH ROAD to DAMBRE CAMP. Rested for balance of day. Casualties: Killed 9 O.R., Wounded, 19 O.R., Missing 2 O.R. July 2 officers for company today.	BELGIUM 27 N.W. 2 N.W. EDN. 3.A.
DAMBRE CAMP				
ROAD CAMP. ST. JANS TER BIEZEN	30		Move at 6.5 a.m. to ROAD CAMP, F.25.C. BELGIUM 27 N.E. 1.20000 near ST. JANS TER BIEZEN, taking over from 1/5th Bn ROYAL HIGHLANDERS showing camp with 1/1st BUCKS Bn. Route: arrival head N. of VLAMERTINGHE YPRES-POPERINGHE road, arrival head N. of POPERINGHE and POPERINGHE -WATOU road. Order H.Q. A,B,C,D Companies at 200 yards interval. Accomodation NISSEN BOW huts, our own in a dry in but. Excellent ground and football ground.	27. N.E. EDN. 2.
			2/LT. HAROLD BARRETT joins and 2/LT. VIVIAN GARLICK rejoins.	

Army Form C. 2118.

WAR DIARY
or
INTELLIGENCE SUMMARY.
(Erase heading not required.)

Place	Date	Hour	Summary of Events and Information	Remarks and references to Appendices
	30		Large reinforcement - 159 OR	
	31		Companies at disposal of commanders for clothing and kit inspections. 2/Lt. A. BENNETT from 1st Bn LEICESTERSHIRE REGT joins. Another draft :- 42 OR. Inter-company football started. Fine and bright.	

A. M. Ashton Lt-Col
Commanding
1/4 Oxford & Bucks Lt. Infty

Army Form C. 2118.

WAR DIARY
or
INTELLIGENCE SUMMARY.

WAR DIARY

1/4TH BN. OXFORD. + BUCKS LT. INFTY.

SEPTEMBER 1917

VOL XXX

WAR DIARY
or
INTELLIGENCE SUMMARY.

Army Form C. 2118.

September 1917

Place	Date	Hour	Summary of Events and Information	Remarks and references to Appendices
ROAD CAMP ST. JANS TER BIEZEN	1		Refitting and clothing - a rest day of interior economy. Later, company football begins on the excellent parade ground.	
	2		Fine and bright. Parade church service at 11am. Brig.-Gen. D.M. WATTS presents Military Medal to #200072 Sgt F. HALEY, #200677 L/c. C.C. GRAY and #200749 Pte. H.S. PEARCE.	
	3		Sunny but overcast showers. Re-organization of companies. Drill on square.	
	4		Warm and sunny. Brigade party gust to sea-side at MARDICK, near DUNKIRK, by motor-lorries. 1 officer, 24 O.R. from battalion. Squad drill, physical training and bayonet fighting. Two officers per company go for three days to Corps School, VOLCKERINGHOVE. 3 D 71, on special course for FLANDERS offensive. Leaves battalion with only one company officer and headquarters officers.	HAZEBROUCK sd 1:100,000 edn 2.
	5		N.C.O. Cadre in training as yesterday. Weather continues fine. Football practice.	
	6		Morning training continues. 2/Lt. J.M. CONSTABLE joins.	
	7		Nothing new, drill chiefly on square. Officers return from Corps School.	

Army Form C. 2118.

WAR DIARY
or
INTELLIGENCE SUMMARY.
(Erase heading not required.)

September 1917.

Place	Date	Hour	Summary of Events and Information	Remarks and references to Appendices
ROAD CAMP	8		Col. ROBERTS O.C. Divisional Train, inspected transport, cookers and water carts. Reports them in very satisfactory condition and adds that much credit is due transport officers of Brigade for this condition. Company training on line of salient taught by Corps School. Later platoon football fixtures. Rifle firing on Brigade 30× range. Parade Church service at 10 a.m.	
	9		Bright quiet day. Parade Church service at 10 a.m.	
	10		Training by companies on special schemes as before. Fine and warm. #General football games played.	
	11		Company training with visibility of 500 yards. Hostile bombing machines overhead at night as usual. Twins prominently. Notice of Brigade horse show for beginning of next week. Carps. Commdrs. Cert Military Medal to #201735. Sgt. W.N. HOBBS and Military Medal to #201736 Pte H.T. FINCH.	
	12		Company training in morning. Officers addressing class under Maj. A.B. LLOYD-BAKER begins with 9 officers. #8013 Clr. Sgt. E. BUCKINGHAM taken on strength as Regimental Sergeant-Major.	
	13		Dull in morning. Continued company schemes. Firing on rifle range. Riding plans continues. Horse preparation for horse show. Defo[...]	
	14		Fine and bright. Coys. straight company training. Notice of move to training area north of AUDRUICQ 2A 15.60 [HAZEBROUCK 5 E 1.00.00.] No detail until 11 p.m. when order for move of part of transport by road. Ready for 2 companies.	

Army Form C. 2118.

WAR DIARY
or
INTELLIGENCE SUMMARY.

(Erase heading not required.)

September 1917.

Instructions regarding War Diaries and Intelligence Summaries are contained in F. S. Regs., Part II and the Staff Manual respectively. Title pages will be prepared in manuscript.

Place	Date	Hour	Summary of Events and Information	Remarks and references to Appendices
ROAD CAMP	15		Clear and bright. Part of transport start at 9am in a brigade unit for BONNINGUES 3 & 25. Company scheme as before. Inter-platoon football reached third round. Battn. for companies.	HAZEBROUCK 5A. 1/100,000 Sheet 2.
	16	10.15 a.m.	Battalion entrained at 10.15 a.m. at HAZEBROUCK in accordance with 145th Inf. Bde. Order No. 249, and proceeded by rail to AUDRUICQ, where it marched into billets at BONNINGUES 7.45 p.m. Part of transport not arriving by road entrained at PROVEN, reaching BONNINGUES a few hours after the battalion. [Ref. BELGIUM & FRANCE, 27 N.E. 1:20,000; CALAIS 13, 1:100,000]	145th Inf. Bde. Order No. 249
BONNINGUES		7.45 p.m.		
	17		Training as usual. Weather fine. Surroundings very pleasant.	
	18		Fine & cool; occasional showers later. Firing by companies on full firing range at QUEMY from 6.30 - 9.45 a.m. in practice attack.	
	19		Battalion took part in a brigade scheme near TOURNEHEM lasting from 9 a.m. to 1.30 p.m. Draft of 62 O.R. arrived. Fine early with rain at night.	
	20		Duce. Battalion training. 2/LT. ERNEST LAURIE and 2/LT. D.S.L. PERKINS joined battalion.	

WAR DIARY or INTELLIGENCE SUMMARY

Army Form C. 2118.

September 1917

Place	Date	Hour	Summary of Events and Information	Remarks and references to Appendices
BONNINGUES	21		Fine. Battalion took part in divisional scheme near NORDAUSQUES, lasting from 10am. to 3 p.m. 2/LT. R.A. BUTTERY joined.	HAZE RROUEN 5½":1:100,000 EDN 2.
	22		Battalion training. Everyone happy with the change of surroundings. 2/LT. A.L. DAVIS, 2/LT. E.G. MAGGS, 2/LT. W.R. VINCE, 2/LT. BERNARD TWELVETREES, 2/LT. W.A. LUCK and 2/LT. L.C. SPAVEN joined battalion.	
LICQUES	23		Reveille. Horse show. Battalion marched to ROAD CAMP field at LICQUES [Ref. CALAIS, 1:100,000]. Battalion were tent and second prizes for officers' chargers, first and second prizes for packhorses, second prize for cooker and three others for vehicles. 2/LT. G.W. D'ARCY and 2/LT. HORACE MILES joined. (2F&6J)	
EST MONT OUEST MONT	24	4a.m. 4.30 P.M.	Transport moved to ESQUELBECQ at 11 a.m. via NORDAUSQUES, EPERLECQUES and WATTEN. The battalion arrived here 5 am, at followed marched to billets at EST MONT and OUEST MONT [3 B77] at	145 Inf. Bde. Order 9.47. AT 99.
	25	6 a.m. 1 p.m.	Transport continued march via WORMHOUDT to PESELHOEK, + 22 dtt. [BELGIUM + FRANCE, 27 N.E. 1:20,000]. Battalion marched to WATTEN starting b.a.m. and entrained at 7a.m. proceeding by rail direct to BRIELEN where detrained. Billeted at REIGERSBURG CAMP where coming under orders of G.O.C. 5th Div. Arrived 1 p.m. 2/LT. R. LEE joined.	145 Iny Bn. Order No. 250 of 24.9.17.

Place	Date	Hour	Summary of Events and Information	Remarks and references to Appendices
	26		Warned that we to ready for move into support positions at Reif-Lewis Cottee. Battalion stood-to. Move cancelled. Resting rest of day.	
ST. JULIEN FRONT – MON DU HIBOU	27		Resting during day. At 6 p.m. the battalion moved from REIGERSBURG CAMP in order A, B, C, D; A and B companies returning via left company of 2/2nd LONDON REGT. of 175TH INF. BDE. C and D companies going 145 LT INF. BDE ORDER with billets at CANAL BANK. Route BATH ROAD to BRIDGE 2 & 3. Final NO.2.61. -board track to ADMIRALS ROAD, ALBERTA AVENUE to MON DU HIBOU. [Ref: BELGIUM 2 F.N.W. and POELCAPPELLE, Edn.3 1:10000] Line taken over extended from D.1.d.5.7. to D.16.4.7. with double company headquarters at HUBNER FARM and battalion headquarters at MON DU HIBOU. Disposition: A company right half B left, each with front and support lines of approximately equal strength. Relief completed at 10 p.m. Casualties: Capt. L.W. BIRT seriously wounded; O.R. 1 killed, 2 wounded.	Map Ref: POELCAPPELLE Edn.3 1:10000
	28		A bright hot quiet day. From 5.30-7 p.m. enemy shell area STEEN-REEK to THE TRIANGLE heavily. From 9.40 p.m. northern edge of ST. JULIEN -POELCAPPELLE road with H.E. and shrapnel, enemy movement. C and D companies moved from CANAL BANK by BRIDGE 4 – GOURNIER FARM – MON DU RASTA – VIELLES MAISON – front line relieving the right companies of 7th YORK + LANCASHIRE REGT.	

Army Form C. 2118.

WAR DIARY
or
INTELLIGENCE SUMMARY.
(Erase heading not required.)

September 1917

Place	Date	Hour	Summary of Events and Information	Remarks and references to Appendices
HUBNER FARM – QUEBEC FARM – BAVAROISE HOUSE.	28		Battalion line now extended to BAVAROISE HOUSE. Outpost groups and supports placed on to A and B companies. Company Reorganisation open. Relief complete at 11.15 A.M. Patrol from right company which left post near D.16.B.3.0.5 at 7.40 A.M. had party of enemy working near D.16.B.7.4 when returning to own lines. Patrol was fired upon from direction YORK FARM. Returned at 9.30 P.M. without casualties. Casualties: Killed. 2 O.R.; Wounded 2 O.R.	
	29		Great patrol left our front at twilight to reconnoitre road to YORK FARM and found it impassable. Fired on from D.16.B.7.4. Returned reply at 2 A.M. Later patrols found that machine guns by gun and close shelling of our F.S. possibly from position lines filling Mon du Hibou, THE TRIANGLE and ST. JULIEN. POELCAPELLE road. GENOA FARM shelled heavily at midday. Slight shelling during of HUBNER Front line generally quiet. From 7 P.M. continuous shelling throughout night of the roads, especially after dusk, settled at midnight. Enemy small patrol attempted reconnaissance but without success in fog?	
			Dispositions: A.C. companies on outpost line, B company front + and D front. B and C support. Round company front + stilted position B.6.D.8 night midnight.	

WAR DIARY or INTELLIGENCE SUMMARY

September 1917

Place	Date	Hour	Summary of Events and Information	Remarks and references to Appendices
THE TRIANGLE — forward of Kortekeer-Cabaret.	29 (contd)		Casualties: Killed 1 O.R., wounded 2 O.R. Enemy artillery quieter than usual. Visibility unusually good after thinning mist. Our heavy artillery could be easily observed in detection shooting. Enemy aircraft was active. Several enemy battalion ones in reverence of Tanks.	Ref: 20SLA.P.E.M. John 3, 1:10000
	30		1/1 st BUCKS Bn. relieved us. Bright moonlight but no interference from enemy. Relief complete at 10.25 p.m. Battalion proceeded into Brigade reserve in CANOPY TRENCH and CALIFORNIA DRIVE, Headquarters at CHEDDAR VILLA (Ref. ST. JULIEN, I.N.W.2, Sh.28a 1:10,000)	Copy of Order No. 52. attached 1/4 th Bn. of
CHEDDAR VILLA			Casualties: Killed 3 O.R., wounded 2 O.R.	

A.M. Bartlett
Lt. Col.
Officer Commanding
1/4 Bn Oxf & Bucks Lt. Inf.

Army Form C. 2118.

WAR DIARY
or
INTELLIGENCE SUMMARY.

1/4 Bn OXFORDSHIRE + BUCKINGHAMSHIRE
LIGHT INFANTRY

OCTOBER 1917

Army Form C. 2118.

WAR DIARY
or
INTELLIGENCE SUMMARY.
(Erase heading not required.)

Instructions regarding War Diaries and Intelligence Summaries are contained in F.S. Regs., Part II. and the Staff Manual respectively. Title pages will be prepared in manuscript.

Place	Date	Hour	Summary of Events and Information	Remarks and references to Appendices
CHEDDAR VILLA	October 1917 1		Quiet day. Bright but low visibility. Slight shelling. Working parties from B and D Companies carrying ammunition to dump E. of ST. JULIEN. Day casualties 1 O.R. wounded.	Map Ref: ST. JULIEN 27 N.W. 2 & 6a 1:10000
	2		Another bright day. Some shelling of company area in CANOPUS TRENCH and CALIFORNIA DRIVE. 5th WARWICKS took over our present battalion area. Relief complete at 8.15 P.M. Battalion moved to REIGERSBURG CAMP. Casualties Day casualties	145 INF BDE ORDER No 264
REIGERSBURG CAMP	3		REIGERSBURG CAMP. Carrying parties from "C" company forward of ST. JULIEN bombed as they found junction of ADMIRAL'S and BUFFS roads coming out. Suffered casualties. Day casualties. 17 O.R. wounded.	
	4		Cloudy. Quiet day in camp. Baths for most of battalion. Heavy rain in early morning. Dull with showers throughout day. 143 Inf Bde. attacked at 6 a.m. 1/5th GLOSTERS and this battalion in divisional reserve for countering enemy counter-attack. 1/5th GLOSTERS, in front, moves to CHEDDAR VILLA. This battalion	48th Div. G.97/204 and F121
CHEDDAR VILLA		7 a.m.	moves to CANAL BANK at 7 a.m., then at 1.50 P.M. leaves for CHEDDAR VILLA. At 4 P.M. moves up to readiness position at ARBRE ridge (D7a), under orders of G.O.C. 143 Inf. Bde. In position	143 Inf Bde. Orders G.O.R. G.O.B.2
ARBRE		6 p.m.	1/5th GLOSTERS joined 143 Inf Bde in continuing attack at 5 p.m., on line WEIRDOM, INCH, BERKS HO, SHAFT HO and OXFORD HD.	

Army Form C. 2118.

WAR DIARY
or
INTELLIGENCE SUMMARY.

(Erase heading not required.)

Place	Date	Hour	Summary of Events and Information	Remarks and references to Appendices
ARBRE	4 October 1917		Morning attack made in areas that was thought further gains might be secured, line remained as at close of yesterday attack roughly; TERRIER FM, COUNTY CROSS ROADS, western end of CEMETERY, western side of WELLINGTON FARM to KRONPRINZ FM, exclusive. More than 200 prisoners taken and several machine guns. Battalion remained in archived position under considerable shelling. Casualties: 3 O.R. wounded. Capt W.H.P.Dillon + present.	
CHEDDAR VILLA	5	4-6 P.M.	Clear but cloudy. Random shelling. Battalion moved back into 143 Inf Bde reserve at CHEDDAR VILLA, CANOPUS TRENCH and CALIFORNIA DRIVE between 4 and 6 P.M. B and D Companies staying by A and C de several carrying parties. Casualties: 2 O.R. wounded.	143 Inf Bde Intelligence present.
	6		More rain and colder. A and C Coys, under Capt. J.E. BOYLE and 2/LT. H. MILES respectively, reinforce 143 Inf Bde in front line for express purpose of defining and, if possible, advancing line. Move into position after dusk, following reconnaissance. "A" Company opposite VACHER FM, "C" in CEMETERY and opposite BURNS HO, "A" "TANK", detailed to capture BURNS HO and then VACHER FM, unable to reach either objective. Operations under command of O.C. 5th R. WARWICKS. 7th R. WARWICKS in conjunction with O.C. 5th R. WARWICKS. "B" Company was covering parties. "D" standing by. 1 O.R. wounded	143 Inf Bde OO B 17 and OO B 30

WAR DIARY / INTELLIGENCE SUMMARY

Army Form C. 2118.

Place	Date	Hour	Summary of Events and Information	Remarks and references to Appendices
	October 1917			
	7	2.30 a.m.	Very cold, occasional showers during the morning. At 2.30 a.m. a patrol of 1 officer and 8 sections, including Lewis gun, from "A" company left D.2.83.3 to reconnoitre lightly held, took VACHER FARM. They proceeded along railway, then for 40 x when a machine-gun fired on them from about D.2.87.7. Replying with L.G. heavy rifle fire from D.3.a.15.50 men opened on them. At 4 a.m. the officer with this patrol detailing approach to VACHER FARM too strongly held to proceed further. There were no casualties. From midnight until dawn "C" company sent out several reconnoitring patrols. They found a concrete emplacement at edge of CEMETERY (V.26.d.25.10) with machine gun post in front, sent a strongly held trench from OXFORD HOUSES to V.26.d.47, about 15 yards from road, and a slight crest, owing to failure of TANKS to reach the company did not advance to RURNS 40 but established a definite line from road at V.26.d.19 through middle of S. edge of CEMETERY. "A" company before dawn also established a definite line E. of WELLINGTON. Both companies relieved in evening orderly night by companies of 1/1 BUCKS and 1/4 R. BERKS and return to CHEDDAR VILLA, 1/4 S. Inf. Bde. taking over Command from 1/43 Inf. Bde. Casualties 3 O.R. wounded.	POLGAPPELLE 1:10000 Sh. 4
CHEDDAR VILLA				1/4 5 Inf Bde. Order No. 257, 1/43 Inf. Bde. Order O.O. 2

WAR DIARY or INTELLIGENCE SUMMARY.

Army Form C. 2118.

Place	Date	Hour	Summary of Events and Information	Remarks and references to Appendices
CHEDDAR VILLA DAMBRE CAMP	October 1917. 8		Working Parties by "B" Company. Companies resting. 144 Inf. Bde. relieves 145 Inf. Bde. Battalion moves to DAMBRE CAMP at 6 p.m. 1/1 BUCKS and 1/4 R. BERKS jointly take over Headquarters at CHEDDAR VILLA, having contact shewn in front line to cover outgoing troops of 144 Inf. Bde. Enemy very active in night. Ruhr canvas Camp replaced nett.	145 Inf Bde Order No 257. Map Ref: POELCAPELLE 1/10,000 Sheet 4. BELGIUM 2TNW 1/20,000
	9		Strong drying wind. Battalion resting. Warning of attack by 144 Inf Bde observed. At 4:30 a.m. warning that battalion may move forward again — by train to ADMIRAL'S ROAD — to pass on attack if continuing. Commanding Officer goes to Conference at Divisional Headquarters. All ready to move. No further word. 1 O.R. wounded.	
	10		Cold and wet again. No movement order after all but preparations none further back. Companies resting interior economy and 1 O.R. wounded. 1 total casualties in HeadQuars - Lindleys 1 killed, Burnell killed.	
	11		Fine most of day but cold wet work. Clothing parades and Kit inspections. A quiet day.	
ROAD CAMP	12		Showery and raw. Battalion moves at 6.45 p.m. to ROAD CAMP, ST. JANS TER BIEZEN. Route: SIEGE JUNCTION, B20 66.5, HOSPITAL FARM, DIRTY BUCKET CORNER, A30 Central, CHEMIN MILITAIRE, ELVERDINGHE - POPERINGHE Road, SWITCH ROAD, POPERINGHE-WATOU Road. Heavy rain and very dark during march. All in at 10.30 a.m.	BELGIUM + FRANCE Sheet 28 1:40,000 and Sheet 27

WAR DIARY
INTELLIGENCE SUMMARY

Army Form C. 2118.

Place	Date	Hour	Summary of Events and Information	Remarks and references to Appendices
ROAD CAMP	October 1917			
	12 (cont)		Following officers joined: Capt. T.S.W. FOX, 2/Lt. T.J. OVENSTONE, 2/Lt. R.S. STENNER, 2/Lt. C.S. STAFFORD, 2/Lt. THOMAS MOORE, 2/Lt. H.J. NORTHCOTT, 2/Lt. J.F. WRIGHT, 2/Lt. J.T. FOSTER, 2/Lt. ARTHUR ROBERTS, 2/Lt. NORMAN GAY, 2/Lt. W.C. GATES. Much reduced strength of officers.	
	13		Cold and wet. Inspection parades only.	
	14		Fine and bright. Warm and sultry. Voluntary Church service. At 6.45 p.m. Battalion marched off & entrained at HOPOUTRE siding S.W. of POPERINGHE. [L.11.d. - BELGIUM + FRANCE, 2/7 N.E. Edn.] 2'. Entraining most hurriedly. Accommodation very poor. Men crowded in cowaril trucks. Chilly night. Started 10 p.m.	
LIGNY-ST.FLOCHEL CAUCOURT	15		Detrained from 6 - 7 a.m. at LIGNY-ST. FLOCHEL after eight hours journey. Breakfasted on high ground S.E. of station. At 9.30 a.m. marched off to CAUCOURT via TINQUES - BETHENCOURT - VILLERS-BRULIN Ft. & G. - BETHONSART. Reached CAUCOURT at 11.30 a.m. Billets found good.	Coun. My Ref. LENS 11.
	16		Brigadier Genl. came to inspect billets in morning.	
	16		Training by companies in morning. Battalion paraded at 1.30 p.m. for brigade parade for presentation of medals at 3 p.m. on high ground N.W. of CAMBLIGNEUL [5 H 25.65]. Brig. Gen. D.M. WATT presented medals. Dull and windy.	LENS 11. 1/100,000

WAR DIARY
INTELLIGENCE SUMMARY

Army Form C. 2118.

Place	Date	Hour	Summary of Events and Information	Remarks and references to Appendices
			October 1917	
CAUCOURT	17		Training by companies and company sports. Fine and bright.	
	18		Morning training as usual. First reconnaissance party to Enemy of our sector in front of VIMY RIDGE, going by light railway from our camp near CAMBLAIN L'ABBE to THELUS. At 3 P.M. Battalion marched to VILLERS CAMP at VILLERS-AU-BOIS via CAMBLIGNEUL and CAMBLAIN L'ABBE. Reached camp 5 P.M. All in comfortable huts.	Map Ref. LENS 11 1/100,000
VILLERS AU-BOIS	19		General training and lectures. Night operations by companies. Battalion covered by "SCOUTS", 2nd CANADIAN DIVISION of Shams.	
	20		Training and clothing parade. Football.	
	21		Fine and bright. Voluntary church services. Festival.	
	22		Company training in musketry, bayonet fighting and drill. Route marches for rifle and Lewis gun Brigade training at 4 P.M. to go into action. Night operations thinly opposed and ply for infantry. Lateness of Reinforcement. Only about outstanding events. Musketry and Lewis gun	
	23			
	24		One company route marching Remainder training on Thursday and practice in rapid musketry. Bright and fine. Cold, high wind. 2/Lts. M.C. ROUCHEFORT, H.D. HOPCRAFT and J.L. MURPHY joined.	
	25			

(A7092). Wt. W12859/M1293. 75,000. 1/17. D.D. & L., Ltd. Forms/C.2118/14.

2/Lts. C.E. MOON and Newjoined.

WAR DIARY
or
INTELLIGENCE SUMMARY
(Erase heading not required.)

Army Form C. 2118.

Place	Date	Hour	Summary of Events and Information	Remarks and references to Appendices
VILLERS-AU-BOIS			October 1917	
	26		Indoor training and lectures because of rain.	
	27		Fine and bright. Outdoor training.	
	28	10 A.M.	Brigade parade for distribution of medals. 2/Lt H. MILES awarded Military Cross for gallant conduct on 8th and 9th inst - when in command of "C" company. Rev BURNS. HOUSE. Church parade for joint service with 1/1 BUCKS at 10.30 a.m. Lecture Lieut C.E. MURRAY, UNITED STATES forces, giving further information and lanterns. Parade in the company areas. Film with lights lowered in evening.	
	29		Wet and stormy. Lectures and work indoors.	
	30		Fine but low visibility. Company training. Working party supplied by Battalion to recent attacked inhabitants of NEVILLE- ST.VAAST in searching for private papers and treasure. Major A.B. LLOYD-BAKER arrived and assumed command in absence on leave of Lt-Col. A.T.W. BARTLETT. Battalion concert in Y.M.C.A. Cinema	
	31			

A. B. Lloyd Baker
Major
for Lt. Col.
Commanding
1/4th OXF. & BUCKS. LT. INFTY.

www.ingramcontent.com/pod-product-compliance
Lightning Source LLC
Chambersburg PA
CBHW080807010526
44113CB00013B/2338